ON THE HOLY SPIRIT

MICHAEL SERVETUS
ON THE HOLY SPIRIT

AN ANNOTATED TRANSLATION OF
THE RESTORATION OF CHRISTIANITY
BOOK 5 ON THE DIVINE TRINITY

translated by
Peter Zerner, Peter Hughes,
and Lynn Gordon Hughes

edited by
Lynn Gordon Hughes and Justo Hernández

Blackstone Editions
Toronto, Ontario, Canada
www.BlackstoneEditions.com

© 2025 by Lynn Gordon Hughes
All rights reserved
Published 2025

978-1-7386994-1-4

Front cover image: *St. Michael and the Dragon*
Walters Art Museum, Baltimore, MD
Creative Commons W.26.131R

*Extrema manus nondum
operibus eius imposita est*

Books in This Series

Volume 1: *On the Trinity and the Bible*
   The Restoration of Christianity:
     On the Divine Trinity, books 1 and 2
     Translated by Peter Zerner and Peter Hughes

Volume 2: *On the Mysteries of the Word*
   The Restoration of Christianity:
     On the Divine Trinity, books 3 and 4
     Translated by Peter Zerner and Peter Hughes

Volume 3: *On the Holy Spirit*
   The Restoration of Christianity:
     On the Divine Trinity, book 5
     Translated by Peter Zerner, Peter Hughes, and
     Lynn Gordon Hughes

Contents

Preface *by Lynn Gordon Hughes*	ix
Key to Annotations, Symbols, and Abbreviations	xiii
A Note on the Text	xx
Introduction	1
The Restoration of Christianity	
On the Divine Trinity, book 5	27
Appendixes	
A. The Paris Manuscript, book 5	85
B. The Galenic Physiological System	125
C. Servetus's Place in Medical History *by Justo Hernández and Peter Hughes*	135
Annotations	181
Bibliography	197
Index of Biblical References	205
Index of Authorities Cited	209

Preface
by Lynn Gordon Hughes

The original translators have passed away, but the work continues.

My husband Peter Hughes and his colleague Peter Zerner started translating Servetus's *Christianismi restitutio* (*The Restoration of Christianity*) in 2005. Their goal was to produce an annotated translation of the first 286 pages of *Restoration*: the five books and two dialogues on the Trinity. They worked on it together until Peter Zerner died in 2019. At that time the project consisted of draft translations, in various states of completion, of books 1 through 5 and dialogue 1. Peter Hughes then took on the task of transforming this unruly body of work into publishable form. There was much to be done: reviewing and polishing the translation, tracking down footnotes and preparing annotations, writing introductions to each volume and a Translator's Introduction to the project as a whole.

I joined the project team in 2022, intending to concentrate my efforts on the aspects of book production that remain to be done after the main text is complete: checking references for accuracy, preparing the bibliography and indexes, and so on. Volume 1 of the series proceeded more or less as planned. But my role was unexpectedly, and sadly, expanded after Peter was diagnosed with cancer in October 2022. As his health declined, I gradually took over more and more of the responsibility for completing the project, as well as

Preface

for the more mundane aspects of his care. Having begun to study Latin in 2020, I was able to help with the revision of the translation. I wrote some of the annotations, especially those that required library research that Peter was no longer able to do. And I completed the introduction to volume 2, which was left unfinished when Peter died in April 2024.

At the time of Peter's death, volume 3 consisted of a draft translation and little else. The footnotes and annotations existed only as rough notes. The introduction had not even been started. I had promised Peter that I would see the project through to publication, at least through volume 3, but how was I to fulfill that promise? Book 5 of *Restoration*, with its famous passage on the flow of blood through the heart and lungs, would require specialist knowledge of anatomy and physiology, both ancient and modern.

Fortunately, help was at hand. Prior to his illness, Peter had been collaborating with a colleague in Spain, Justo Hernández, on a series of articles exploring the claims that have been made over the years for Servetus as a medical pioneer, and the reality behind those claims. Shortly before he died, Peter suggested adapting the unfinished articles as an introduction for volume 3. As it turned out, the information in the articles was far too detailed and extensive to serve as an introduction. But I saw that we could use a small part of this material in the introduction, and turn the rest into an informative appendix. Justo agreed to this use of the articles and, most importantly, he agreed to become a co-editor of volume 3. So, with this volume, it is my pleasure to introduce a new contributor to the project.

Justo Hernández is a medical doctor and professor of history of medicine at the Faculty of Medicine of the University of La Laguna in Tenerife, Canary Islands, Spain. After finishing his medical career, he got a master's degree in classical studies in Italy and then decided to dedicate himself to studying and researching the history of medicine. To this end, he trained in the departments of history of medicine at the University of Navarra, with Professor Juan Antonio Paniagua, and at the University of Valencia with Professor José María López Piñero. He defended his doctoral thesis on Spanish Renaissance medicine at the University of Valencia. He was always fascinated by

Preface

Michael Servetus and has extensively studied Servetus's life and work, trying to distinguish between who he really was and what historians of medicine have said about him.

Peter and Justo met in New York in 2014, at a meeting of the Renaissance Society of America, where Peter delivered a paper on Servetus as a geographer. They discovered that they shared a common interest in the way Servetus has been depicted over the years, and the extent to which the current image of Servetus is a product of the Enlightenment.

For this volume, Justo has not only contributed his research on Servetus's place in medical history, but has used his expertise in medicine and medical history to revise and supplement the annotations dealing with anatomy, physiology, and the history of ideas about the structure and function of the human body. Without his help, it would not have been possible to produce this volume in anything like its present form. We are lucky to have him as part of the team.

Key to Annotations, Symbols, and Abbreviations

Bible Books, Chapters, and Verses

In referring to the books of the Bible we have adopted the names commonly used in English Protestant Bibles. In particular, the four books called 1-4 Kings in the Vulgate we call 1-2 Samuel and 1-2 Kings.

For the convenience of readers who would like to track down Servetus's biblical citations and allusions, we have provided verse numbers, to the extent that they can be ascertained. Since Servetus wrote before versification had become established, he did not have the same sense of pinpoint location that later writers would develop. Some of his references are to a whole chapter, or to several verses scattered throughout. In quotations he occasionally stitched together several disjoint phrases from different verses in a particular chapter, adding connecting words of his own.

Sometimes chapters within books of the Bible are divided in different places in various versions of the Bible. In particular, there are two ways of numbering the Psalms: Roman Catholic Bibles use the Septuagint numbering, while Protestant Bibles follow the Masoretic Hebrew numbering. In most cases the Protestant psalm numbers can be obtained by adding one to the number that

Servetus cited. In the translation, we have retained the numbers that Servetus used, but in our footnotes we refer the reader to the English Protestant chapters and verses.

> another, heavenly fire. For God, who lit the first lamp in us, again turns our darkness into light, as it says in Psalm 17[a] and 2 Samuel 22.[b] And this is what Elihu also teaches in chapters 32 and 33 of Job.[c] Zoroaster, [Hermes] Trismegistus, and Pythagoras, as I will soon

> inhalation, the love of God is kindled in our hearts by the Holy Spirit. The heart, in addition to housing
>
> ---
> [a] Ps 18:28.   [b] 2 Sam 22:29.   [c] Job 33:28, 30 (not Job 32).
> [d] On page 180.

Servetus cited Psalm 17 (Vulgate numbering), but the footnote is to Psalm 18.

Abbreviations

The following abbreviations are used when referring to frequently-cited works and collections of works.

Calvini opera	*Ioannis Calvini opera quae supersunt omnia* (vol. 29-87 of *Corpus Reformatorum*, 1863-1900)
Errors	Servetus, *De Trinitatis erroribus*
Galen, FN	Galen, *De facultatibus naturalibus*
Galen, PHP	Galen, *De placitis Hippocratis et Platonis*
Galen, UP	Galen, *De usu partium corporis humani*
PG	*Patrologia Graeca*, ed. J.-P. Migne (1857-1866)
PL	*Patrologia Latina*, ed. J.-P. Migne (1841-1855)
Restoration	Servetus, *Christianismi restitutio*

Key to Annotations, Symbols, and Abbreviations

Typographical Conventions and Punctuation

The following conventions are used in all translated text.

Page Numbers

Page numbers in the translation of *The Restoration of Christianity* show the location of page breaks in the original 1553 publication. Page numbers are printed in boldface and enclosed in square brackets, e.g. **[10]**.

Note that **all** references to page numbers in *Restoration* (in annotations, cross references, index, etc.) use these standard page numbers.

Headings and Other Text Supplied by the Editors

Square brackets are used to identify text added to the translation to improve clarity. This includes section headings and subheadings that have been added in order to bring out the structure of the text.

> [*The Brain*]
>
> [*Animal Spirit*]
>
> Thus the vital spirit is poured from the left ventricle of the heart into the arteries of the entire body in such a way that the part of it which is more rarefied moves toward the upper part [of the body], where it is further elaborated. [It moves] especially into the

In this passage, square brackets designate two different levels of headings and additional text added by the editors.

Quotations

Quotations from the Bible are printed in italics. Quotation marks are used for non-biblical quotations.

Cross References

Marginal notes are used to cross-reference passages from *Restoration* to parallel passages in *On the Errors of the Trinity*.

Key to Annotations, Symbols, and Abbreviations

> Hence, after the Holy Spirit descended, Christ said, *You will see the angels of God ascending, and descending upon the Son of Man* (John 1).[a] In one [account of Jesus's baptism] it says *angels descending*, in another is says *the Spirit descending*, and in a third *the Holy Spirit descending*.[b] In [the story of the conversion of the eunuch] in Acts 8 [the Holy Spirit] is first called an angel, then the Spirit, and finally the Spirit of the Lord.[c] Isidore [of Seville], speaking about the Paraclete,[d] says, "He will announce future events to you." He supposes [the Paraclete] to be an angel,

In this passage, the quotations from the Bible are shown in italics. The quotation from Isidore is in quotation marks.

> Among the [ancient] Jews the flesh was sanctified, but now the spirit is holy. The anointing which we receive from Christ is of the Spirit (2 Corinthians 1, 1 John 2, and Acts 10).[c] True Christians are governed by an internal anointing and sanctification which is done in the spirit and by the [Holy] Spirit. This is why we call the Spirit holy, and for this reason we are baptized *in the name of the Holy Spirit*,[d] which was unknown to the Jews, so that being *dead to the Law*[e] and buried [with Christ] in the flesh,[f] we should be ever mindful

Err, 65r

Err, 61r

This passage is related to material on pages 61r and 65r in Errors.

Annotations and Footnotes

Annotations are explanatory notes, varying in length from a few sentences to multi-paragraph mini-essays. Annotations are used only in translated text, where they are identified by superscript numbers. They are located at the end of the volume, after the appendixes.

Footnotes are found in translated text and also in editorial content, such as the introduction and annotations. In translated text, footnotes are identified by superscript letters, starting over with "a" on every page. In editorial content, footnotes are numbered sequentially within each document and identified by superscript numbers.

> cloud, as if on fire. And all of this in one substance: because there is one primary substance of these three elements,[b] which is corporeal, spiritual, and shining with light.[2] In one mode of divine dispensation, the elementary substance <u>of the cloud</u> becomes a tangible

In translated text, superscript numbers indicate annotations and letters indicate footnotes.

When annotations are referenced (in other annotations or in footnotes) they are identified as follows:

> After all the [sensory images] have been illuminated in the middle ventricle, the doorkeeper [vermis cerebelli][a] allows the <u>spirit itself</u> to reach the fourth ventricle, located in the parencephalon [cerebellum], and a bright image is kindled in the light of the soul itself. There, in what is actually the base of the
>
> ―――――――――――
> [a] See A.R5.23.

In this example, A.R5.23 indicates annotation 23 for Restoration book 5.

Identification of Works Cited

Works cited in footnotes may be identified in several different ways.

1. The most frequently cited sources are identified by abbreviations, e.g. *Calvini opera* or *Restoration*. See the list of abbreviations above.

2. Works that are listed in the bibliography are identified by author and title, sometimes in shortened forms. Full publication details are found in the bibliography.

3. For works not in the bibliography, full publication details are supplied in the footnote.

Titles of works written in Latin (or in other languages using the Latin alphabet) are given in the original language in the footnotes, even though they are referred to in the main text by their English translations. For works written in languages using other character sets, such as Greek and Hebrew, English titles are used in footnotes.

Most of the primary sources cited in this book use some type of section numbers, so that a passage can be identified without having to specify a particular edition. Where this is not possible, page numbers are used; the edition is specified in the Bibliography. For works that are in the standard collections *Patrologia Latina* (PL) or *Patrologia Graeca* (PG), the location information is included in the footnote.

The Paris Manuscript

There is a manuscript, located in the Bibliothèque Nationale in Paris, which contains a draft of part of the "On the Trinity" section of *The Restoration of Christianity*. The manuscript has been transcribed and translated by Peter Hughes. The translation of book 5 from the manuscript is included in this volume as an appendix.

Most of the typographical conventions used elsewhere are also applicable to this appendix. However, in the appendix, two sets of page numbers are shown. Page numbers in the manuscript are printed in boldface and enclosed in triangular brackets, e.g. **<10>**. To aid in matching the manuscript text with the corresponding text in the printed version, page numbers from the printed edition are also shown. Where the text of the manuscript is different from the final version, the variant text is underlined in both the appendix and the main text.

Although most of the footnotes and annotations found in the main text are also applicable to the manuscript, they are not repeated in the appendix. Any footnotes in the appendix point to references or features that are specific to the manuscript.

Key to Annotations, Symbols, and Abbreviations

world.ᵃ On the contrary, the body is actually the food of the spirit. [The body] is truly united to our spirit as one substance, bound together by the spirit of regeneration. Truly the flesh of Christ is food — much more truly than [ordinary] outward food. There is no truth, as the paradox says, in our ordinary food; rather, the truth is in that [heavenly] food, in which there is unchanging and immaculate purity. This is the true food of the ever-living life that is in us.

One might wonder, if the Holy Spirit was originally in Christ alone, how did it [195] descend on him at the Jordan River?ᵇ I reply that before the Resurrection Christ had not yet acquired the full glory and power of God.ᶜ By a special dispensation of God, this was reserved until the Resurrection. At the Jordan, the

is no truth in the bodies of this world. On the contrary, the body is actually the food of the spirit. [The body] is truly united to our spirit as one substance, <32> bound together by the spirit of regeneration. Truly the flesh of Christ is food—much more truly than [ordinary] outward food. There is no truth, as the paradox says, in our ordinary food; rather, the truth is in that [heavenly] food,ᵃ in which there is unchanging and immaculate purity. This is the true food of the ever-living life that is in us.

The question may arise, if the Holy Spirit was originally in Christ alone, how did it [195] descend on him at the Jordan River? I reply that before the Resurrection Christ had not yet acquired the full glory and power of God. By a special dispensation of God, this was reserved until the Resurrection. At the Jordan, the new power and glory of the

This is the same passage, as it appears in the printed version of Restoration (A) and in the Paris manuscript (B).

- *The variant text ("One might wonder" vs. "The question may arise") is underlined in both places.*
- *(A) shows the page number from the printed version [195]. (B) shows this number and also the page number from the manuscript <32>.*
- *(A) includes footnote superscripts a, b, and c. These are not repeated in (B), although they are relevant to the manuscript. (B) includes footnote superscript a, which points to a footnote that is applicable to the manuscript only.*

A Note on the Text

The Restoration of Christianity

Only three copies of the original printing of *Christianismi restitutio* are known to remain in existence. They reside at the Bibliothèque Nationale in Paris, the Österreichische Nationalbibliothek in Vienna, and the University of Edinburgh. In 1790 a transcription based on the Vienna copy, made to match the original pagination, was published in Nuremberg by Christoph Gottlieb von Murr. This was reprinted by Minerva of Frankfurt in 1966.

Until recently most scholars who have consulted *Restoration* have used the Murr transcription, which contains a number of copying mistakes, a few of which are significant. Fortunately, the Paris copy is available online on BnF Gallica, the web site of the Bibliothèque Nationale. The first 576 pages of the Vienna copy are reprinted in *Miguel Servet: Obras Completas*, vols. 5 and 6 (ed. Ángel Alcalá). As these two copies of *Restoration* are defaced or damaged in different ways, it is helpful to be able to inspect both.

The Paris Manuscript

The Paris manuscript is available online on BnF Gallica, as Latin manuscript 18212.

Introduction

With this volume we reach the end of our annotated translation of "Five Books on the Trinity," the first 198 of the 734 pages of Servetus's final and most important theological work, *The Restoration of Christianity* (*Christianismi restitutio*).

The first two volumes in this series each covered two books of *The Restoration of Christianity*. This volume covers just one: book 5, "Concerning the Holy Spirit." It is an unusual book, with a history somewhat different from that of the rest of *Restoration*.

To begin with, we must acknowledge that, ever since its initial publication in 1553, *The Restoration of Christianity* has been *read about* more than it has actually been *read*. As soon as it was printed, a determined effort was made to suppress it. From the point of view of the Protestant and Catholic authorities, destroying the book was just as important as destroying its author. When Servetus was convicted of blasphemy and heresy in October 1553, he was sentenced by the Council of Geneva to be "attached to a stake and burned with your book to ashes." The Inquisition in France also condemned him to death, and burned him in effigy along with five bales of blank paper representing his book. In the end, out of 1000 printed copies of *Christianismi restitutio*, only three survived.[1]

---

[1] Bainton, *Hunted Heretic*, 103, 112-113, 141-142. The story of the three surviving copies is told in Lawrence and Nancy Goldstone, *Out of the Flames* (New York: Broadway Books, 2002), 221-283.

Introduction

Even after *The Restoration of Christianity* was reprinted in 1790, few people read it. It is a long text, and a difficult one.[2] Although the story of Servetus's life and death continued to be told as a cautionary tale about religious intolerance, his ideas, for the most part, seemed doomed to languish in obscurity. The first complete translation of *Restoration* into English was not published until 2010.[3]

There was, however, one exception to this obscurity. Book 5 contains a short passage — only three pages — that was destined to take on a life of its own. As part of his depiction of the activity of the Holy Spirit, Servetus made use of what we now recognize as new and ground-breaking anatomical and physiological information. Seventy-five years before William Harvey published his revolutionary description of the circulation of the blood, Servetus became the first European to publish an accurate description of the path of the blood through the heart and lungs.[4] Once this became known, Servetus acquired a new set of admirers: medical doctors and students of the history of medicine. The passage on the pulmonary transit has been extensively studied and written about.[5] Decades before the rest of *Restoration* was translated into English, multiple translations of this passage were available, with accompanying commentary.[6]

---

[2] On the difficulty of understanding Servetus's thought, see Hughes, introduction to *On the Trinity and the Bible*, 2-4.

[3] *The Restoration of Christianity: An English Translation of Christianismi Restitutio, 1553*, translated by Christopher Hoffman and Marian Hillar, with notes by Marian Hillar, was published by The Edwin Mellen Press in 2007. Three additional volumes were issued as *Treatise on Faith and Justice of Christ's Kingdom* (2008), *Treatise Concerning the Supernatural Regeneration and the Kingdom of the Antichrist* (2008), and *Thirty Letters to Calvin, Preacher to the Genevans, and Sixty Signs of the Kingdom of the Antichrist and His Revelation Which Is Now at Hand* (2010).

[4] Some three hundred years earlier, the Arab physician Ibn al-Nafis (1213-1288) had given a description of the pulmonary transit in *Commentary on the Anatomy of the Canon* (c.1242), but this was not known in Europe.

[5] In an unpublished paper, included in this volume as appendix C, Justo Hernández and Peter Hughes report having surveyed over 200 references to this passage, from the eighteenth century to the twenty-first.

[6] O'Malley, *Servetus's Geographical, Medical and Astrological Writings*, 195-208. Pagel, *William Harvey's Biological Ideas*, 136-153.

Introduction

All of this creates special challenges for translating, annotating, and even introducing Servetus's work on the Holy Spirit. In this volume, we have tried to strike a balance, acknowledging the special importance of those three pages while also situating this passage within the context of the rest of book 5, the rest of *The Restoration of Christianity*, and Servetus's larger project of reforming Christian belief. But we begin where most people do: with Servetus's description of the pulmonary transit.

Servetus as a Medical Pioneer

To understand what was (and what was not) revolutionary about Servetus's description of the working of the heart and lungs, it is necessary to know something about the model of human anatomy and physiology that was current in his day.

In the sixteenth century, the works of the second-century anatomist and physician, Galen, were considered authoritative in medicine, just as the works of Aristotle were considered authoritative in most branches of philosophy and science. In the Galenic physiological system, blood flows through the body, but it does not circulate. Instead, as it makes its way through the body, it is consumed for the nourishment of the bodily tissues. A continuous supply of new blood is therefore required, and this is formed in the liver, from ingested food. This blood flows through the body via the veins, which were believed to originate in the liver. A small amount of blood flows from the liver to the heart, where it mixes with inhaled air to form "vital spirit." Blood charged with vital spirit is then distributed to the tissues of the body via the arteries. A small amount of this blood flows to the brain, where it is further refined and transformed into "animal spirit," the stuff of the mind and soul.[7] (The word "animal" derives from the Latin word for soul, *anima*. It is somewhat unfortunate that this was the term adopted in English for the highest and most ethereal form of spirit, because

---

[7] Galen described his system most fully in *De usu partium* (UP). Brief modern expositions of the Galenic view may be found in, among other places, Singer and Rabin, *Prelude to Modern Science*, xxxviii-xxxix; Pagel, *William Harvey's Biological Ideas,* 127-136; and Harris, *Heart and Vascular System*, 267-396.

the word "animal" in English is more likely to conjure up an image of something sub-human rather than super-human. A better term would be soul spirit or — from the Greek word for soul — psychic spirit.) A more detailed description of the Galenic system, showing how it differs from both Servetus's version and the modern view of the circulatory system, is found in appendix B, "The Galenic Physiological System."

Servetus accepted most of Galen's model. But he described a different pathway for the transit of blood from the right to the left side of the heart. Galen believed that blood seeped through imperceptible openings in the septum between the left and right sides of the heart, before mixing with air from the lungs in the left ventricle.[8] Servetus, however, rejected the idea of imperceptible openings. He described the flow of blood from the right ventricle, through the pulmonary artery to the lungs, where it is transformed through aeration, then through the pulmonary vein to the left ventricle, whence it enters the aorta and is distributed throughout the body via the arteries.

People who know Servetus primarily as a medical pioneer often ask: Who was this heretic Michael Servetus, so original in his thoughts on both religion and medicine? Why did he choose to publish a medical discovery of this magnitude in the middle of a theological tome?

As this is the third volume of our annotated translation of *The Restoration of Christianity*, it might seem unnecessary to introduce Servetus at this point. But as noted above, book 5 of *Restoration*, because of its significance in medical history, has always attracted its own special set of readers. For the benefit of those who may be coming to this volume without much prior knowledge of Servetus, before proceeding to a discussion of book 5 as a whole, we begin with a brief summary of what is known about Servetus's life, and the relation between his medical writing and his overall theological project.

---

[8] Galen, UP 6.17. No such openings are visible in dissection, but Galen explained that this was because the openings are very small, and because a dead animal is "chilled and shrunken" compared to a living one. FN 3.15.

Additional questions arise specifically out of Servetus's description of the pulmonary transit. How did he, not otherwise known to be a great medical pioneer, come to be in possession of this revolutionary information? How much credit does he deserve in medical history for discovering and/or revealing the flow of the blood through the lungs? Was his knowledge confined to the section of the cardiovascular system that he explicitly described, or did he know about the circulation of the blood before William Harvey? Alternatively, was his knowledge so thoroughly embedded in the ancient Galenic model of physiology that it could not properly be called a discovery at all? These questions will be addressed in appendix C, "Servetus's Place in Medical History."

Who Was Michael Servetus?

The details of all but the last few months of Servetus's life are shrouded in mystery. What passes as his biography has been put together from bits and pieces of contradictory testimony that he gave to inquisitors in France and interrogators in Geneva while on trial for his life.

The central fact of Servetus's life, what he is most remembered for, is that, because of his critique of orthodox trinitarian theology and his opposition to the practice of infant baptism, he was convicted of heresy and blasphemy and burned at the stake by the Protestants of Geneva under the guidance of John Calvin.[9] The execution of a prominent dissident by representatives of the Reformed Church was a controversial, even shocking move, for a group that had, up to then, advocated a policy of religious toleration. There were a number of protests against Servetus's execution, most famously by Sebastian Castellio. His book *On Whether Heretics Should Be Persecuted* (1554), which quoted Calvin's own words

---

[9] *Calvini opera* 8:827-830. Servetus mistakenly thought that he was on trial for heresy alone. But with the charge of blasphemy the Genevans felt themselves on firmer legal ground. The ambiguity between blasphemy and heresy allowed them to sentence Servetus to death although, by a strict application of either ancient or more modern law, heresy was not a capital offence. See Standford Rives, *Did Calvin Murder Servetus?* (Charleston, SC: Booksurge, 2008), 323-332.

against such persecution, is considered a foundational work in the history of religious toleration.[10]

Here is what we can reasonably conjecture to be the outline of Servetus's life.[11] Miguel Servet was born in Spain, most likely c.1506.[12] He was raised in a small town in Aragon, Villanueva de Sijena, and received parts of his early education at the studium in Zaragoza and at the University of Toulouse.[13] In the course of his youthful experiences Servetus was attracted by evangelical Christianity and Erasmian humanism. Under these influences he began to study Hebrew and Greek in order to read the Bible in its original languages. Inspired by his reading of the early Church Fathers, Servetus felt called to restore Christian theology to its earliest form, prior to the introduction of the orthodox trinitarian formula at the Council of Nicaea in 325. He hoped, among other things, to create a non-trinitarian Christianity that would be palatable to Muslims and Jews, paving the way for a voluntary union of the various branches of the children of Abraham.[14]

---

[10] Sebastian Castellio, *De haereticis, an sint persequendi* (Magdeburg, 1554), 107-108.

[11] A large portion of the evidence upon which we base our conjectures about Servetus's life story is derived from the records of Servetus's interrogations in Vienne and Geneva, which are collected in *Calvini opera*, vol. 8. Roland Bainton's biography, *Hunted Heretic*, first published in 1953, remains a reasonably reliable source, less speculative than most. Also well-balanced is Ángel Alcalá's introduction to *Miguel Servet: Obras Completas*, vol. 1, as well as his introductions to subsequent volumes. A recent book by Miguel González Ancín and Otis Towns, *Miguel Servet en España* (2017), presents documents that shed new light on Servetus's family constellation and early education. The authors rightly question some of the assumptions that others, including Bainton, have made; yet they engage in speculation of their own, notably on the question of Servetus's birth and ancestry. See also Hillar, *Michael Servetus*.

[12] The date of Servetus's birth has long been controversial. It is most often given as 1511, sometimes 1509. But recent scholarship shows that it is likely to be around 1506. See Hughes, "Early Years of Servetus," 36-39; Ancín and Towns, *Miguel Servet en España*, 29-53.

[13] Alcalá, introduction to *Obras Completas*, vol. 1, l-li. Ancín and Towns, *Miguel Servet en España*, 189-234. Hughes, "Early Years of Servetus," 42-48.

[14] Hughes, "Early Years of Servetus," 54-85. See also Hughes, introduction to *On the Trinity and the Bible*, 46-48.

Introduction

Aspiring to bring about a radical reformation of the Church, which would go beyond what he considered to be the mere institutional tinkering of the other reformers, in 1530 Servetus travelled to Switzerland and Germany, where he visited and conversed with various Protestant reformers, but was unsuccessful at bringing then over to his radical point of view.[15] In 1531 he published *On the Errors of the Trinity*, his challenge to the orthodox formulation of the doctrine of the Trinity. This theological manifesto attracted very few sympathizers and alienated many readers.[16] In 1532 he issued a revised and softened version of his teaching, *Dialogues on the Trinity*, but it fared no better. As these books scandalized both the reformers and the Roman Catholic authorities, he felt compelled to go into hiding. In order to protect himself from the Inquisition while living in France, he fabricated a new identity, Michel de Villeneuve.

As Villeneuve, Servetus lived and worked in Lyons and Paris during the 1530s. In Lyons he supported himself by working as an editor and proofreader. There he met the humanist Symphorien Champier, who introduced him to Neoplatonism and encouraged him to study medicine.[17] By the end of 1536 he was studying mathematics and medicine at the University of Paris. He became expert in the works of Galen and studied Arabic medicine.[18] An early result of his new expertise was *On Syrups* (1537). In this monograph he took a largely philological approach, surveying and examining ancient texts.[19]

---

[15] Alcalá, introduction to *Obras Completas*, vol. 1, xxxiv, lvii-lxi. Bainton, *Hunted Heretic*, 25, 32-35. Hillar, *Michael Servetus*, 13-19.

[16] Alcalá, introduction to *Obras Completas*, vol. 1, lxii-lxiv. Bainton, *Hunted Heretic,* 38-44. Hillar, *Michael Servetus*, 26-29, 34-36.

[17] Servetus, *In Leonardum Fuchsium apologia*, A2r. Alcalá, introduction to *Obras Completas*, vol. 1, lxx-lxxiii. Bainton, *Hunted Heretic*, 87. Hillar, *Michael Servetus*, 52-54.

[18] Winter von Andernach, Dedicatory Epistle to *Institutionum anatomicarum*. Servetus, *Syruporum, passim*. Francisco Javier González Echeverría, *El amor a la verdad: Vida y obra de Miguel Servet (*Gobierno de Navarra, 2011), 194-204.

[19] María T. Santamaría, "La medicina filológica de Miguel de Villanueva," in *KOINÓS LÓGOS: Homenaje al profesor José García López*, vol. 2, edited by E. Calderón, M. Morales, and M. Valverde (Murcia: Universidad, 2006), 963-972.

Introduction

At Paris Servetus also lectured on "judicial astrology," the forecasting of future human events based upon celestial phenomena. Although astrology was considered part of natural philosophy and was used in medicine, its use to foretell the future was considered dangerous. Ordered by the university to desist, Servetus countered by defending himself in a tract justifying astrology on the authority of Galen, Hippocrates, Aristotle, Plato, and other ancient writers. The work was banned and Villeneuve was ordered to respect the authority of the university. He chose to leave the city soon afterward.[20] Although he later claimed to be a "doctor of medicine from Paris," there is no evidence that he ever received a medical degree there.[21]

After engaging in a perfunctory period of further medical study at the university in Montpellier, and possibly obtaining a medical degree,[22] Servetus established himself as a physician, first in the town of Charlieu, then — at the invitation of Pierre Palmier, Archbishop of Vienne, who had attended his lectures in Paris — in Vienne.[23] At the same time he continued to work for the Lyons publishers. He edited the second edition of the Bible as translated into Latin by Santes Pagnini, published in 1542. Servetus's familiarity with Pagnini's Hebrew scholarship helped to guide the new biblical studies that informed and inspired *The Restoration of Christianity*.[24] This work, largely written in the early 1540s, set Servetus on the path towards destruction.

In 1546, in the course of a brief epistolary debate with John Calvin, Servetus sent a draft of *The Restoration of Christianity* to the

---

[20] Jean Dupèbe, introduction to *Michel Servet: Discussion Apologétique pour l'astrologie* (Geneva: Droz, 2004), 1-29. Alcalá, introduction to *Obras Completas*, vol. 1, lxxiii-lxxviii. Bainton, *Hunted Heretic*, 74-77. Hillar, *Michael Servetus*, 77-85.

[21] *Calvini opera*, 8:767. Alcalá, introduction to *Obras Completas*, lxxix-lxxxi. Bainton, *Hunted Heretic*, 77.

[22] Alcalá, introduction to *Obras Completas*, vol. 1, lxxx.

[23] *Calvini opera*, 8:767. O'Malley, *Servetus's Geographical, Medical and Astrological Writings*, 189-190, 192. Alcalá, introduction to *Obras Completas*, vol. 1, lxxix.

[24] Alcalá, introduction to *Obras Completas*, vol. 1, lxi, xcii-xciii. Bainton, *Hunted Heretic*, 63-65.

Introduction

Geneva reformer.²⁵ The main result of this debate was to convince Calvin that, if Servetus ever came into his power, he would have him destroyed.²⁶ When Calvin was advised that *The Restoration of Christianity* had been put into print, he arranged for Servetus to be betrayed to the French Inquisition.²⁷

After escaping from imprisonment in Vienne, Servetus turned up in Geneva, where he was immediately arrested, accused by Calvin, interrogated, tried, and finally, after several months of miserable confinement, condemned and executed. The Catholics in France had to content themselves with burning him in effigy.²⁸

Why Publish a Medical Breakthrough in a Book of Theology?

Servetus, like many intellectuals of his time, was what we would call a polymath, or a "Renaissance man." Learned people in his time did not usually specialize as academics do today. Fields that we now see as entirely separate existed on a continuum and had extensive overlap. Servetus was, at various times, occupied with theology, medicine, mathematics, astrology, and geography.²⁹ He considered all of these subjects to be aspects of one general field of study. Mathematics was critical for astrology and geography; medical practice had to take geography and astrology into account; and astrology and medicine provided macroscopic and microscopic windows on the divine.

Servetus was not alone in combining medicine with theology. Other writers on medicine, both in Servetus's time and earlier, often added theological reflections to their descriptions of the human

---

[25] Calvin, *Defensio*, 38-57. *Calvini opera*, 8:xxx-xxxi. Alcalá, introduction to *Obras Completas*, vol. 1, xcvii-xcviii. Bainton, *Hunted Heretic*, 96-97. Hillar, *Michael Servetus*, 89-91. The epistolary debate took place in February 1546. Servetus later published an additional thirty letters to Calvin, which Bainton and Alcalá claim were sent, while Hillar more plausibly contends that they were, in effect, literary essays, meant only for publication.

[26] Calvin to Guillaume Farel, 13 Feb 1546, in *Calvini opera*, 12:283.

[27] *Calvini opera*, 8:837, 8:842. Cavard, *Le procès de Michel Servet*, 94-114.

[28] *Calvini opera*, 8: 725-830, 8:850-851. Cavard, *Le procès de Michel Servet*, 131-144.

[29] See Hughes, "Michael Servetus's Britain," 85-109.

Introduction

body. One such was Galen, who was forever marveling at the great foresight of the Creator, or of Nature, in fashioning the various parts or features of the body.[30] Other theologians monitored developments in medicine, looking for opportunities to explain religious doctrine. For example, in his study of the soul, the prominent Lutheran, Philip Melanchthon, commented on the anatomists Galen and Vesalius.[31] Thus, Servetus may not have thought he was doing anything unusual when he used a result drawn from medicine to illustrate a theological point.

Nonetheless, the extent to which Servetus combined theology and physiology was unusual, even in his time. For Servetus, in addition to being a polymath, was a person with multiple identities. In the outer world he was the physician Michel de Villeneuve, very careful not to ruffle Roman Catholic feathers. At the same time, inwardly, he was still the theologian and radical reformer, Michael Servetus. And this inner self was the driving force of his life and of the work that he felt called to accomplish. Thus, while to most physicians or medical writers, theology shed light on the human body, to Servetus information drawn from physiology was primarily a tool for understanding and participating in God's plan for humankind.

Still, there is something mysterious about the sheer amount of medical and anatomical information Servetus included in book 5 of *The Restoration of Christianity*. He introduced the description of the pulmonary transit with, "So that you, reader, may have a complete understanding of how the soul and the spirit function, I shall here add divine philosophy, which you will easily understand if you have been trained in anatomy."[32] This raises the question of who he imagined his readers to be. There are many indications that the people he most wanted to reach were the Protestant reformers. After all, he sent a draft of the book to Calvin in 1546, and tried to engage Calvin in

---

[30] See, for example, Galen, UP 6.20.
[31] Philip Melanchthon, "Epistola dedicatoria" in *De anima* (Wittenberg, 1552). Melanchthon made many references to Galen in the earlier editions of the 1540s.
[32] *Restoration*, 169.

a prolonged discussion of it. When Calvin stopped answering his letters, he appended "Thirty Letters to Calvin" to the final version of *Restoration*. He also included an "Apology to Melanchthon," a response to the Lutheran leader's criticism of his earlier writings. Servetus had no reason to believe that these or any of the other leading theologians of the day had been trained in anatomy.

Overview of Book 5

Book 5 of *The Restoration of Christianity* is often discussed in the context of Servetus's contribution to medical science. But the discussion of the heart, lungs, and blood occupies less than ten percent of book 5 — a little over three pages out of 36. It seems that those three pages are of greater importance to later generations than they were to Servetus himself. Therefore, let us consider the structure and content of book 5 in its entirety.

As this book, "Concerning the Holy Spirit," is the last of the "Five Books on the Trinity," we might expect it to talk about the place of the Holy Spirit in the Trinity. Actually, this is hardly mentioned. In book 1, Servetus argued that the Holy Spirit is not a being but an activity, or even an "accident," of God — that is, it is not an essential part of God's nature. In book 5, Servetus still described the Holy Spirit as an activity, mode, or dispensation of God, but he was no longer interested in using this to show that trinitarians are wrong to include the Holy Spirit in the Godhead. As Jerome Friedman says, in his insightful study of Servetus's theology, "In 1531 [when he wrote *On the Errors of the Trinity*] Servetus was primarily concerned with Christology from the point of view of disproving the trinity. By 1553 his interests ... encompass the entire restructuring of Christian belief."[33]

The evolution of Servetus's thinking can be seen by comparing *The Restoration of Christianity* with *On the Errors of the Trinity*. Book 1 of *Restoration* stays close to the material covered in *Errors* — so much so that, in the first volume of this series, we included book

---

[33] Friedman, *Michael Servetus*, 63.

1 of *Errors* side-by-side with book 1 of *Restoration*, for purposes of comparison. In books 2 and 3 of *Restoration*, the overlap with *Errors* is still substantial, though no longer as systematic. Books 4 and 5, however, have only a few isolated instances of overlap with *Errors*, amid a mass of new material. Moving in a direction that is more mystical but also more materialistic, in book 5 Servetus was interested in exploring the connections between air, breath, the breath of God, the Holy Spirit, and the human spirit, mind, and soul. These are all different things, but at some level, for Servetus, they are all one.

Let us consider how the topics addressed in book 5 contribute to Servetus's project of restructuring Christian belief.

The Word, the Spirit, and the Light (pages 163-168)

The opening section of book 5 is a continuation of topics discussed in book 4, such as the Word of God and the Holy Spirit, and their role in the begetting of Christ. It recapitulates the discussion in book 4 about the physical and metaphysical structure of the universe. Servetus presents ancient Greek ideas — for example, that all created things are composed of matter and form, and that matter is composed of four elements — and weaves them into a Christian narrative. Forms are made of light; God is light; the Word, the Spirit and the light are present in Christ. Also in this opening section, Servetus introduces a theme that will run throughout book 5: that the Holy Spirit may be thought of as a substance. Like a substance, it can be bestowed on people, or removed from them, or divided among many people; some people have more of it, and others less.

After this introduction, the book is divided into three sections: the relationships among the human body, soul, and spirit; the nature of the Holy Spirit, considered from different points of view; and the final destiny of humankind, which was, Servetus believed, to become divine.

Blood, Breath, and Spirit (pages 168-171)

This is the most famous part of the book, in which the pulmonary transit is described. First, however, Servetus must establish the equivalence of spirit and breath, pointing out that, in Hebrew and

Introduction

Greek as well as Latin, the same word is used for both. This lays the groundwork for the argument that when we breathe in air, we are breathing in Spirit. Servetus briefly summarizes the Galenic understanding of the role of the liver, the heart, the brain, the veins, the arteries, the nerves, vital spirit, and animal spirit. It is this context that he introduces the idea that the blood passes through the lungs, where it is charged with Spirit from the air — "a truth of which Galen himself was not aware."[34] He supports his new understanding of the pulmonary transit with arguments from anatomy, but the purpose of the discussion is to "understand the generation, as a substance, of the vital spirit itself."

> [Vital spirit] is composed of, and nourished by, the air that is inhaled, and the most rarefied blood ... It is generated in the lungs from a mixture of inhaled air with fine-textured, elaborated blood, which the right ventricle of the heart transmits to the left [through the lungs].

"So," he concludes, "transmission from the arterial vein [pulmonary artery] into the venous artery [pulmonary vein] in the lungs occurs for the sake of the spirit."[35]

The Brain (pages 171-177)

In view of how much attention has been focused on the three pages dealing with the heart and lungs, it may come as a surprise that a second, rarely discussed, physiological section, on the brain, is over twice as long.

The discussion of the brain begins with a description of the refinement of vital spirit in the smallest and most delicate blood vessels of the brain, to produce animal spirit. Just as vital spirit is transmitted through the arteries, animal spirit is transmitted through the nerves, which were believed to be hollow tubes much like the blood vessels. This section continues with a long and extremely technical description of the anatomy of the brain, drawn

---

[34] *Restoration*, 171.
[35] *Restoration*, 170-171.

almost entirely from Galen. This includes descriptions of the bones of the skull, the cranial nerves and blood vessels, and the various layers of the membrane surrounding the brain. It discusses details of structures that are, even today, unlikely to be familiar to a lay audience: the fornix, the infundibulum, the vermis cerebelli, and the quadrigeminal bodies. However, the only structures of the brain that are really relevant to Servetus's argument are the ventricles, or cavities in the brain.

In living animals the ventricles contain cerebrospinal fluid, but neither Galen nor Servetus describe them as fluid-filled; this may not have been apparent in the dissection of dead bodies. Servetus repeatedly refers to the ventricles as "empty spaces."[36] The ventricles — including the choroid plexus, which is a complex of blood vessels located in the ventricles — are described as the site of everything interesting that happens in the brain. They contain the mind, the spirit, and the soul. (The "soft mass" of the brain outside the ventricles is described as "cold and without sensation ... a cushion for the above-mentioned vessels, so that they do not rupture."[37])

The ventricles were thought to be open to the air, through the nose, so that air and spirit could be inhaled, and waste products exhaled. The action of the mind was conceived as a kind of combustion, requiring a supply of air to keep it alight. The ventricles were also places of spiritual warfare, since evil as well as good spirits could be inhaled from the air. The four ventricles were believed to have specialized functions: the first two for the reception of air, spirit, and sensory data; the third for thinking; and the fourth for memory.

The Substance of the Soul (pages 178-182)

This is the section of book 5 most influenced by Servetus's study of Hermetic and Neoplatonic writings. In this section, but nowhere else in book 5, Servetus cites Plato's dialogues and works attributed

---

[36] *Restoration*, 172, 174, 175, 176.

[37] *Restoration*, 172.

Introduction

to Zoroaster, Hermes Trismegistus, and Pythagoras, all mediated through the writings of the Neoplatonist philosopher and translator Marsilio Ficino.

As he explained in the sections on the blood and the brain, Servetus sees the soul as both matter and spirit — united to the Holy Spirit and the ethereal world of archetypes, and also united to the material world below. For this reason, the soul can be "seduced" by the body and the senses, but it can also rise to realize its kinship with heavenly things. The heavenly, spiritual side of the human soul is what makes it possible for us to be reborn, or illuminated by the Holy Spirit. This leads to a discussion of regeneration, but since this is thematically more closely related to the final section of the book, it will be discussed below.

Finally, Servetus shows that not just the human soul, but all of creation is suffused with divinity: the Holy Spirit fills creation, as the soul fills the body.

The Nature of the Holy Spirit (pages 182-195)

The central section of book 5 is devoted to a series of meditations on the nature of the Holy Spirit. The cumulative effect of the series is to suggest that the Holy Spirit can never truly be grasped by the human mind, but only approached indirectly, through alternative models — all true, and all inadequate. The Holy Spirit is present in encounters with angels. The Holy Spirit is a divine person, just as the Son is — not, Servetus hastens to add, in the way trinitarians understand "persons," but God himself as seen through human eyes. The Holy Spirit is a mode of the divine. The Holy Spirit is a spirit of justice, convicting the world for its sin, revealing the truth of Christ and the falsehood of Satan. The Holy Spirit is God acting in the world. The Holy Spirit is the spirit of Christ in us, causing us to be born again, to know ourselves as brothers and sisters of Christ and beloved children of the Heavenly Father.

The Spirit of Regeneration (pages 181-182 and 195-198)

It is in his discussion of rebirth or regeneration that Servetus makes his boldest claim, which amounts to nothing less than a blurring of the distinction between humanity and God. "The [human] soul is not God, but through [the Spirit of grace] the soul is made God."[38] "Our very own spirit is God, proceeding and being born from God, just as Christ is God, having proceeded and been born from God."[39] "We are one with him in substance, just as he is one with the Father."[40]

Servetus speaks of a "hypostatic union" between the Holy Spirit and the human soul — language that is usually used only for the union of the divine and human natures of Christ.

> The soul is in the Holy Spirit and the Holy Spirit is in the soul. Just as God is in Christ, Christ is in God, and Christ is God while remaining a human being, so the soul, by its rebirth on high, becomes the Holy Spirit through hypostatic union, yet remains the soul. In this way a human being becomes God and becomes one with God.[41]

All of the preceding sections of book 5 — on the Holy Spirit, the human mind and soul, and the way the spirit functions in the body — have been leading up to this. The implications are far-reaching, and will be explored further in the discussion below.

Key Concepts in Book 5

The Higher Elements and the Substance of God

Servetus's claim that human beings can become God is sensational, but it grows naturally from a seed planted inconspicuously in book 4 of *Restoration*. "Water, air, and fire possess a kind of heavenly matter distinct from earthy matter ... [This is] something unknown to all philosophers, and is related to knowledge of Christ."[42]

In book 5, Servetus expanded this, connecting the three higher, or "heavenly," elements with the Word, the Spirit, the begetting of

---

[38] *Restoration*, 181.
[39] *Restoration*, 197.
[40] *Restoration*, 195.
[41] *Restoration*, 195.
[42] *Restoration*, 159.

Christ, the soul, light, and the archetypes or forms that are made of light. Binding all of these together is the image of the cloud of the oracle of God. This is the pillar of cloud that guided the Israelites through the desert, and from which God spoke to Moses; the cloud that overshadowed Mary at the begetting of Christ; the cloud from which the voice of God said, "This is my beloved son"; and the cloud in which the Son of Man will appear in glory after the Great Tribulation.[43]

> The Word brought forth by breath was truly the Word spoken from the cloud; it was the seed of the begetting of Christ, containing in itself the Spirit in substantial form ... The cloud of the Word and the Spirit of God was, in its inner substance, the archetype of this watery and airy cloud. And it was a shining cloud, as if on fire. And all of this is one substance: because there is one primary substance of these three elements, which is corporeal, spiritual, and shining with light. In one mode of divine dispensation, the elementary substance of the cloud becomes a tangible solid body; in another it becomes a breath of wind. It is the very same substance, always possessing an innate light. In one mode God appeared as the Word in the cloud. In another he was there sending forth his Spirit ... In either mode he is always light, truly and substantially.[44]

This passage, so rich in symbolic and allusive language, sounds like poetry, so that it is easy to miss the extraordinary claim contained within it: "there is one primary substance of these three elements, which is corporeal, spiritual, and shining with light."[45] In other words, there is a substance, made of the familiar elements of water, air, and fire, that is both corporeal and spiritual. Mixed with the lower element of earth, it is the stuff of our everyday world. In its

---

[43] See Ex 13:21-22, Num 14:14 (pillar of cloud); Ex 33:9 (God speaks to Moses); Luke 1:35 (begetting of Christ); Matt 17:5, Mark 9:7, Luke 9:35 (voice from the cloud); Matt 21:27, Rev 14:14 (Son of Man coming in glory).

[44] *Restoration*, 164-165.

[45] The word translated here as "shining with light" is *splendens*. It is related to another key term, *splendor*, which Servetus introduced in book 4 as one of the basic components of the universe. See A.R5.2.

pure form, it is the stuff of the Word, the Spirit, and the soul — the stuff of God. Servetus is very insistent on this point. Note how many times the words "substance," "substantial," and "substantially" appear in this passage. Indeed, "substance" could be said to be the key word of book 5.

The idea of a substance that is both earthly and heavenly underlies the physiological sections of book 5. If the Holy Spirit is a substance, it can fill the air around us; it can be breathed into our lungs; and it can be incorporated into the human body, mind, and spirit. "In us there is a threefold spirit — natural, vital, and animal — formed from the substance of the three higher elements."[46] "The vital spirit ... is a bright vapour made from very pure blood, containing in itself the substance of water, air, and fire."[47] Memories "are stored in the very substance of the soul, as if in some material substance."[48]

For Servetus, there is no unbridgeable gap between God and not-God. Rather, there is more of a continuum, mediated by the three higher elements. Moreover, all of this is without reference to Christ or Christianity. It is the natural condition, not just of the human body, but of all creatures, great and small. In fact, not just living things, but all of creation is suffused with divinity.

Calvin, for whom the difference between God and not-God was infinitely great, was quick to react to this aspect of Servetus's thinking. In a famous interchange at the Geneva trial, Calvin accused Servetus of pantheism.[49] Here is Calvin's version of the story:

> When he asserted that all creatures are of the proper essence of God and so all things are full of gods (for he did not blush to speak

---

[46] *Restoration*, 169.

[47] *Restoration*, 170.

[48] *Restoration*, 177.

[49] Servetus was not a pantheist, because he did not identify God with the universe. He is more properly described as a panentheist, a term coined in the nineteenth century for one who believes that the divine is present in every part of the universe and also exists apart from creation. Servetus expressed this idea when he wrote, "the Holy Spirit, a mode of the Divine, is understood to be separate and apart from creation, but nevertheless the whole ... is one Holy Spirit ... Deity in a stone is stone, [deity] in gold is gold, and [deity] in wood is wood." *Restoration*, 182.

and write his mind in this way), I, wounded with the indignity, objected: "What, wretch! If one stamps the floor would you say that one stamped on your God? Does not such an absurdity shame you?" But he answered, "I have no doubt that this bench or anything you point to is God's substance." And when again it was objected, "The devil then will be substantially God?" he broke out laughing and said, "Can you doubt it? This is my fundamental principle: that all things are a part and portion of God, and the nature of things is the substantial spirit of God."[50]

Human Nature and Original Sin

Servetus's view of human nature was Pelagian. Pelagius (c.355-c.420), a contemporary and opponent of Augustine, taught that human beings are free to choose either sin or righteousness — though in practice all people choose sin, at least some of the time. Pelagius thought that we need divine grace to strengthen us and help us to choose the good, but not to overcome a hereditary taint caused by Adam's sin, that prevents us from even willing the good. Pelagianism was condemned as a heresy at the Council of Carthage in 418.

Like Pelagius, Servetus denied original sin. This is only touched upon briefly in book 5, but it is discussed at greater length elsewhere in *Restoration*. In book 5, Servetus writes, "Humankind, which was once justly punished by God, is now justly freed by Christ's mercy."[51] He then dismisses the subject, saying, "We will explain all of this in more detail in the book on original sin, since here, in the section on the Holy Spirit, is not the right place for it." Upon turning to "the book on original sin,"[52] we find in the very first paragraph a ringing denunciation of the whole idea:

---

[50] *Calvini opera* 8:496. Translated by Roland H. Bainton in *Hunted Heretic*, 127.

[51] *Restoration*, 189. In book 3 Servetus explained that Adam's sin had the effect of causing the face of God to be hidden, as by a veil. In the incarnated and risen Christ, the veil is torn away, and we can once more see the face of God, as we were meant to see it. Christ, the second Adam, has effectively healed the damage done by the first Adam. See *Restoration*, 94.

[52] The "book on original sin" is "On the Destruction of the World, and its Restoration by Christ," the first of the "Four Books on Heavenly Regeneration and the Kingdom of the Antichrist." *Restoration*, 357-409.

> Various ideas have been put forth by many people, concerning the primal sin of Adam, by which our first parent lost the world; and concerning [the idea that all human beings are consequently] marked by the guilt of original sin. Some say that children possess certain qualities, others say that they lack certain qualities; however, all affirm that on account of these qualities they will be cast into eternal hell. But I will accept only what is clearly taught in the Gospels and in Genesis. I cannot condemn these little ones to a future hell, when neither the Israelites themselves, nor the Ninevites, nor the other barbarians, are thus condemned in the Scriptures. The unbaptized little ones are blessed by Christ. How could he — the mildest and most merciful Lord, who freely bore the sins of the wicked — so harshly condemn those who have done nothing wrong?[53]

Of course, human beings can and do commit sinful actions. But Servetus set quite a high bar for declaring an action to be sinful. In order for an act to rise to the level of a sin, it must be committed wilfully, with full understanding that it is wrong. This requires a person to be capable of understanding the difference between good and evil, which Servetus thought took place around age 20.[54] He also believed that God reveals himself differently in different times and places, so that what is sinful for the Israelites may not be sinful for the Ninevites, and what is sinful for Christians may not be sinful for Jews.[55]

Servetus's view of human nature explains his opposition to infant baptism, which most Christians view as a sacrament for washing away original sin. As an Anabaptist — which he was by the time he wrote *Restoration* — he believed that baptism is a personal covenant with God that can only be made by someone sufficiently mature to understand what it means. But he did not believe that this was sufficient; he argued that baptism also requires repentance and renunciation of sin, which presupposes that the person has lived in the world long enough to experience sin and evil firsthand.[56] He

---

[53] *Restoration*, 357.

[54] *Restoration*, 363.

[55] *Restoration*, 359. Jerome Friedman sees in this the seeds of cultural relativism and universalism. Friedman, *Michael Servetus*, 57.

[56] *Restoration*, 368.

therefore recommended baptism at age 30, following the example of Christ.[57]

Given what Servetus has said in book 5 about the Holy Spirit, we can understand why original sin had no place in his world view. For Calvin and the Reformed tradition, the consequence of Adam's sin is separation or alienation from God.[58] But is it really possible to be separated from God, if we are taking in the Spirit of God with every breath?

Regeneration and Deification

The idea that Christians can share in Christ's divinity has a long history and is, is fact, entirely orthodox. It holds a central place in the Eastern Orthodox tradition, where it is called *theosis*, or deification: a union with the risen Christ so complete that the believer shares in Christ's deity and immortality. The Roman Catholic catechism asks, "Why did the Word become flesh?" and answers:

> The Word became flesh to make us *"partakers of the divine nature"*: "For this is why the Word became man, and the Son of God became the Son of man: so that man, by entering into communion with the Word and thus receiving divine sonship, might become a son of God." "For the Son of God became man so that we might become God." "The only-begotten Son of God, wanting to make us sharers in his divinity, assumed our nature, so that he, made man, might make men gods."[59]

Although Servetus's language of deification is similar to that used by the Church Fathers, there is a subtle, but very important

---

[57] *Restoration*, 526-528.

[58] According to Calvin, the consequence of Adam's sin is "estrangement from God." *Institutes*, 5th ed. (1559) 2.1.5. This is echoed in the Westminster Shorter Catechism (1648), a foundational document of the Reformed tradition in the English-speaking world: "All mankind by their fall lost communion with God."

[59] *Catechism of the Catholic Church*, 2nd ed. (Washington, DC: United States Catholic Conference, 1992, rev. 2016), par. 460. https://www.usccb.org/sites/default/files/flipbooks/catechism/ accessed 5 Mar 2025. This is supported by references to the Bible (2 Pet 1:4); Irenaeus, *Adversus haereses* 3.19.1 (PG 7 939); Athanasius, *De incarnatione* 54.3 (PG 25 192B); and Thomas Aquinas, *Opuscula* 57.1-4.

difference. Mainstream Christians are careful to specify that human beings may, by the grace of God, become adopted children of God, heirs of Christ, or members of the body of which Christ is the head.[60] However, they can never truly become God, or gods, or children of God in the same way that Christ was the Son of God. Augustine explained the difference:

> If we have become children of God, we have also become gods: but this is by virtue of having been adopted by grace, not begotten by nature. For only the Son of God, our Lord and Saviour Jesus Christ, is God — one God with the Father, the Word that was in the beginning, the Word that was with God, and the Word that was God. The others that are made gods are made by his grace, not born from his substance ... For we are not like God in the same way as [Christ] is. He is like the one by whom he was begotten. We are similar, not equal; he is equal, and therefore similar.[61]

Since Servetus saw the material world as interpenetrated with the substance of God, he saw no reason why Christians should not be united with God in substance as well as in spirit. "Through Christ," he wrote, "the creature is united with the Creator: conformed to him, intermingled and joined with him in the flesh as in the spirit, made hypostatically one with God. This is the great mystery: our union in substance with the Father through the Son."[62]

A human being is united with God by being regenerated, or reborn, with the aid of the sacrament of the Lord's Supper. Servetus thought of this as a physical, material process, affecting the flesh as well as the spirit. The regenerated spirit contains the same "super-elemental" substance that is found in "the spirit of God, which is the spirit of the begetting of Christ, from which angels and souls emanated."[63] Through this union, the regenerate person shares in Christ's incorruptibility and immortality. Servetus uses the key

---

[60] See Rom 8:14-17; 12:4-5; Gal 4:5; Eph 1:5.
[61] Augustine, *Enarratio in psalmum* XLIX (PL 36 565).
[62] *Restoration*, 166.
[63] *Restoration*, 181.

words "elements" and "substance" to indicate that this incorruptibility and immortality is of the body as well as the soul.

> There is born within us a new, substantial, and immortal human being, made from blood and bone, who is in substance one with the soul ... After our regeneration, the spirit of Christ remains in us forever, with eternal elements as they are in the resurrected [Christ], just as his eternal flesh remains in us.[64]

This emphasis on the Lord's Supper as the means of regeneration and deification is consistent with the mature Servetus's understanding of the nature of Christ. In *On the Errors of the Trinity*, and in the parts of *The Restoration of Christianity* that stay close to *Errors*, Servetus insisted that Jesus was a real human being. It is this (along with the often-misunderstood title, *On the Errors of the Trinity*) that has led to the idea that Servetus had a "low" Christology — that he was an Arian or proto-unitarian.[65] Even in *Errors*, however, Servetus asserted that Christ was both the Son of God and God himself.[66] By the time he wrote the new parts of *Restoration*, Servetus's Christology was very "high" indeed. The man Jesus is all but forgotten.[67] Servetus's Christ does not have a dual nature, divine and human. He is the human face of God — the only way that the infinite God can be seen and known by the finite human mind — but his true nature is entirely divine.[68] Not just his spirit, but his flesh is of "divine substance, in the heavenly elements and the substantial form of light."[69] When human beings partake of this celestial Christ in the Lord's Supper, it is no wonder that they are infused with divinity.

---

[64] *Restoration*, 196.

[65] Hughes, introduction to *On the Trinity and the Bible*, 36-42.

[66] *Errors*, 2r-6r.

[67] In book 5, Servetus mentions Jesus only four times, and three of these are in quotations from the Bible (pp. 167, 190, and 192). The only other use of the name "Jesus" is on p. 186, where Servetus says that the Father manifests himself and communicates to the world "through Jesus Christ alone."

[68] Hughes, "The Christology of Michael Servetus." See also Hughes, introduction to *On the Mysteries of the Word*, 3-6.

[69] *Restoration*, 194.

Introduction

An Ending and an Invitation

And so we arrive at the end of the "Five Books on the Trinity," and of our project of producing an annotated edition of this opening section of Servetus's *magnum opus*. It has been the intent of the translators and editors to introduce readers to the thought of Servetus and to situate it in the context of the religious and philosophical ferment of his times. Then we can know him not just as a victim of religious intolerance, but as a bold and original thinker. And perhaps we can reflect on whether and in what ways we might consider him a spiritual ancestor.

Book 5 is the keystone of *Restoration*. It is the link that connects the books on the Trinity to the sections that follow: on the difference between the Law and the Gospel, on the sacraments, and on the mysteries of regeneration. It bids us not to stop here, but to continue learning about Servetus and his world. It leads on.

THE RESTORATION
OF CHRISTIANITY

DE TRINITATE
DIVINA LIBER QVINTVS,
in quo agitur de Spiritu Sancto.

DE spiritu sancto sermonem distulimus, donec esset cognita hypostasis verbi prolatione patefacti: quoniam relationem ad verbum hic passim faciemus, in verbo spiritum cognituri. Quemadmodum Dei essentia, quatenus mūdo manifestatur, est verbum: ita quatenus mundo communicatur, est spiritus: estq́ manifestationi annexa communicatio. Quemadmodum in verbo erat idea princeps creati hominis, ita in spiritu erat idea princeps creati spiritus. Erat spiritus in archetypo, spirationis constitutio certa, sempiternè in Deo constans, & inde velut exiens. Prodibat cum sermone spiritus, Deus loquendo spirabat. Sermonis & spiritus erat eadem substantia, sed modus diuersus. Ad quam rem sunt aliquot similitudines, si hoc benè prius cogites, Deū immensum, qui creaturis vniuersis est essentialiter conformatus, & exhibitus, se homini multò magis conformasse, & essentialiter exhibuisse, per sermonem & spiritum. Ob idq́ sermonis & spiritus Dei imago ab initio fuit sermo & spiritus noster, seu sermo & halitus noster. In sermone nostro est spiritus, & re ipsa nō differt à sermone spiritus, sed dispensationis modo, ita in Deo. Si virtute Dei fieret, vt me loquente tu in voce mea hominem videres, id videres, quod vox ipsa significat, diceres, in sermone meo visibili esse spiritum inuisibilem, auditu perceptibilem. Diceres quoque, in spiritu esse sermonem, in substantia spiritali situm. Ad eūdem modum, in sermone Dei erat spiritus,

On the Divine Trinity

Book 5

Concerning the Holy Spirit

[163] We have postponed the discussion of the Holy Spirit until we were familiar with the hypostasis[1] of the Word, revealed by its utterance — because we will here be making frequent reference to the relation [of the Spirit] to the Word. For it is through the Word that we shall come to understand the Spirit.

<u>Just as the essence of God, insofar as it is manifested to the world, is the Word; so insofar as it is communicated to the world, it is the Spirit.</u>[a] <u>And this communication is closely connected with that manifestation.</u> Just as the original ideal form of the creation of humanity was present in the Word, so too the original ideal form of the creation of the [human] spirit was present in the Spirit. <u>This was the Spirit as an archetype, a certain arrangement of breath, which is eternally present in God, and [forever] coming forth from him.</u> The Spirit proceeded with the Word, since God breathed out as he was speaking. The Word and the Spirit were the same substance, but their modes of activity were different.

---

[a] See the opening paragraph of *Restoration*: "The manifestation of God himself through the Word, and his communication by means of the Spirit, both become substance in Christ alone."

[*The Word, the Spirit, and the Light*]

To begin with, if you think about it carefully, you will see a number of similarities [between the Word and the Spirit]. For the infinitely great God, who, in his essence, conforms himself to every created thing, conformed himself far more to a human being, and thus revealed his essence far more, by means of the Word and the Spirit. For this reason, our own word and spirit — that is to say, our speech and our breathing — were, from the beginning, an image of the Word and the Spirit of God. In our speech there is spirit, and in itself, except in the manner of its dispensation, it does not differ from the speech of the Spirit in God. If, by God's power, when I speak to you, you could see a human being in my voice; if you could see what the voice itself signifies, then you would say that, in my visible speech, there is an invisible spirit which is audibly perceptible. You would also say that in my spirit there is a word, located in spiritual substance. In the same way, the Spirit was in the Word of God, **[164]** and the Word was in the Spirit—the visible Word and the perceptible Spirit. For just as in God there was a man, so too in God there was the spirit of this man. The whole mystery of the Word and the Spirit blazed forth in the glory of Christ. When God breathed out Christ, through him he breathed out everything that is, and fulfilled all things when he revealed the fullness of his own Spirit.

Here is another similarity to the Word and Spirit of God: the image of the heavenly Word, or the cloud of the oracle, is the cloud of [earthly] elements. This is the substance of the wind, which goes everywhere in the wind. Thus God is both Word and the Spirit, Word and Spirit being variously distributed into the body and the soul.

A third likeness [to the Word and the Spirit] is the generative seed, which is the substance of the

Spirit. For in Christ was both the seed of the Word and the substance of the Spirit from a single deity. Scripture teaches these likenesses; the very nature of things also teaches us, guiding us from created things to the Creator. <u>Why is it any cause for wonder that God took the form of a human being, when he has already conformed himself to every created thing? This omniform essence had the power to present itself however he wished. This presentation, which contained breath,</u> the Word brought forth by breath, was truly the Word spoken from <u>the</u> cloud; it was the seed of the begetting of Christ, containing in itself the Spirit in substantial form.

Light has always been considered to be shared by the Word and the Spirit. The cloud of the Word and the Spirit of God was, in <u>its inner</u> substance, the archetype of this watery and airy cloud. And it was a shining cloud, as if on fire. And all of this is one substance: because there is one primary substance of these three elements,[a] which is corporeal, spiritual, and shining with light.[2] In one mode of divine dispensation, the elementary substance <u>of the cloud</u> becomes a tangible <u>solid</u> body; in another it becomes a breath <u>of wind</u>. It is the very same substance, always possessing an innate light. In one mode God appeared as the Word in the cloud. In another he was there sending forth his Spirit. In either mode he was always light—truly without any illusion. In one mode, he is the Word in the flesh; **[165]** in another he is the Spirit in the soul. In either mode he is always light, truly and substantially.[3]

Just as God was the Word, the Spirit, and the light in the cloud, so too are the Word, the Spirit and the light now present in Christ. God united all of these <u>in</u>

---

[a] That is, the three "higher" elements: water, air, and fire. See A.R5.35 and *Restoration*, 159 (book 4).

Christ, hypostatically and substantially, in flesh and in spirit. In Christ God united his own uncreated light with created light, and it was a single form—just as, as I have said, one form is made from combining solar and aqueous light.[a] Also, in the generation of the one Christ, the lower [elements] are united in substance with the higher elements of the archetypal world.[b] Thus, to sum up: the recapitulation[4] of all things is gathered as one in Christ.[c] With the divine Word as the dew of Christ's begetting, intermingling with the created elements of the earth through the activity of the Spirit of God, the body of Christ came into existence. When both divine and human breath had coalesced and been implanted in his soul, a single hypostasis of his spirit came into existence, which is the hypostasis of the Holy Spirit, revealing [for the first time] the true hypostasis of the Holy Spirit itself, which has always been the divine breath. The same light was shared by both the body and the spirit, and glorified the human elements taken from Mary, in one hypostasis with God. Behold, all things are one in Christ.

Notice that in archetype, the Word, the Spirit, and the light are one and the same; and the same cloud is simultaneously watery, airy and fiery.[d] In the book of Genesis, however, the Word and the Spirit are mentioned before the light, and water and air before fire. God made use of the dispensation of the Word and the Spirit before the light appeared (Genesis 1[e]—because the light of Christ was to be revealed at

---

[a] See A.R5.2. [b] See A.R5.35. [c] Eph 1:10. [d] See *Restoration*, 159: "Just as our paternal seed is watery and filled with an airy and fiery spirit, so too [was] the cloud of the oracle of God, acting as if it were watery, airy, and fiery." [e] Gen 1:1-3. The word of God is not mentioned in Genesis 1, unless it is the "said" in "God said, let there be light." Spirit is mentioned in Gen 1:2: "the spirit of God was hovering over the face of the waters."

a later time. Water and spirit are mentioned in this passage, but not fire, which was subsequently composed of both spirit and light.[a]

The Jews were acquainted with two heavens, the watery one and the airy one, but not the fiery third heaven <u>which is within us</u>.[b] Among the Jews there was no regeneration <u>of baptism</u> by water, spirit, and fire. Christ, the Light of the World, revealed to us the true light which was hidden from the Jews. Therefore it is not without mystery[c] that [mention of] fire was omitted by Moses [in chapter 1 of Genesis].[d] For that fire was sent down to us. **[166]** It is not without mystery that God made use of the dispensation of the Word and the Spirit, before he revealed the light. God <u>has always</u> bestowed the Word and the Spirit on humankind, but not the light made manifest [in Christ]. In former times God revealed himself to humanity through his word[e] and communicated with humanity through his spirit, as though he were then keeping the light of Christ hidden. *God created all things through Christ,*[f] who — in the Word, the Spirit, and the hidden light — was then with God. It was he who, coming at a later time, gave us a new birth by the Word and the Spirit, revealing the light itself, and illuminating us [with it], in order that the greatness of the glory and the grace of Christ might be visible to us. In the same way as, in the first generation, God gave the Word and the Spirit to humanity to

---

[a] See *Restoration*, 155 (book 4), where fire is said to be made from "airy matter and light." [b] On the watery and airy heavens and the third heaven, see *Restoration*, 157 (book 4). [c] In this paragraph Servetus twice uses the expression "It is not without mystery" (*non est sine mysterio*). However, the sense of the argument seems to be the reverse: it is no mystery. [d] See *Restoration*, 159 (book 4): "Moses does not mention the third heaven because [it] does not have a particular location. It is within us and, like fire, pervades everything." [e] That is, the word of God that came to the prophets. [f] Eph 3:9.

a greater degree than to other living beings, so too did he in after times give us a new birth in word and spirit by means of the Gospel. Like Christ, we are born by the Holy Spirit through the Word of God.

Making use of these two dispensations from the beginning, God created bodies by the Word and gave them life by the Spirit; just as the heavens were made by his word and all the power in them by <u>his spirit</u>. The material of <u>human beings</u> was created by his word, and the soul was put in by the Spirit. In resurrection, the parts of the body were <u>reassembled</u> by the Word or voice of God, and the soul was put in by the Spirit (Ezekiel 37).[a]

Thus God distinguishes these things, and so do we. In God, the workings of the Word and the Spirit were once of this kind, these dispensations and modes of activity being identical with God. But later, when God's mysteries were revealed in Christ, a greater distinction [between Word and Spirit] became apparent, because of a more abundant manifestation of divinity—both of them now appearing joined together in a body made of flesh and born of spirit. Through Christ, the creature is united with the Creator: conformed to him, intermingled and joined with him in the flesh as in the spirit, made hypostatically one with God. This is the great mystery: our union in substance with the Father through the Son.

The dispensation of the Spirit is the same as God [himself], and not a third metaphysical being. Although I have already demonstrated this, arguing against Peter Lombard towards the end of the first book,[b] I will now show it again. Just as what God made through the Word **[167]** is said to be made

---

[a] Ezek 37:1-14. [b] *Restoration*, 28-29, where Servetus cites numerous Bible passages that mention the Father and the Son, but no third being (e.g. Matt 23:9-10, 1 Cor 8:6, 1 John 1:3).

by himself, because God was the Word, so too when scripture speaks of things made by his Spirit, it is saying that they are made by God himself, because *God is Spirit*.[a] When the Holy Spirit spoke, it was God who was speaking *through the mouths of* the saints and *prophets* (Acts 3, Hebrews 1).[b]

Thus those things that are done by means of the Holy Spirit, are, in some way, to be attributed to God himself. To receive *the Holy Spirit* means to *receive power from on high* through the arrival of a heavenly messenger (Luke 24 and Acts 1).[c] The Holy Spirit is God's anointing. *God* himself *anoints us* and God *is Spirit* (2 Corinthians 1 and 3).[d] God himself is the Holy Spirit in us, *because God said, I will dwell in them*, and because he said, *you are the temple of God* (1 Corinthians 3 and 6 and 2 Corinthians 6).[e] [Scripture also speaks of] *the dwelling place of God in the Holy Spirit* (Ephesians 2 and Isaiah 57).[f] *Whoever scorns us, scorns God*, because *he gave his Spirit to us* (1 Thessalonians 4).[g] Anyone who lies to the Holy Spirit is lying *not to men but to God* (Acts 5).[h] For the Holy Spirit is a mode of deity, and acts in Christ and through Christ, by [God's] dispensation. This is proven because it is called *the Spirit of Christ* and *the Spirit of the Son* (1 Peter 1 and Galatians 4).[i] Likewise it is written in Romans 8 that *the Spirit of God dwells in you. But if anyone does not have the Spirit of Christ, he does not belong to him.* <u>Because</u> *if the spirit of him —* <u>namely,</u> the Father — *who raised Jesus [from the dead dwells in you, he who raised Christ from the dead will also give life to your mortal bodies through his Spirit who dwells in you]*.[j]

---

[a] John 4:24.   [b] Acts 3:18, 21; Heb 1:1.   [c] Luke 24:49; Acts 1:8.
[d] 2 Cor 1:21-22; 3:17.   [e] 1 Cor 3:17; 6:19; 2 Cor 6:16.   [f] Eph 2:22; Isa 57:15.   [g] 1 Thess 4:8.   [h] Acts 5:3-4.   [i] 1 Pet 1:11; Gal 4:6.   [j] Rom 8:9-11. Servetus's text ends with "who raised Jesus, etc." The remainder of Rom 8:11 is shown here in square brackets.

On the basis of these words, when Hilary, speaking metaphysically, <u>that is,</u> about a real, invisible Son, says "through the Holy Spirit" in books 2 and 8 of *On The Trinity*, he sometimes means the Father, sometimes the Son, and sometimes a third being.[a] Athanasius says similar things about the spirit of these <u>three</u> beings at the beginning of the *Dialogues*.[b] But I think all <u>these</u> things can be easily understood without resorting to metaphysical beings, because the Spirit of God is said [by scripture] to be enlarged or diminished, and divided in some way. For instance, God says to Moses, *I will remove, or cut off, some of your spirit, and give a share to seventy men.*[c] Let me repeat this: in Numbers 11 [God was] removing or taking the spirit that was in Moses and giving it to seventy men. A portion <u>of [Moses's] spirit</u> was given to them, without any diminution, through a mode of divine distribution.

<u>We say that</u> the partitioning, enlargement, and diminution of God's spirit **[168]** ought to be understood according to the modes of divinity. And this is also the case when [spirits] that are truly divided are joined together.[d] The division of ministries and activities [in the early church] was made according to [God's] varied dispensation (1 Corinthians 12).[e] Also, according to [God's] dispensation, *the Spirit* is said to be *greater in Daniel* than in others (Daniel 6),[f] and the apostles were many times *filled with the Holy Spirit* (Acts 2 and 4).[g] To give the Spirit of God means, as

---

[a] Hilary, *De trinitate* 2.30, 8.25-26 (PL 10 70B-71B, 254A-255B).   [b] [Athanasius], *De unitate sanctissimae trinitatis* 1 (PL 62 240C- 241C).   [c] Num 11:16-17, 25.   [d] Possibly a reference to the unity of all believers, e.g. John 17:21, Acts 4:32, Gal 3:28.   [e] 1 Cor 12:4-11.   [f] Dan 6:3. Most modern translations say that Daniel had an excellent spirit, but the Vulgate and Pagnini's translation use the word *amplior*, greater or larger.   [g] Acts 2:4; 4:8, 31.

[scripture] says, *I will give them heart,* understanding, and intelligence.[a] Wisdom was given to Solomon,[b] which is the Holy Spirit, the spirit of wisdom. *The spirit of wisdom, counsel, knowledge,*[c] piety, and other gifts is given [by God].

[*The Human Body, Soul, and Spirit*]

[*Blood, Breath, and Spirit*]

God is said to give us his spirit, not only because of gifts like these, but because he alone breathes soul into us (Genesis 2 and 6).[d] Our soul is a lamp of God (Proverbs 20).[e] It is like a spark of the spirit of God, an image of the wisdom of God — created, of course, but very similar to [God's] spiritual wisdom — implanted in [us] and possessing the innate light of the divine. It is a spark of [God's] primal wisdom, and the very spirit of the divine. The spirit of the divine was implanted in human beings even after the sin of Adam, as God himself bears witness in Genesis, chapter 6, mentioned above.[f] Through [God's] grace, the dispensation of our life is given and sustained by his breath (Job 10, 32, and following chapters;[g] Isaiah 2;[h] and Psalm 103[i]). God himself sustains the breath of life in us by his Spirit, *giving breath to the people who live on earth, and spirit to those who walk upon it,*

---

[a] Jer 24:7; 32:39; Ezek 11:19; see also Job 32:8; Ps 119:130; Prov 2:6, etc.   [b] 1 Kg 4:29.   [c] Isa 11:2.   [d] Gen 2:7; 6:17; see also Gen 7:15, 22.   [e] Prov 20:27.   [f] In Gen 6:3, God says that his spirit may remain with a human being for 120 years. On Servetus's rejection of the doctrine of original sin, see A.R5.32.   [g] Job 10:12; 32:8; 33:4; 34:14. See also Job 27:3.   [h] Isa 2:22 is a warning to reject the idolater, "whose breath is in his nostrils" (i.e. who is but a mortal man). Servetus may have given the verse a more metaphorical interpretation, based on the Latin of the Vulgate ("whose spirit is in his nostrils") and Pagnini ("whose soul is in his nostrils").   [i] Ps 104:29.

so that we may *live, move, and have our being* in him (Isaiah 42 and Acts 17).[a]

When God summons wind from the four winds and breath from the four breaths, the bodies of the dead live again (Ezekiel 37).[b] From the breath of the air itself, God brings forth the souls of those [dead] human beings, in whom life is born from the breathing of air. Hence in Hebrew the word for soul is the same as the word for breath.[5] From the air God brings forth the soul. With that very soul he brings forth air, and the spark of the Deity himself, which fills the air. The saying of Orpheus is true: "The soul is carried by the winds, and enters [the body] from the universe by means of the breath," **[169]** as quoted by Aristotle in *On the Soul*.[c] Ezekiel teaches that the soul contains something of the elemental substance [air],[6] and God himself teaches that [the soul is in] the substance of the blood.[d]

I shall now explain this subject at greater length, so that you may understand that the substance of the Holy Spirit itself is, in its essence, united to the substance of the created spirit of Christ. I call the air "spirit," since in the sacred language [Hebrew] there is no other special name for air.[e] This shows that divine breath is in the air, which is filled with the spirit of the Lord.

So that you, reader, may have a complete understanding of how the soul and the spirit function, I shall here add divine philosophy, which you will easily understand if you have been trained in anatomy.

---

[a] Isa 42:5; Acts 17:28.   [b] Ezek 37:1-10, esp. 37:9.   [c] Aristotle, *On the Soul* 1.5 (410b). Aristotle disagrees with the Orphic saying, on the grounds that there are living things, such as plants and fish, that do not breathe. It is not known what "Orphic" work Aristotle had in mind.   [d] Gen 9:4; Lev 17:11, 14; Deut 12:23. On p. 170, Servetus himself identifies these as the chapters where God teaches that the soul is in the blood.   [e] See A.R5.5.

Book 5

[*Blood, Vital Spirit, and Animal Spirit*]

It is said that in us there is a threefold spirit—natural, vital, and animal[7]—formed from the substance of the three higher elements.[a] [Alexander of] Aphrodisias calls them three spirits.[8] Actually <u>there</u> are not <u>three, but two</u> distinct spirits. Vital spirit is transmitted through anastomoses[9] from the arteries to the veins, where it is called natural spirit.[10] First, therefore, is the blood, whose seat is in the liver and in the veins of the body. Second is the vital spirit, whose seat is in the heart and in the arteries of the body. And third, like a ray of light, is the animal spirit, whose seat is in the brain and in the nerves of the body. In all of these is the energy of the one spirit and light of God.

The development of human beings in the uterus teaches us that natural spirit is transmitted from the heart to the liver. This is because an artery, joined to a vein, passes through the umbilical cord of the fetus. Likewise, after [birth], this artery and vein remain joined together.[11] The soul, having been breathed into Adam by God, is in the heart before it is in the liver, and is transmitted from the heart to the liver. It is by breathing in through the mouth and the nostrils that the soul is brought [into the body]. The breath, however, is directed <u>to</u> the heart. The heart is the first organ to come to life and is the source of heat in the middle of the body.[b] From the liver [the heart] receives the liquid of life [blood] as its matter, and in turn gives life [that is, vital spirit, to the whole body]; just as liquid water supplies matter to the higher elements, and is brought to vigorous life by [these elements], together with light.[c]

---

[a] See A.R5.35. [b] Galen, UP 6.2. [c] See *Restoration*, 156 (book 4): "[Water supplies] the higher elements with matter, and receives from them, in turn, formative power."

[*The Soul Is in the Blood*]

The matter of the soul comes from the blood of the liver by means of a marvelous elaboration, **[170]** of which you will now hear. Hence the soul is said to be in the blood, and the soul itself is blood, or a sanguinary spirit. The soul is not said to be primarily located in the walls of the heart, or in the body of the brain, or in the liver. Rather it is in the blood, as God himself teaches in Genesis 9, Leviticus 17, and Deuteronomy 12.[a]

In this regard, we must first understand the generation, as a substance, of the vital spirit itself. It is composed of, and nourished by, the air that is inhaled, and the most rarefied blood. The vital spirit originates in the left ventricle of the heart, with the lungs greatly assisting in its generation.[b] It is a rarefied spirit, elaborated by the power of heat, of a bright colour and a fiery potency.[c] It is a bright vapour made from very pure blood, containing in itself the substance of water, air, and fire. It is generated in the lungs from a mixture of inhaled air with fine-textured, elaborated blood, which the right ventricle of the heart transmits to the left.

This transmission is not through the middle wall of the heart, as is commonly believed,[12] but, rather, this fine-textured blood is led, by consummate artistry, over a long course through the lungs. It is prepared by the lungs and rendered bright in colour, and then poured from the arterial vein [pulmonary artery] into the venous artery [pulmonary vein]. Next, in the venous artery, [this blood] is mixed with inhaled air, and by exhalation it is cleansed of dark impurities. And, at last, the entire mixture, suitable material for

---

[a] Gen 9:4; Lev 17:11, 14; Deut 12:23. [b] Galen, PHP 6.6.
[c] Galen, PHP 6.4.

Book 5

the production of vital spirit, is drawn by diastole into the left ventricle of the heart.[13]

The communication <u>and the various interconnections</u> in the lungs, between the arterial vein [pulmonary artery] and the venous artery [pulmonary vein], <u>show that the communication and preparation [of the blood]</u> is accomplished by the lungs. This is confirmed by the remarkable size of the arterial vein [pulmonary artery], which would neither be made the kind of vessel it is, nor be as large as it is, nor would it drive such a great quantity of the purest blood from the heart to the lungs, merely to nourish them. Nor would the heart serve the lungs in this way—especially since, in the embryo, the lungs received nourishment from another source. For the little membranes or **[171]** valves of the heart do not open until the moment of birth, as Galen teaches.[a] Therefore, it is for another purpose that blood begins to be poured so copiously from the heart into the lungs at the moment of birth. Likewise, it is not just air, but rather air mixed with blood, that is sent from the lungs to the heart through the venous artery [pulmonary vein].

Therefore, the mixing [of air with blood] takes place in the lungs. The bright colour is given to this spiritous blood by the lungs, not by the heart. The left ventricle is not large enough for such copious mixing, nor is there room to elaborate [the blood] sufficiently to produce its bright colour. Finally, the middle wall [of the heart], being devoid of vessels and any means [of communication between the ventricles], is unsuited for the transmission or elaboration [of blood], although some blood may possibly seep through.[b] By the same

---

[a] Galen, UP 15.6. See also A.R5.11.　[b] The word translated here as "seep" is *resudare*, literally "sweat." Vesalius used the same word in *Fabrica* (1543), 589. See appendix C.

artistry by which transmission from the portal vein to the vena cava occurs in the liver for the sake of the blood, so also, in the lungs, transmission from the arterial vein [pulmonary artery] into the venous artery [pulmonary vein] occurs for the sake of the spirit. If anyone compares what I have just said with what Galen writes in books 6 and 7 of *On the Usefulness of the Parts [of the Body]*, he will fully understand [that what I am describing is] a truth of which Galen himself was not aware.

[*The Brain*]

[*Animal Spirit*]

Thus the vital spirit is poured from the left ventricle of the heart into the arteries of the entire body in such a way that the part of it which is more rarefied moves toward the upper part [of the body], where it is further elaborated. [It moves] <u>especially</u> into the retiform plexus,[14] which is located beneath the base of the brain, close to the seat of the rational soul. It is further <u>refined</u>, elaborated and perfected by the fiery power of the mind in the very fine vessels, or capillary arteries, which are located in the choroid plexuses.[a] [These plexuses] contain the very mind itself. They penetrate into all the innermost spaces of the brain, and cover the inside of the ventricles of the brain. These vessels, enfolded and interwoven, extend right up to the place of the origin of the nerves, in order to produce in them the power of sensation and movement.

---

[a] The choroid plexus is a complex of arteries, veins, and capillaries located in the ventricles of the brain. The vessels of the choroid plexus are lined with specialized cells that produce cerebrospinal fluid and serve as a barrier between the blood and the brain.

Although these vessels, so finely interwoven in such a wondrous way, are called arteries, they are actually the ends of arteries which, **[172]** with the assistance of the cerebral membranes [meninges], extend to the place of the origin of the nerves. This is a special kind of vessel. For, just as there is in the lung a special kind of vessel, made from a vein and an artery, for transmitting [blood] from the veins to the arteries, so, too, there is a special kind of vessel for transmitting [spirit] from the arteries to the nerves. It is formed from the outer layer of an artery and the meninges — especially since the meninges themselves maintain their outer layers in the nerves.[15] Nervous sensation is not [located] in the soft matter of the nerves, just as [it is not located in the soft matter of] the brain. All of the nerves terminate in filaments of membrane which possess the most delicate sensing ability. It is for this reason that spirit is always transmitted in them. From these small vessels of the membranes or choroids, therefore, the luminous animal spirit, like a ray of light, is poured, as from a fountainhead, <u>through the nerves</u> into the eyes and the other sensory organs. By the same path, but in a reverse direction, the <u>luminous</u> images of the objects of sensation, arriving from without, are sent to the same fountainhead, as if penetrating inwardly through the luminous medium [of spirit].[16]

From all of this, it is evident that it is not correct to say that the soft mass of the brain is the seat of the rational soul, since it is cold and without sensation. Rather it serves as a cushion for the above-mentioned vessels, so that they do not rupture. And it protects the animal spirit, so that it does not blow away when it needs to be transmitted to the nerves. It has to be cold in order to temper the fiery heat contained in these vessels.[17] Hence, also, so that the nerves may act as faithful protectors of the spirit, the previously mentioned vessels maintain a shared outer layer with the membrane in the inner cavity.[a] And [the brain is surrounded] by a thin membrane [pia mater], as also by a thick outer layer [dura mater].

[The Brain, the Mind, and the Soul]

Furthermore, those empty spaces in the ventricles of the brain, which philosophers and physicians regard with wonder, contain nothing less than the soul itself. But the main reason that these ventricles were created is to receive, like sewers, the waste products of the brain, as shown by the passages [from the ventricles] to the palate and the nose, from which unhealthy discharges flow. And when the ventricles become so filled with mucus that the arteries of the choroid plexus are immersed in it, **[173]** apoplexy quickly develops. If a noxious humour, whose vapour infects the mind, obstructs a part [of the brain], epilepsy is produced, or some other disease near that part [of the brain], in which the expelled [humour] settles.

Thus we can say that the mind is located in that place, where we can clearly observe it being afflicted. Excessive heating of these vessels, or inflammation of the meninges, causes unmistakable delirium and madness. Hence we conclude—from the accidents and diseases [that affect them], from their location and substance, from the force of heat and the ingenious beauty of the vessels that contain it, and from the actions of the soul that are evident in them—that the small vessels are of the greatest importance, because all the rest [of the vessels] serve them, and because the sensory nerves are attached to them, so that they receive their power from them. Finally, [we can perceive the

---

[a] See A.R5.15.

importance of these vessels] because we can observe the intellect working there, when, deep in thought, we see the pulsing of the arteries that lead to the temples. Anyone who has not observed the place [where this happens], will hardly understand this.

These ventricles were also created for another reason: so that a portion of inhaled air, drawn by diastole into the very vessels of the soul, penetrating the hollow spaces through the ethmoid bones,[18] might renew the animal spirit contained within, and provide ventilation for the soul. In these vessels are the mind, the soul, and the fiery spirit, which require constant fanning. Otherwise, [the mind and spirit] would suffocate, as an ordinary fire does when it is covered up. Like a fire, [the mind] requires fanning and ventilation, not only to obtain fuel from the air, but also to expel its impurities. Just as external elemental fire, having the fluid of a body as fuel, and being ventilated, maintained, and nourished by the air, is bound to a dense earthly body because of shared dryness and a shared form of light; in the same way our fiery spirit and soul, having blood for fuel, and ventilated, maintained, and nourished by an airy spirit through our inhalation and exhalation, are bound to our body, forming a unity with it. Thus we have twofold nourishment, spiritual and corporeal.

Here, in the same luminous place where the spiritual [fire] is kindled, just as spirit is drawn to this place when we inhale, it is certainly fitting that the nature of our spirit should be inspired **[174]** by another holy, heavenly, and luminous spirit, exhaled from the mouth of Christ. It is fitting that the place in which our understanding and luminous soul are located should be further illuminated by the light of another, heavenly fire. For God, who lit the first lamp in us, again turns our darkness into light, as it says in

Psalm 17[a] and 2 Samuel 22.[b] And this is what Elihu also teaches in chapters 32 and 33 of Job.[c] Zoroaster, [Hermes] Trismegistus, and Pythagoras, as I will soon show,[d] taught the same thing.

The formation and tempering of the vessels [where the soul resides] produces a healthy state of mind, because the soul is in a better state when those [vessels] are better arranged. However, just as the light which is implanted in us by a good spirit shines brighter and brighter, it is also darkened by an evil one. If a dark and wicked spirit forces its way into the vessels of the brain that contain the luminous spirit of our soul, you will see demonic madness, just as clear revelations are produced by a good spirit. Those vessels are easily attacked by a wicked spirit, which dwells <u>nearby in</u> the deep watery pits and hollows of the ventricles of the brain. That wicked spirit, whose power is of the air, <u>freely</u> enters and exits these empty spaces along with the air we breathe, so that, within those vessels, which are like the citadel [of our soul], it is in constant struggle with our spirit. Indeed, it besieges [the soul] from all sides, so that [the soul] is scarcely able to breathe, except when the light of the spirit of God arrives, driving away the evil <u>spirit</u>.

See how perfectly suited this location is to the workings of the mind, the spirit, revelation, and understanding, whether inborn or acquired — and also for the battle against the greatest temptations, not to mention lesser ones. By means of a similar kind of inhalation, the love of God is kindled in our hearts by the Holy Spirit. The heart, in addition to housing the principle of life, is the seat of the will. Because of

---

[a] Ps 18:28. [b] 2 Sam 22:29. [c] Job 33:28, 30 (not Job 32).
[d] On page 180.

the temptations of the intellect and the excitements of the flesh, it is the chief source of sin. This accords with Matthew 15.[a]

But before we move on to the heart, let us first conclude the description the brain. The activities of the mind vary according to the diversity of the brain's vessels, so that **[175]** there are different organs [of thought] in the various ventricles. These I will now explain.

A small portion of the air we inhale is transmitted, through the ethmoid bones, to the fiery animal spirit contained in the choroid vessels, and from there to the two anterior ventricles of the brain, situated on the right and left sides of the sinciput [upper part of the skull]. Here the capillaries of the choroid artery expand to draw in air to ventilate the soul. There the two optic nerves, having come together, deliver their clear visual images. The auditory and other sensory nerves are covered by a common membrane, providing the safest and most secure protection. For if, in those empty spaces [ventricles], images and spirits were to drift together with the soul, everything would be expelled when we blow our noses, or, at any rate, when we sneeze.

If the soul were [in the ventricles] it would no longer be in the blood, since there is no blood outside the vessels. Thus the mind is very securely situated in the choroidal vessels. The membrane is very secure, and the principal sensory nerves extend into the vessels which are located in the anterior ventricles. So this is the beginning of the "common sense,"[19] the common understanding of the external senses, or the imagination: the senses are brought together and begin to be combined. The air that is breathed into the brain is

---

[a] Matt 15:18-19.

carried from the two anterior ventricles to the middle [ventricle], which is, rather, a common passageway. [The air from the anterior ventricles] comes together beneath the psalloid,[20] where we find the purest and most luminous part of the mind, containing the seeds of ideal forms, which are divinely implanted in us. <u>From the images the mind has already grasped, it can think new thoughts, or</u> organize and combine images: to deduce things from other things, to distinguish between things and, illuminated by God, to grasp the pure truth.

The [middle] ventricle is smaller and the reasoning of the intellect is <u>more excellent</u>. This is because the choroid arteries, which draw in the fiery spirit by diastole, are more abundant here. And the apprehensions of the common sense lead to more <u>and more</u> brilliant reasoning, with <u>that spiritual</u> light penetrating inward through the vessels, and deity <u>itself</u> **[176]** shining there. There is not as much empty space here as in the other ventricles. Perhaps one ought to call it a passageway rather than a ventricle, or even the long and winding path of rational inquiry. It been fashioned wisely, to suit the difficult task of rational inquiry. This ventricle is smaller [than the anterior ventricles] because this is a purer and clearer part of the mind, so it does not accumulate as much waste material. And what [waste material] is produced here flows easily and directly into the infundibulum[21] underneath, lest it extinguish or impede the light of the mind.

The blood vessels are more numerous around the conarium [pineal body],[22] with more pulsations of the arteries, producing a more powerful activity of the mind and of the fiery spirit here. Also here, near where the pulse pounds more powerfully at the temples, we can detect the working of the intellect, on the outside as well as the inside. This single observation points us directly to the exact location of the mind. In addition, this place is closer [than any other] to the sense of hearing, which is the sense of learning. The composition of the human body is a tremendous miracle!

Many and long are the winding pathways leading to the cerebellum, so that it requires careful scrutiny to investigate every twist and turn, and to illuminate the darkness. Using the imaginative faculty, what <u>was previously</u> stored away in memory can also greatly assist in this task. Here, <u>where thought is concentrated</u>, the kindling of the inhaled air is held back <u>and to a certain extent enlarged</u> by the wormlike doorkeeper [vermis cerebelli][23] and the sinuous "buttocks" [quadrigeminal bodies],[24] until, fanned and impelled by the pulsation of all the arteries of the mind, a thought is perfected, and everything is <u>clearly</u> illuminated. Thus this fiery place is especially suited for the mind, which is itself fiery and which shares in God's light. And when it conceives an idea, this is likewise a ray of light and a kind of luminous image. Even the external, perceptible likenesses of <u>things</u> that are sent to the eyes are luminous. Coming from a luminous object, or having the form of light, they are sent through a luminous medium.[a] By this means the mind itself becomes more and more enlightened.

[*The Senses*]

The intellect is not only adorned with the sense of sight, which shows us the many differences among things, but also by the objects perceived by the other senses, which all have an affinity with our luminous spirit. **[177]** This affinity derives from the substantial form of all things, which is light, as well as from the spiritual component of the action of each [of the senses].

---

[a] See A.R5.16.

Sound and odor are like spirit. They are perceived as spirit, and act in us the same way that spirit does. Perception of sound occurs at the membrane of the ear, when an external spirit strikes the internal spirit, which contains the light of the soul and the concord of spiritual harmony, regulated by the diastole and systole [of the heart]. The way in which odors are perceived is very similar. Things that are tasted and touched, although they are corporeal, nevertheless have the power to alter the soul. <u>Things that are tasted do this by means of moistness; things that are touched do it by pressure.</u> [The soul is altered] by the common form <u>of light, by means of</u> its various effects upon the spirit. By means of light, all substances act upon the soul, <u>when they</u> impress upon it the ideal form of all things. The sophists, who once taught that there was nothing to be seen either in God or in us except qualities and masks, now see the substances themselves. But we who see the substantial light in Christ, also look for a vision of the true light in other things.

After all the [sensory images] have been illuminated in the middle ventricle, the doorkeeper [vermis cerebelli][a] allows the <u>spirit itself</u> to reach the fourth ventricle, located in the parencephalon [cerebellum], and a bright image is kindled in the light of the soul itself. There, in what is actually the base of the brain, the vessels steadfastly stand guard over the treasure trove of memory, and store away the things which have been discovered by the senses and reasoning. These things are not attached to the walls [of the ventricle], but are stored in the very substance of the soul, as if in some material substance. <u>There the soul has</u> stronger vessels <u>to hold back the spirit</u>, so that memory does not flow away <u>too</u> easily.

---

[a] See A.R5.23.

Here I briefly mention that it is by this pathway that the faculty of movement of the entire body is transmitted to the muscles, radiating the animal spirit through the large nerves of the spine. <u>Accordingly there are four ventricles in the brain and three internal senses. For the first two ventricles together produce one common sense, which is the receiver of images. The middle one is for thinking and the last is for memory.</u> So much for the portion of <u>spirit</u> drawn into the brain, the organs of the brain, <u>and their powers</u>.

[*The Substance of the Soul*]

[178] Most of the inhaled air is drawn through the trachea into the lungs. It then proceeds into the venous artery [pulmonary vein], in where it is mixed with bright, fine-textured blood and further elaborated. Then the entire mixture is drawn by diastole into the left ventricle of the heart, where it is perfected by the power of the strong life-giving fire contained there. After all the impurities resulting from elaboration are exhaled, it becomes vital spirit. All this is, as it were, the matter of the soul itself.

Besides this mixture [of blood and spirit] there are two components of the soul: something created by the <u>living</u> breath, or produced by its matter; and spirit itself, or divinity instilled by breathing. All of this is one and makes up one soul. What we normally call the soul is breath and spirit, both united in its essence with the [Holy] Spirit. It is an ethereal substance, similar to its super-elemental[a] archetype, and also to this world below. It is a single natural soul: vital and animal.

---

[a] The word "super-elemental" (*superelementaris*) is used in book 3 to denote the cloud that went before the children of Israel in the desert (Ex 13:21-22; 14:24; Num 14:14). See *Restoration*, 120: "It was super-elemental, of uncreated matter, shining from within."

Behold the whole explanation of <u>the soul, and why</u> *the soul of all flesh is in the blood,* and *the soul itself is blood,* <u>as God says</u>.[a] By the breath of God, a gleam of the heavenly spirit, or spark of the ideal, was inhaled through the mouth and nostrils into the hearts and brains of Adam and his progeny. Within them, it joined its essence to the spiritual matter <u>in the blood</u>, and made a soul in their innermost parts (Genesis 2, Isaiah 57, Ezekiel 37, and Zechariah 12).[b] Following the Chaldaeans, the Academics taught that such dissimilar substances could be united in this way. They said that aether[25] was united by God to the elemental air, so that the divine mind could be sent into this solid body. The sacred scriptures teach this very clearly, speaking of the breath of God and the elemental breath.[c]

In *Timaeus*, Plato clearly teaches that the substance of the soul is a mixture of elemental and divine substances.[d] There is [in us] a third, intermediate substance, which shares in both of these. For the soul bears the signs of deity and of the world of elements. If this were not the case, a soul could not possess the powers of an intelligent mind, and also the life-giving **[179]** faculties of the body.

Hence it happens that when the soul pays heed to the senses, it is seduced by the body, loving its kinship [with the body]. But at other times, it soars on high, more influenced by its kinship with heavenly things, which it had previously neglected. In *Cratylus*

---

[a] Lev 17:11; Deut 12:23. [b] Gen 2:7; Isa 57:15-16; Ezek 37:6; Zech 12:1. [c] There are several references in the Bible to the breath of God, or to God breathing life into someone (e.g. Gen 2:7; Ezek 37:9; Job 4:9, 27:3, 33:4; Rev 11:11). There are no references to elemental breath. "Elements" in the Bible generally means worldly or corruptible things (e.g. Gal 4:3,9; 2 Pet 3:10,12). [d] Plato, *Timaeus* (69c).

Book 5

the soul, ψυχή (*psyche*), is said to be refreshed by breathing, ἀναψυχή (*anapsyche*).[26] Nevertheless, in a human being, [the soul is said] to be from the divine mind.

Just as the soul gives life to the body, so God breathes life into the soul. Isaiah teaches that spirit, which is from God, is wrapped in a breath of air.[a] And so God created passages [in the body] for the breath, because souls are clothed in air. Zechariah says that the spirit of the soul is made in a certain fashion in the innermost parts of a human being.[b] The words of Genesis confirm this. For it is not simply said that the soul is the breath of God, but rather that a living soul was formed within [the human being] by inhaled breath.[c]

In the elements of the body, just as in a seed,[d] there is a substantial symbol of the soul that is to be brought forth, as we will show further, beyond what has already been shown. There are two things in semen, which are essential for the soul, which cause the soul of a child to be similar to the soul of its father. These are: the formal or formative faculty, and the material of the spirit. The formal and formative faculty is light itself and the ideal form. The souls of other animals, and those of human beings as well, are clearly brought forth from semen. In human beings, there is the breath of the divine mind, in that ideal form which the nature of the seed requires; and the soul is formed in accordance with this.

The breath of God enters the heart and brain of a human being through the face: the mouth and nostrils. In this way the soul is formed according to the ideal

---

[a] Isa 42:5.   [b] Zech 12:1.   [c] Gen 2:7.   [d] The Latin word *semen* means both seed and semen; in this paragraph, when either word is used, it should be understood that both meanings are intended.

form of humanity. Thus God, like a potter, is called the maker of the soul (Zechariah 12).[a] [God] himself fashions the soul in the heart of each human being (Psalm 32).[b] God is called the maker of light (Isaiah 45).[c] For he actually makes the substantial forms of things in light itself, just as he makes ideal forms in the light of his mind. So God formed the soul in light, just as the soul itself later forms and fashions other images in light.

Finally, God is called *the maker of all things* (Jeremiah 10),[d] since he created nothing to which he did not give a definite form. God, the maker of all things, even gave definite forms to angels and souls. Even before we existed, God shaped us both inwardly and outwardly with wondrous artistry and manifold wisdom (Psalm 138).[e] First of all, God, conceiving all things in his mind, shaped them from eternity as patterns based upon the ideal forms in his own [divine] light. Then, bringing each of them out into the world, **[180]** he formed them as he had already pre-formed them [in his mind].

If, by inferior [human] reason, you can understand these actions, you will understand that Christ first had his form in God. From this we have [in turn] received our own [forms], formed in external, created light. In this created light, God gives a real and substantial form to all things, impressing the stamp of his light, or his ideal forms, on all things, and also infusing into humanity the breath of the divine mind. That breath of the soul, sent into us by God, is a kind of lamp or spark of [divine] light. God himself is the fire and God is the spirit, who is the source of the fiery

---

[a] Zech 12:1. The image of God as a potter is found in Isa 29:16, 64:8; Jer 18:16; Rom 9:21.   [b] Ps 33:15.   [c] Isa 45:7.   [d] Jer 10:16.   [e] Ps 139:13-16.

and spiritual soul in our fiery and airy vital spirit. The original ideal form of souls and other things is in the light [of the divine mind], and in light is the natural life, as John says.[a] It is the very light of God, *that* naturally *illuminates every human being* born *into the world* (John 1).[b]

The fountain of the soul is in the luminous Word of God, and *in his light we see light* (Psalm 35).[c] According to this understanding, the Holy Spirit given in rebirth is beautifully united with our soul, like light with light and fire with fire. Otherwise we could not speak of the rebirth of the spirit except in the likeness of the first birth and breath of God. And the new illumination is superior to the old.

Zoroaster the Chaldaean sage taught this in *Oracles of Wisdom*.[d] There [he says that] the soul, which is sent down into us from the light of God, yearns to return to that same light, to be illuminated by it, and to become fire again. He says, "You must ascend to the light itself and to the Father's rays, from which soul, wrapped in the abundant light of the mind, flows into you."[e] And, "[The soul], through the power of the Father, becomes a brilliant flame."[f] In *Pimander*, Hermes Trismegistus says, "God the Father, from whom man is born, is light and life. Therefore, if you comprehend that you yourself are made of life and light, you will climb upward again to life and light."[g] In his [*Golden*] *Verses* Pythagoras says, "Take courage, because there exists a divine race of human beings to whom sacred

---

[a] John 8:12: "I am the light of the world." [b] John 1:9.
[c] Ps 36:9. [d] That is, the Chaldaean Oracles. See A.R5.25.
[e] Chaldaean Oracles no. 7 (frag. 115), quoted in Ficino, *Theologia Platonica* 10.8.4. [f] Paraphrase of Chaldaean Oracles no. 12, 21, 15b (frags. 96, 112, 158), quoted in Ficino, *Theologia Platonica* 13.4.16. [g] *Corpus Hermeticum* 1.21.

nature reveals all things by bringing them forward into the light."ᵃ

[*The Spirit of Regeneration*]

There is a hidden light within us, a light that reveals itself in another, greater light by means of God's baptism. By the **[181]** light of Christ's life, the life of our soul goes forth at birth, as does the life of our spirit in rebirth. There is another way [of life for us], just as there was a new and different spirit in Christ himself. [The Holy Spirit] itself, which was once the spirit of Elohim, is now the spirit of the mouth of Christ, generating and regenerating (Psalm 103).ᵇ However, [it accomplishes these things] in different ways. Regeneration differs from generation, as the Spirit of grace differs from the soul we are born with. This spirit is God. The [human] soul is not God, but through [the Spirit of grace] the soul is made God. The vital spirit of the soul, and the elements which compose it, are subject to corruption. The elements of the new spirit are incorruptible, like the vital spirit that Christ now possesses in heaven. Thus the soul of all flesh is confined within limits ordained by God. The soul originates as a kind of vital vapour in the blood. The human soul originates as a kind of breath of the mind [of God] in the blood. However, the Holy Spirit of regeneration is a new breath of the Deity with the renewed elements of the regeneration of Christ.

Do not be afraid to say that both our soul and the Holy Spirit of Christ are essentially united with such an [incorruptible] elemental substance, just as the

---

ᵃ *The Golden Verses of Pythagoras* is a list of moral precepts or proverbs, authorship and date of composition unknown. It is not by Pythagoras, who left no writings. This quotation uses verses 63-64 as translated by Ficino, *Theologia Platonica* 11.5.3. See also Steuco, *De perenni philosophia* 9.21.   ᵇ Ps 104:30.

Book 5

Word is united with the flesh. The fire of our soul, and the fire of our spirit, are inseparably connected to this substance. They are sustained and nourished by it, just as the fires that we can see are sustained and nourished by liquid and air. Just as a fire is extinguished when these [substances] are lacking, so [without the elemental substance] the soul is extinguished within us, unable to perform its vital activities. Indeed, the substance of the soul, which comes from God — considered by itself, apart from these mundane elements — is like something elemental, as is also the substance of angels. For the spirit of God, which is the spirit of the begetting of Christ, from which angels and souls emanated, contained such an elemental, or superelemental, substance in the archetypal world. The spirit of the incarnated Christ now contains [this substance], along with a human spirit. The spirit of our regeneration contains this same substance, when we are born [again] by water, spirit, and the fire of heaven.[a] **[182]** Here in [the world of] created things we are to understand that there are also uncreated things. And all of these things come together into one substance [composed] of soul and spirit.

Consider the kind of substance Christ in heaven contains within himself today, what kind of breath he has, and what kind of vital spirit. For he himself is the Holy Spirit, containing these incorruptible elements within himself, united hypostatically to himself. Just as the Word of God is hypostatically a man, so too is the spirit of God hypostatically the spirit of a man. By the power of the Resurrection, however, all the elements of his body and spirit are renewed, glorified, and made incorruptible. And Christ shares all these things with us in [the sacraments] of baptism and the Lord's Supper, sharing his whole self with us. The Holy Spirit is the

---

[a] John 3:5.

breath of Christ's mouth (John 20).[a] In the same way that God breathes forth the soul together with air, so Christ breathes forth the Holy Spirit together with air.

[Divinity in Creation]

In summary, you ought to keep in mind that, just as the soul is understood to be separate and apart from air or fire, but nevertheless the whole is one soul, one idea, and one entity; just so, the Holy Spirit, a mode of the Divine, is understood to be separate and apart from creation, but nevertheless the whole — the Holy Spirit, the vital spirit of Christ — is one Holy Spirit. The addition of Deity to these things, or the addition of these things to God himself, does not change the name [of the things]. Deity in a stone is stone, [deity] in gold is gold, and [deity] in wood is wood, <u>according to their own ideal forms. Again</u>, deity in a human being is a human being, although on a more exalted level, and [deity] in spirit is spirit. So too, the addition of a human being to God is [still] God, and the addition of <u>a human</u> spirit to [the Holy Spirit] is the Holy Spirit.

[The Nature of the Holy Spirit]

[The Holy Spirit as an Angel]

The Holy Spirit is thought of as being present not only in the breath of Christ, but also in angels. Therefore one ought to consider whether an angel is the Holy Spirit, and who is this other [being], the Paraclete.[27] The ministry of an angel is associated with the outpouring of the Holy Spirit, as, for example, when a dove or tongues <u>of fire</u> were seen (Matthew 3 and Acts 2).[b] For the same reason [appearances of God in the Old Testament] are said to be by the ministry of an angel, for

---

[a] John 20:22.   [b] Matt 3:16-17; Acts 2:2-4.

events in the Law that happened by the word of God took place through the agency of angels. [For example] an angel in the person of God appeared to Moses in a burning bush (Exodus 3 and Acts 7).[a] The voice of God spoke to Moses through an angel, saying, *I am the God of your fathers.*[b] The substance **[183]** of God in the Word was present there in the manifestation of the angel, just as the substance of God in the [Holy] Spirit was present at the Jordan River, and over the Apostles [at Pentecost].[c] An angel in the person of God spoke and appeared to Abraham (Genesis 18 and 22),[d] Hagar (Genesis 16 and 21),[e] and Jacob (Genesis 31 and 32).[f] See also Joshua 5 and 6,[g] and Judges 2 and 6.[h]

In Exodus 23 God provides the explanation for this: he was the divinity, or *the name of God*, in the angel, and whoever heard the voice of the angel was hearing the voice of God.[i] Thus, just as [God's] voice from heaven was transmitted through an angel, saying, *I am the God of your fathers*, so too was [God's] voice from heaven transmitted through an angel when he said, *This is my son.*[j] Indeed, this was the voice of the Holy Spirit (Matthew 3 and Luke 3).[k] <u>For a third</u>

---

[a] Ex 3:2; Acts 7:30. [b] In Ex 3:2 an angel appears to Moses in the burning bush, but the voice that says "I am the God of your father" in Ex 3:6 is identified as that of God. This is typical of the way God and angels are treated as interchangeable in the Torah.
[c] Matt 3:16-17 (and parallel passages Mark and Luke); Acts 2:2-4.
[d] Three men (presumably angels) speak to Abraham in Gen 18:2-9. An angel speaks to Abraham in Gen 22:11, 15-18. [e] Gen 16:7-12; 21:17-18. [f] An angel speaks to Jacob in Gen 31:11-13. In Gen 32:24 Jacob wrestles with a "man," who is later revealed to be God. [g] The "Commander of the Army of the Lord" speaks to Joshua in Josh 5:13-15. In Josh 6:2-5 the Lord speaks to Joshua in his own person. [h] An angel speaks to the children of Israel in Judg 2:1-4, and to Gideon in Judg 6:11-22. [i] Ex. 23:20-23. In Ex 23:21 God commands the people to obey the voice of the angel "for my name is in him." [j] Matt. 3:17; 15:5; Mark 9:7; Luke 9:35. See also Mark 1:11; Luke 3:22. [k] Matt. 3:17; Luke 3:22.

<u>being could not have spoken the words, "*This is my son.*"</u> Therefore, the Holy Spirit was not a third being, but was a dispensation of the Deity through an angel.

Err, 61r

Hence, after the Holy Spirit descended, Christ said, *You will see the angels of God ascending, and descending upon the Son of Man* (John 1).[a] In one [account of Jesus's baptism] it says *angels descending*, in another is says *the Spirit descending*, and in a third *the Holy Spirit descending*.[b] In [the story of the conversion of the eunuch] in Acts 8 [the Holy Spirit] is first called an angel, then the Spirit, and finally the Spirit of the Lord.[c] Isidore [of Seville], speaking about the Paraclete, says, "He will announce future events to you." He supposes [the Paraclete] to be an angel, because the word "angel" means "messenger," and the Holy Spirit delivers many messages through angels.[d]

Err, 61r

All angels are ministers of the spirit (Psalm 102).[e] And Hebrews 1: God *makes his angels spirits and his ministers fiery flames.*[f] God revealed many things to the good prophets by means of his good angels, just as he chose to deceive the evil prophets by means of evil spirits (3 Kings 22, 2 Chronicles 18 and Ezekiel 14).[g] Angels entered the souls of the prophets as spirits, as, for instance, in Ezekiel and Zechariah.[h] Angels are called the spirit of falsehood, the spirit of truth, or the spirit of God.[i] An angel in human form spoke to

---

[a] John 1:51. [b] John 1:51; Matt 3:16; Luke 3:22. [c] Acts 8:26, 29, 39. [d] Isidore, *Etymologiae* 7.3.9 (PL 82 268C-D). [e] Ps 103:20-21. [f] Heb 1:7, quoting Ps 104:4. [g] 1 Kg 22:13-19; 2 Chr 18:4-22; Ezek 14:6-11. [h] Angels appear to Zechariah, e.g. in Zech 1:9-19; 2:3; 4:1-5. Cherubim appear to Ezekiel in Ezek 9:3; 10:1-19; 11:22. [i] The spirits that inspire prophets may be truthful or lying (see the story of Ahab in 1 Kg 22). We are instructed to test all spirits, to distinguish the spirit of truth from the spirit of error (1 John 4:6). None of these spirits are explicitly called angels.

the centurion, but it spoke to Peter and the others as the Holy Spirit (Acts 10, 11 and 13).[a] The Holy Spirit could not speak to the centurion, because he did not know Christ. However, in the human being who is reborn [in Christ] all things are said to be [done] by the Holy Spirit operating within. Hence in Acts, chapter 16, it is called the Spirit and the Holy Spirit,[b] <u>and</u> in [Paul's] dream of the Macedonian man an angel is <u>revealed</u>.[c] In the Bible, angels and spirits are spoken of separately. They are really the same, but there is a difference in the manner [in which they appear], just as there is a difference between the Word and the Spirit. **[184]** The Word and angels appear in a human mode, while the Spirit appears in a spiritual mode.

It is not surprising that the words or deeds of an angelic spirit may be said to be [the work of] the Holy Spirit, for the words or deeds of an apostle are [also] <u>called</u> the words or deeds of the Holy Spirit.[d] Therefore, an angel is not properly called the Holy Spirit, except in the sense in which, [in Old Testament times], an angel was called Jehovah.[e] What was done by the Word of God under the Law was done by angels. But an angel is not, on that account, said to be the Word of God—except as a kind of semblance and ministry, nor is it said to be God, except as a semblance and ministry. We attribute far less divinity to angels than did the Jews, by whom angels were once worshipped as gods.[f] Hence we conclude that neither in relation

---

[a] Acts 10:1-6 (angel); Acts 11:4-17; 13:2-10, 52 (Holy Spirit).
[b] Acts 16:6-7.   [c] Acts 16:9-10. The man in Paul's vision is not explicitly called an angel.   [d] For example, Acts 2:4; 4:8, 31.
[e] There is no place in the Bible where an angel is specifically called Jehovah/Yahweh, but there are several places where the names "Yahweh" and "angel of Yahweh" are used interchangeably. See, for example, Gen 16:7-13, Ex 3:2-4, Judg 6:11-22.   [f] See *Restoration*, 101-102 (book 3).

to Christ nor with respect to ourselves, can an angel rightly be called the Holy Spirit, but only a minister acting in the service of the Holy Spirit.

[*The Holy Spirit as the Comforter Sent by Christ*]

Thus the Holy Spirit, the Comforter, whom Christ promises will be with the apostles in the future,[a] and who was given to them in Acts 2,[b] is not primarily understood to be an angel, although <u>an angel shares</u> in its ministry. But Christ promises them another, internal Comforter in place of this external Comforter, <u>a new Holy Spirit to come</u>, which did not then exist, but which is to be given to them after the Resurrection, and will gloriously participate in an angelic ministry.

This [Holy Spirit], which is truly said for many reasons to be different from the Son, is also separate from the angelic ministry. First of all, the Spirit differs as greatly from the Son as breath does from a human being. <u>Moreover</u>, setting aside this created breath, the substance of the Holy Spirit is truly different from the substance of the Son. [The Holy Spirit] is said to be another person [*alius*] and another being [*aliud*] than Christ.[28] But if <u>the expression</u> "another being" <u>denotes to you</u> something discordant, then I will not grant that the <u>comforting</u> Spirit is another being than the Son. Indeed, they are one, just as Christ and the Father are one.[c] For they are in harmony, and they are one and the same Deity. The Deity acts now in one mode, and now in another.

Under the [Old Testament] Law, <u>such</u> a Spirit—with such an essence, distinct and visible, joined together with a human spirit in one everlasting hypostasis—was not given [to humanity]. Therefore it is now more separate [from the former angelic ministry], and

---

[a] John 14:16, 26; 15:26.   [b] Acts 2:2-4.   [c] John 10:30.

is called "another person."[a] Before the Word became a human being, the Holy Spirit, in itself, was actually **[185]** a substantial mode of the Deity, not hypostatically united with the spirit of a human being. Now it has a substantial and everlasting union with the human spirit of Christ.

Christ also spoke of the Spirit as another person than himself, since he did not possess the Spirit at the time [of his earthly ministry].[29] But, as promised by the Father, Christ received at his resurrection a new spirit of glory, which he afterwards transmitted to the apostles.[b] He calls the Holy Spirit another person, because of its surpassing glory, which had never been seen before.

[Christ says:][c] [The Holy Spirit] will be another person than the spirit which you apostles have already received. It will be a person other than me. Indeed I shall be another person, and a new human being. The quality[d] of glory in [the Holy Spirit] will be very different from what it is now.

This is why [Christ] says, *He* [the Spirit of truth] *will glorify me.*[e] After the Resurrection, so great is the glorified Christ, and the new glory of his Holy Spirit, that the angels, as Peter bears witness, would *desire to look into it*,[f] and would be struck dumb with amazement. This is because the angels, who were themselves gods among the Jews, had never beheld such a dispensation of deity under the Law. Through

---

[a] In this and the following two paragraphs, the word *alius* ("other" in the masculine gender) is translated as "another person." The word "person" is not explicitly present in the Latin. See A.R5.28.
[b] See 2 Cor 3:18; 1 Pet 4:14.   [c] This paragraph is written in the voice of Christ, but it is not a quotation or even a paraphrase of anything in the Bible. It is Servetus's imaginative reconstruction of something that Christ might say.   [d] The word translated here as "quality" is *gustus*, litreally "taste."   [e] John 16:14.   [f] 1 Pet 1:12.

Christ, a new knowledge of the Holy Spirit was given to the angels, as well as a new knowledge of God. The angels learned things about the Kingdom of Christ, which they did not previously know (Ephesians 3).[a] The Kingdom of Christ, which is given to us, is the kingdom of the Spirit. And it is said that in the spirit all things are revealed to us,[b] all things come about, and thus [all things] come about through the Holy Spirit. The Father honoured the Son with such glory, that not only is he God from God, but he also is God, from whom another God proceeds.[c] But if you find the phrase "another God" offensive, then say "another Comforter" and another person of the Deity. Christ is God, from whom other gods proceed and are born. For we are gods, proceeding from [God] himself and *born of God* (John 1).[d]

But why does Christ say about the Holy Spirit, *He will not speak on his own authority*?[e] It is because the Holy Spirit does not supply anything to anyone which is not in harmony with the Word of God. Didymus [the Blind], in the second book of *On the Holy Spirit*, explains it thus: [Christ says] *He will not speak on his own authority*, that is, not without me, but rather the mode of the divine breath will be from my will and the will of the Father.[f] Here we must ascend gradually to the source from which Christ came, **[186]** so that, through his gift, we may drink from that very source. Keep in mind, reader, that God in himself, considered apart from Christ, is so hidden, and so transcends everything, that he has nothing in common with us — nor with the angelic spirit, which he infinitely exceeds. Remember: the angels themselves do not see

---

[a] Eph 3:10. [b] John 14:26; 16:13; 1 Cor 2:10. [c] Language from the Nicene Creed: Christ is "God from God," and the Holy Spirit "proceeds from the Father and the Son." [d] John 1:13.
[e] John 16:13. [f] Didymus, *De spiritu sancto* 34.

God, nor do they have communication with his Spirit, beyond what is given [to them] through Christ. For no one sees the Father, except [the Son] alone[a] and those to whom he wishes to reveal [the Father]. And God communicates to no one by means of the Spirit, except through [the Son].

[*The Holy Spirit as a Mode of the Divine*]

Of course, there are [multiple] divine modes of vision and communication, by which the Father manifests himself to the world, and which he communicates through Jesus Christ alone. And just as he now shows [these divine modes] to us, he preformed them from eternity in accordance with the wisdom of Christ. The Holy Spirit, and its fullness in Christ, is a substantial divine mode, eternal in God. <u>This eternal mode was preformed in the mind of God.</u> This <u>shows</u> the preformation of the spirit of Christ in God. If that portion, or spark, or measure, or breath, or mode of the spirit, which was in Peter or Paul,[b] was once substantially in God, how much <u>more</u> is the fullness [of deity][c] in Christ himself? When the Holy Spirit was given to Peter and Paul, no change in God occurred, nor was anything then actually removed from him. But in receiving the [gifts of the Holy Spirit] that had been prepared for them, [Peter and Paul] were changed through union with and reception of [the spirit] that was intended for them. The spirit that was given to them was received from Christ, and prepared for them in Christ. <u>What immense preparation, and what indescribable modes!</u> *<u>The eye has not seen nor the ear heard the things that have been prepared for us.</u>*[d]

---

[a] Matt 11:27; Luke 10:22; John 14:9.   [b] Acts 4:8 (Peter), Acts 13:9 (Paul).   [c] See Col 2:9: "For in him dwells all the fullness of the Godhead bodily."   [d] 1 Cor 2:9.

Certainly the actual substance of the Holy Spirit was in the apostles. It was given to them in a certain measure, which had been prepared for them from eternity. They are said to have been truly filled with the Holy Spirit (Acts 2 and 4).[a] For [the spirit that] was in them <u>then</u> so filled them and moved them that they burst into miraculous actions. Yet the Spirit was not in them in its full plenitude and *without measure*. That was reserved for Christ alone (John 3, Romans 12, 2 Corinthians 10, and Ephesians 4).[b] Therefore we speak of a certain measure [of Spirit] as being in this **[187]** spirit, in that one, and in yet another one, and all of them being one spirit. Do not be surprised, then, if Christ said "*another Paraclete*" and "*another spirit*,"[c] since even you may speak of one here, another there, and yet another somewhere else. If you take away the sophistical realities,[30] everything will be easy.

To sum it all up, the Holy Spirit can be defined in a few [words]. The Holy Spirit is a substantial mode of the divine, adapted to the spirits of angels and human beings. Although the Holy Spirit forms a substantial unity with the sanctified creation of the Spirit that is in Christ, nevertheless, in itself, it is understood to be pure deity. In accordance with the mode of [divine] dispensation, deity is from deity, according to the succession of divine distribution; just as in branches, leaves, and flowers there is divinity from the divinity of seeds and roots, and in a sprout there is divinity from the divinity of the vine. Therefore, the Holy Spirit is truly a substantial mode [of the divine], distinct from the Father and the Son: proceeding, subsisting,

---

[a] Acts 2:4; 4:8. [b] John 3:34; Rom 12:3; 2 Cor 10:13-15; Eph 4:7. [c] John 14:16 (another Paraclete); 2 Cor. 11:4 (another spirit).

Book 5

perceptible by the senses, speaking and acting, now here and now there.

The Holy Spirit is distinct from God the Father, so that we may say that God is in the Holy Spirit, just as God was in the Word and God was in the light. The Holy Spirit is born from God, just as light is born for us from God. God is the father of the Holy Spirit, just as he is *the father of light*,[a] and *the father of glory*.[b] By the same figure of speech God is called the father of wisdom and the father of the Word — as long as you do not understand [his fatherhood] in human terms. God dwells in spirit, and *God is spirit*;[c] God dwells in fire, and God is fire. God dwells in light, and God is light. God is in the mind; he inhabits the mind; and God is mind itself.

Perhaps you will object that according to us, God's glory does not seem to be greater now than it was [before the Incarnation]. For the Spirit of God from eternity contained only the divine hypostasis, or the substantial mode of divinity, like the primal ideal form of the elemental breath in God; and now it should [also] have the elements of the human spirit of Christ, united with him in a single essence at the Incarnation. [Furthermore] the glory of God must be greater after the Resurrection than it was when Christ was active on earth. I answer that the glory of God in himself can neither be increased nor diminished. The more he glorifies us, so much greater is the glory in us. In the resurrection of Christ, God showed that his power and glory were so great, that he could create **[188]** incorruptible things from corruptible human elements. And for our glory, he could unite them to his deity with elements like his own, so gloriously that, together with

---

[a] James 1:17.   [b] Eph 1:17.   [c] John 4:24.

God, they form substantially a single spirit, which is the Holy Spirit. Anything that is in Christ is, in substance, one with God. As [Christ] himself says, *I and the Father are one*.[a]

Just as the body of Christ is so closely joined to God, that it is substantially one with him, so too is his spirit — and <u>the</u> spirit <u>of humanity</u> through him — so joined and attached to God, that it is one spirit with him (1 Corinthians 6).[b] <u>The spirit is given through Christ alone, and it is the spirit of Christ, made human, that is joined to us.</u> The eternal vital spirit of Christ himself is substantially joined to us, as the very flesh of Christ. But after reading the books on baptism and the Lord's Supper,[31] you will understand these things <u>more clearly</u> than I can possibly [explain them] here. For now it will be enough for you to understand that the substance of the Holy Spirit is divine substance, which can be united to our spirit through Christ, by means of a certain kinship, thereby sanctifying our spirit.

[*The Justice of the Holy Spirit*]

Now that you understand the essence of the Holy Spirit, and the gift of our sanctification, we must also briefly touch on another gift. Accordingly we will now explain what Christ said in John 16: The Paraclete spirit *will convict the world for its sin, according to my justice, and pass judgement* on my enemy.[c] Behold the wonderful gift of the Holy Spirit!

[Christ says] *the Spirit will convict the world for its sin, because it does not believe in me*.[d] The Spirit will clearly reveal that it is a manifest sin not to believe in [Christ] — he who was pointed to by the prophets

---

[a] John 10:30.   [b] 1 Cor 6:17.   [c] John 16:8. See A.R5.27.
[d] John 16:9.

and signs from heaven, who performed so many great miracles for our salvation, suffered so much for our sake, and fulfilled so many divine mysteries.

[Christ says:]ᵃ [The Holy Spirit] will clearly *convict the world according to* my *justice*, proving that I am just, whom the unjust world falsely accused and called a deceiver. The Spirit will teach that I did everything justly, because I am received by the Father. I would not be received if I were unjust. Not only am I received [in heaven], but I will dwell there forever, so that from now on *you will not see me*.ᵇ This is my righteousness, which is also **[189]** to be communicated to you, and by means of which I will carry you to the Father. Likewise, [the Holy Spirit] will disclose to the world the judgement that was rightly passed against Satan and which [the world] has not understood. He will teach that I have justly overcome and cast out the enemy, who oppressed the world and held it captive in hell.

The judicial power of this judgement is great. For the devil seemed to hold humanity captive by force of law. Having become the slave of sin because they had sinned, human beings were condemned to death by sentence of God. But the Spirit shall teach that the devil acted unjustly in everything, and always acts unjustly, betraying the beloved image of God by so many seductions. For humankind, which was once justly punished by God, is now justly freed by Christ's mercy. We will explain all of this in more detail in the book on original sin,³² since here, in the section on the Holy Spirit, is not the right place for it.

ᵃ This entire paragraph is written in the voice of Christ. Like a similar passage earlier (p. 185), it is Servetus's imaginative reconstruction of things that Christ might have said. ᵇ John 16:10.

[*The Holy Spirit Proceeds from the Father through the Son*]

For now, all that needs to be added is that many people are tormented needlessly, [asking] whether the Holy Spirit proceeds from the Father [alone], or from the Father and the Son. But I can easily explain this.

The Spirit of truth, which proceeds from the Father, is what the Father gives. For he is the original source, and he gives the good spirit to those who seek him. However, pay careful attention to the sense in which the word "proceed" is to be taken here, lest you become vainly preoccupied with an imaginary meaning.

The word "proceed" in Greek is ἐκπορευομένων (*ekporeuomenon*), that is, set out or go forth.[a] It is not a metaphysical sending forth of beings within [the Deity]. Rather, it is going forth [into the world] to do the work of God. There was not a real intrinsic procession [within God], such as the sophists devise. Rather there was an eternal preformation in the archetypal world, a kind of manifestation.

The first remarkable manifestation of the Word and the Spirit was at the Creation. The substantial modes of divinity were directed toward the origin of all substantial things, and the begetting of Christ. In truth, prior to the Creation there was no motion in God himself, nor was there action or being acted upon. There was no actual begetting, no emanation, no breath of life, no breath of the spirit, no bringing forth [of anything]. No one breathed and no one was breathed into. For all of these words indicate kinds of motion, action, and being acted upon.

---

[a] The word ἐκπορευομένων is used once in the New Testament, in Matt 20:29, where it means "departed," "went out," or "left."

Therefore, having set aside **[190]** the intrinsic motions of those three invisible beings, we say that [the Holy Spirit] is a dispensation of God, by means of which he unites the spirit of a human being to himself. This is truly what it means to give and to send forth [God's] spirit: when he takes a human being to himself, and unites [a human] spirit to himself. And since God does this through Christ, the Spirit truly proceeds from Christ, especially since in [Christ] is all of [God's] original abundance.[a]

We have said that deity proceeds from deity, according to the mode of divine distribution. We grant that these words for the sending forth [of the Holy Spirit] may be attributed to God, [who acts] through the dispensation of a created being and in a particular mode. The Holy Spirit is said to proceed visibly, to move, and to descend in the manner of an angel (Matthew 3 and Acts 2).[b] Nevertheless, the substance of God himself, which was in that angel, is not moved. The Spirit of God, which fills all things, illuminates this or that. Thus it moves, while [God] himself does not move. The Holy Spirit proceeds, departs, and goes out from the mouth of Christ, since Christ endows us with this gift by the distribution of his breath.

The Holy Spirit proceeds from the Father and the Son, and it [proceeds] from the Father through the Son. God *poured the Holy Spirit upon us through Jesus Christ* (Titus 3).[c] *And having received from the Father the promise of the Holy Spirit*, Christ *has poured* it upon us (Acts 2).[d] Christ r*eceived gifts* from the Father *when he ascended on high and gave* them *to human beings* (Psalm 67 and Ephesians 4).[33] Christ received these

Err, 62v

---

[a] See Col 2:9. [b] Matt 3:16; Acts 2:2-4. [c] Titus 3:5-6. [d] Acts 2:33.

gifts in the Resurrection. He did not have them before, since *he was not yet glorified*. At that time, the *holy spirit* of regeneration, glorifying and restoring humankind, *was not [yet]* in existence (John 7).[a]

The <u>very</u> spirit that is from the Father is from Christ, having become his own, part of his essence and his nature. Hence Christ said, [*The Comforter*] *whom I shall send to you from the Father* (John 15).[b] When Christ sends [the Spirit] from the Father, he sends it [also] from himself. <u>And when he sends it from himself, he sends it from the Father.</u> For the Father is in him.[c] First, Christ gave honour to the Father by saying that the Spirit is given by the Father.[d] Then he added [a reference] to himself, saying that he will be giving [the Spirit]. Although [when he spoke] Christ did not yet have such great [power], nevertheless he said, *I shall send* [the Comforter] and *he* [the Spirit of truth] *will take what is mine and declare it to you. All that the Father has, is* always *mine*.[e] For that reason, [Christ] said, [the Spirit of truth] *will take what is mine*; that is, he will take of my <u>very</u> substance, **[191]** and of my deity. He will impress upon you the character of my substance, and the ideal form of the Son received by me. And he will now teach you [God's] prescribed order, as he does not speak for himself.[f] I shall communicate [the Holy Spirit] to you from my substance even as *I lay down my life* for you.[g] Therefore the Greeks [in the Eastern church] are wrong when they deny that the Holy Spirit is from the Son, <u>because Christ is the one source from which the Holy Spirit emanates. Truly</u> the Holy Spirit is <u>the life</u>, the soul, and the mind of Christ.

Err, 62r

---

[a] John 7:39. [b] John 15:26. [c] See John 10:38. [d] Luke 11:13. [e] John 15:26; 16:14-15. [f] John 16:13. [g] John 10:15.

[*The Holy Spirit Is Christ in Us*]

Through the spirit of Christ we possess the very mind of Christ, so that we can live the life of Christ himself. Now we can no longer live, unless Christ lives in us. In us is the spirit of Christ, which comes from his inmost substance and the depths of his heart, and which for this reason is called *the love of God in our hearts* (Romans 5).[a] [The Spirit] is given to us from the depths of his heart, so that, through it, Christ may be truly formed in our hearts, and we may be truly transformed into his image. With powerful reasoning Paul shows the Galatians that, because [the Holy Spirit] is the *Spirit of the Son*, through it we are made *children* [of God]. For it impresses on us the very sonship of the Son of God, so that, as brothers of Christ, we may *cry out* along with him, "*Abba! Father!*"[b]

The Spirit itself contains the ideal form of the Son, just as the soul [is the ideal form] of the body. <u>It makes the impression of the Son upon us.</u> It forms the Son in us. <u>It is truly called</u> the spirit of υιοθεσίας (*huiothesia*, adoption):[c] <u>the spirit of sonship,</u> which causes us to be born again. In addition [Christ's] very body — blood, flesh, and bones — is afterwards given to us in the Lord's Supper. This was never given to anyone under the Law, nor [was it ever given] prior to the resurrection of Christ. At that time no one was called the brother of Christ, nor a co-*heir* of his kingdom.[d] Such a *spirit* of regeneration and glorification *did not yet* exist *because* Christ *had not yet been glorified* (John 7).[e] Hence, after his resurrection, Christ himself calls us brothers (Matthew 28, John 20).[f]

---

[a] Rom 5:5.   [b] Gal 4:6.   [c] See Rom 8:15, 23; 9:4; Gal 4:5; Eph 1:5.   [d] Rom 8:17; Gal 4:7.   [e] John 7:39.   [f] Matt 28:10; John 20:17.

[*The Holy Spirit and the Spirit of God*]

What I have just said explains why the term "Holy Spirit" is so frequently used in the New Testament but not in the Old.[a] The reason for this difference is that under the Law there were sanctifications of the flesh, but not sanctification of the spirit. <u>At that time there certainly was spirit, but not as it exists now.</u> Therefore they did not know the Holy Spirit nor had they *ever even heard that there was a Holy Spirit* (Acts 19).[b] <u>This new, or unfamiliar, expression ["Holy Spirit"], **[192]** and the new powers [associated with it], showed that there was something new — truly a new spirit.</u>

Although the spirit that was in the prophets was the spirit of Christ, nevertheless the spirit was different in them than it is in us. The dispensation of deity was different, and the spirit acted in a different way. We can say that the Holy Spirit spoke through the prophets, because it is eternal, yet in truth they were actually sanctified in a different way than we are. They imbibed a different spirit, or, rather one that operated in a different way. *<u>For</u>* [at that time] <u>*Jesus* Christ *had not yet been glorified*</u> (John 7).[c] They *received the spirit of servitude in fear,* but *we receive the Spirit* that makes us *children of God* (Romans 8 and Galatians 4).[d] Therefore Christ calls them servants, while he calls us friends and brothers (John 15 and 20).[e] Therefore, in the new covenant, a new spirit was given, and this is the reason for the new expression ["Holy Spirit"].

The [ancient] Jews had material sanctifications, which occurred by means of external anointing and

---

[a] The term "holy spirit" is found a few times in the Old Testament, e.g. Psalm 51:11 and Isa 63:10-11. In these passages it is a synonym for "spirit of God," with no suggestion that there is an entity called the Holy Spirit. [b] Acts 19:2. [c] John 7:39. [d] Rom 8:15; Gal 4:3-7. See also 1 Cor 2:12, 1 John 3:1-2. [e] John 15:14-15; 20:17.

touching. Whatever *touched [the sacrificial flesh] was sanctified* (Exodus 29 and Leviticus 6).[a] By *touching an unclean thing*, a person's sanctity was polluted (Leviticus 5 and 11).[b]

Among the [ancient] Jews the flesh was sanctified, but now the spirit is holy. The anointing which we receive from Christ is of the Spirit (2 Corinthians 1, 1 John 2, and Acts 10).[c] True Christians are governed by an internal anointing and sanctification which is done in the Spirit and by the [Holy] Spirit. This is why we call the Spirit holy, and for this reason we are baptized *in the name of the Holy Spirit*,[d] which was unknown to the Jews, so that being *dead to the Law*[e] and buried [with Christ] in the flesh,[f] we should be ever mindful only of the sanctification of the Spirit. No Jew was *born again by water and the* Holy *Spirit*.[g] Sometimes we read [in the Old Testament] of the *spirit of holiness*,[h] a special kind of breath from a holy being. But this is a breath of this world, not the Holy Spirit of regeneration, the new Spirit composed of incorruptible elements. If it says in the Law that the spirit of God is in someone, this does not refer to the Holy Spirit of regeneration, as it would among us, but to some kind of understanding, prophetic power, or strength (Exodus 28, 31, and 35; Numbers 24 and 34; and Judges 14).[i]

Err, 65r

Err, 61r

In the holy scriptures the wind is rightly called the breath of God, because of its **[193]** great power, both literally and spiritually.[34] For there was, in the very breath of the air itself, a life-giving energy, which revealed a mystery: the true substance of the Holy

---

[a] Ex 29:7; Lev 6:27.   [b] Lev 5:2; 11:24-28.   [c] 2 Cor 1:21-22; 1 John 2:20, 27; Acts 10:44-45.   [d] Matt 28:19.   [e] Rom 7:4.   [f] Rom 6:4; Col 2:12.   [g] John 3:5.   [h] Isa 63:10-11; Ps 51:11. Translations of these verses often use the expression "holy spirit." See note a on previous page.   [i] Ex 28:3; 31:3; 35:31; Num 24:2; Judg 14:6, 19. The spirit of God is not mentioned in Numbers 34.

Spirit, and the divine life-giving <u>breath</u> of Christ. For this reason God is said to bring forth the wind from his storehouses (Psalm 134, Jeremiah 10 and 51).[a] The wind that moved upon the waters, in Genesis 1, is called the Spirit of God. And because it was great and vigorous, it was used to dry up the waters and force them, as it were, into a heap (Psalm 32).[b] By evaporation, this also produced the airy expanse of the heavenly firmament.[c]

[In the account of creation] it is said that the Spirit of God, by some complex mystery, was already present in God himself and in the Christ who was to come. The Hebrews were also aware of this. They knew of the energy of the Spirit of God, which enlivens, stirs up, and fills all things. The Spirit of God enlivened the waters, so that they might, in turn, enliven the earth for the generation of living things. Inquiring further about the Spirit in the *Bereshit Rabbah*,[d] we find that [the rabbis] said that the Spirit that stirred the waters was the spirit of the Messiah himself, which stirred up and enlivened all things from eternity.[e] Thus [the Hebrews] rightly understood [the Spirit of God], without the fantasies of our Trinitarians, which were not known by anyone in those days. For being learned in the Law and the Prophets, they knew that in the future the Spirit of God himself would come to rest upon the Messiah, and that this Spirit had existed from the very beginning and had always shaped events.

---

[a] Ps 135:7; Jer 10:13; 51:16.   [b] Gen 1:2; Ps 33:7. In neither case is the force identified as the wind.   [c] See *Restoration*, 155-156 (book 4).   [d] A rabbinic commentary on the Book of Genesis, compiled between the third and fifth century CE. Servetus appears to have obtained his information about *Bereshit Rabbah* from a secondary source.   [e] *Bereshit Rabbah* 2. https://www.sefaria.org/Bereshit_Rabbah.2.4

[*The Spirit and Flesh of Christ*]

Regarding the Holy Spirit of Christ, it remains to be observed that, although in us there is no sanctification of the body, there is, nevertheless, a special sanctification in the body of Christ, as it is said that he was *born of the Holy Spirit* and *by the Holy Spirit* (Matthew 1).[a] [He was born] of the substance of the Holy Spirit, just as [he was born] of the substance of the Word. In the archetypal world, the substance of the spirit of God contained, and even now contains, the same elements of the Word—of which, as we said, there are three higher ones[35]— or the substantial pattern of them. The substance of the Word and the substance of the Spirit were, in God, the same substance, <u>whereby God reveals himself</u>.

Now also, although the flesh and the spirit of Christ **[194]** are truly different, nonetheless both have a true participation in the elemental substance — united just like our own flesh and spirit. The flesh of Christ, when it was in the tomb, had its own divine substance, in the heavenly elements and the substantial form of light. The spirit of Christ, which he committed to God as he was dying,[b] contained in itself, and even now contains, the elements of our regeneration, which are the same elements of the Word. And so the three higher elements are common to the body and the spirit. The soul is tied to the earthly body in a common bond, both in Christ and in ourselves. But in us there are only created elements, resulting from the generation of created beings. In Christ there are both created and uncreated [elements], which derive from the propagation of the substances of the Creator and of creation.

---

[a] Two translations of Matt 1:20: the Vulgate ("of the Holy Spirit") and Pagnini ("by the Holy Spirit"). [b] Luke 23:46, quoting Ps 31:5.

Thus on account of this common and substantial bond between flesh and spirit, we clearly perceive that the flesh of Christ was begotten in Mary out of the substance of the Holy Spirit.

Whatever is in Christ is holy. In him there is holiness of body and spirit, and immaculate flesh. In Christ alone the sanctification of flesh, and the begetting [of it], takes place by means of the substance of the Spirit of God. And the substance of the Spirit of God is communicated to his flesh in substantial form. Therefore, the body of Christ, <u>which is truth itself,</u> is not included in the [Platonic] paradox cited previously: that there is no truth in the bodies of this world.[a] On the contrary, the body is actually the food of the spirit. [The body of Christ] is truly united to our spirit as one substance, bound together by the spirit of regeneration. Truly the flesh of Christ is food — much more truly than [ordinary] outward food. There is no truth, as the paradox says, in our ordinary food; rather, the truth is in that [heavenly] food, in which there is unchanging and immaculate purity. This is the true food of the ever-living life that is in us.

<u>One might wonder,</u> if the Holy Spirit was originally in Christ alone, how did it **[195]** descend on him at the Jordan River?[b] I reply that before the Resurrection Christ had not yet acquired the full glory and power of God.[c] By a special dispensation of God, this was reserved until the Resurrection. At the Jordan, the new power and glory of the regeneration of baptism was revealed, just as Christ in his regeneration [at the Resurrection] received a new spirit of glory. By the

---

[a] Ficino, *Theologia Platonica* 11.6.3; see Plato, *Timaeus* (49d-e). Previously discussed at *Restoration*, 148 (book 4).   [b] Matt 3:16; Mark 1:10; Luke 3:22; John 1:32.   [c] John 7:39.

Incarnation, the <u>supreme</u> divine form was cast into a <u>lowly and</u> servile condition; by the Resurrection it was glorified. Therefore, now Christ alone hypostatically contains [within himself] the entire glory of the Word and the Spirit.

[*As He Is, So We Are*]

[*Union with Christ*]

The Holy Spirit is truly and substantially implanted in [Christ] alone. And <u>then</u>, by his <u>grace</u>, it comes to us from him alone. Thus we are <u>one with him</u> in substance, just as he is one with the Father.

<u>Again</u>, one might ask, if the substance of the Holy Spirit unites with our soul to form one thing, what is that one thing? I reply that it is the soul, and it is the Holy Spirit. Where the deity is located does not change the name of either the species or the individual. The soul is in the Holy Spirit and the Holy Spirit is in the soul. Just as God is in Christ, Christ is in God, and Christ is God while remaining a human being, so the soul, by its rebirth <u>on high</u>, becomes the Holy Spirit through hypostatic union, yet remains the soul. In this way a human being <u>becomes God and</u> becomes one with God. You will clearly understand that this whole is a single substance—just as fire combines with fire and light with light, as we said earlier[a]—if you remember that Christ's entire vital spirit, in which there is both soul and the Holy Spirit, is a single entity. Moreover, the very air that we breathe is made one substance with our soul, after <u>its essence</u> has been joined to our vital spirit, deep inside our hearts.[b]

---

[a] On p. 180. [b] Literally, not just metaphorically. See pp. 169-170.

We have shown that supervening forms are one with the form of light already in us.[36] We have also said that supervening ideas are one in essence with the soul, like light with light and spirit with spirit.[a]
[196] Just as Christ is one with God, as he himself says, so we are made one with him by the Holy Spirit. Indeed, we become part of a greater unity. There is born within us a new, substantial, and immortal human being, made from blood and bone, who is in substance one with the soul. You will see this happen in baptism and the Lord's Supper. It is no trifling thing to take communion with Christ and eat his flesh. The rebirth of the spirit is not trifling, but sublime. Christ shares his eternal vital spirit with us in substance, just as he does his flesh. He truly shares his whole self with us.

Now we know the <u>true</u> reason why Christ said that the new spirit, and *eternal life*[b] itself, will *remain in us forever.*[c] The spirit was at one time given to the Jews, in corruptible elements of the soul, when those elements had not yet been made incorruptible through Christ.[d] After our regeneration, the spirit of Christ remains in us forever, with eternal elements as they are in the resurrected [Christ], just as his eternal flesh remains in us. Thus, before the Incarnation, God was not united with a human being, as the spirit of the human Christ is now united [with us]. <u>For it was</u>

---

[a] On p. 180 Servetus said that the holy spirit given in rebirth is united with the soul "like light with light and fire with fire."
[b] The expression "eternal life" is used many times in the New Testament. Among the most relevant in this context are John 3:15; 6:54;10:28; Rom 6:23; Titus 3:7.   [c] See, for example, 2 Cor 1:22; 2 Tim 1:14; 1 John 4:13.   [d] In the 1790 edition, this sentence reads, "The spirit was at one time given to the Jews, in elements of the soul." The full sentence is found in the 1553 edition.

through his coming [into the world] that, for our sake, the Spirit made human was created, so that in this way the Spirit could be united with us. True incorruptibility enters our soul at our regeneration, and the Holy Spirit remains with the incorruptible *human being within us*,[a] inseparably and forever.

The seed of Christ is said to be incorruptible, and the *human being within us* is incorruptible (1 Peter 1 and 3).[b] That human being is incorruptible *who is born not of blood, nor of* the pleasure of *the flesh, but of God* (John 1 and 3, and 1 John 3).[c] From this John concludes that *in this world we are as* Christ is in heaven (1 John 4).[d] As Peter says, by sharing in the deity of Christ, we truly become gods, true *partakers of the divine nature*.[e] In a foreshadowing of this truth, [God] once said, *I said you are gods*.[f] The *human being within us* is God, from heaven, and of the **[197]** substance of God.

When you understand divine regeneration — heavenly regeneration — all this will be better understood. Then you will understand the heavenly *human being within us*; then [as Virgil prophesied] "a new generation will be sent down from heaven on high."[g] A divine generation of Christians will be born, which Isaiah regards with wonder.[h] Human beings will be born, and *will never die* any more.[i]

---

[a] *Internus homo* or *interior homo* (Eph 3:16), often translated as "the inner man."   [b] 1 Pet 1:4, 23; 3:4.   [c] John 1:13; 3:5-6; 1 John 3:9.   [d] 1 John 4:17: "...as He is, so we are in this world."
[e] 2 Pet 1:4. See also Irenaeus, *Adversus haereses*, prologue to book 5 (PL 7 1123B).   [f] Ps 82:6; quoted by Jesus in John 10:34.
[g] Virgil, Eclogue 4.7. This poem predicts the birth of a child who will usher in a new golden age. Beginning in late antiquity, it was seen as a prophecy of the birth of Christ.   [h] For example, Isa 62:12; 63:8; 65:17-19; 66:22.   [i] John 8:51; 11:26.

[*The Spirit and the Word*]

Before we end this book, let us once more compare the Spirit with the Word, as it once was and as it now is, by recapitulating what has already been said. <u>God was manifested in the world in substance, just as he is shared in substance.</u>

Just as God is the Logos, so too is he the Spirit. By means of the Word he commands something to be; by means of the Spirit he gives it life. By means of the Word, bodies are created in heaven and on earth; by means of the Spirit they are given life; and at the same time, the form of light is introduced into these things. Nothing is made without the Word, <u>or</u> has any power without the energy of the Spirit and of light. In the Word itself there is spirit and light. The Spirit comes forth with the Word, and God breathes it out in speaking, just we ourselves are unable to speak without breathing. <u>For this reason</u> it is called the spirit of [Christ's] mouth, the spirit of [his] lips. Just as the substance of the Word was visibly manifest in the corporeal elements of Christ, and substantially contained in his natural body, so also the spirit of God is seen in Christ's spiritual elements, and is substantially contained in his natural spirit.

Just as, in Christ, the Word of God is *one body* in substance with the substance of humanity, (Ephesians 2),[a] so the spirit of God and the spirit of humanity are *one spirit* (1 Corinthians 6).[b] God dwells in the Son, and the Son is God. God dwells in the Holy Spirit, and the Holy Spirit is God. Our very own spirit is God, proceeding and being born from God, just as Christ is God, having proceeded and been born from God. He was the first born, and through him we are

Err, 66v

---

[a] Eph 2:16.   [b] 1 Cor 6:17.

the second. The spirit of regeneration comes to us from the very mouth of Christ. With the sublime gift of his substance, <u>both corporeal and spiritual,</u> Christ gives us more than was given to the Jews.

Before the coming of Christ, no hypostasis of the spirit was visible. **[198]** But Christ wished this [hypostasis] to be shown to the apostles, first at his baptism, then after the glory of his resurrection, so that we might thus be better able to evaluate the effect, and grace, of his coming. Once Christ had been seen and heard, the Holy Spirit was seen and heard, and we became aware of the Comforter within us. Not only did we see the Spirit as a dove and as fire, but we heard it (John 3)[a] and felt it within ourselves (John 14).[b] Thus in Acts 2 *tongues of fire* were seen, <u>*a mighty rushing sound* was heard,</u> and the inward power [of the Spirit] was felt.[c]

In addition, the incarnation of the Word bears a resemblance to the sending forth of the Spirit, through which we become like the Son of God. The Word descending makes Christ descend from heaven, just as, through <u>the Spirit's</u> descent, we ourselves descend from heaven. We also ascend with Christ. For Christ himself is called the Word of God, as if the [divine] oracle departed from God and came into a human being, when the Word was made flesh. But it did not really depart. Rather, Christ ascended to God. In the same way, the Spirit seemed to depart from Christ when it was sent to the apostles (Acts 2). But it did not really depart. Rather we climb up to Christ himself, and begin to take our places in heaven with him. There we already reign with him. Would that we might reign [there with him] forever! Amen.

Err, 92v, 109v

---

[a] John 3:8.   [b] John 14:17.   [c] Acts 2:2-4.

Appendixes

Appendix A

The Paris Manuscript

This appendix contains an alternate version of book 5, taken from the so-called "Paris manuscript." This manuscript, located in the Bibliothèque Nationale in Paris, contains a partial draft of the "On the Trinity" section of *The Restoration of Christianity*, consisting of variant versions of books 3, 4, 5, and dialogue 1.

The date and provenance of the manuscript are unknown. It is a copy of the draft, not Servetus's original, but we do not know when it was copied, or why, or by whom. The original of the manuscript was clearly written earlier than the printed version of *Restoration*, because it lacks certain material that was added at a late stage of composition. Internal evidence shows that it was composed no earlier than 1548.[1]

In this volume, where the text of the manuscript is different from the final version, the variant text is underlined in both the appendix and the main text. This allows the reader to compare the two versions and see what Servetus added, removed, or changed between the date of the manuscript and the final publication.

---

[1] On the dating of the manuscript, see *On the Mysteries of the Word*, 133-134. The topic is also discussed in appendix C, where it is concluded that the manuscript is of little use in helping to establish the date of Servetus's description of the pulmonary transit.

Appendix A

Comparison of the Manuscript and the Final Text

Many of the differences between the manuscript and the final printed version are trivial—just the sort of minor editorial changes that an author routinely makes when revising a text. However, there are some significant additions, deletions, and revisions. The following are among the most noteworthy.

1. Text has been added to the beginning of the final version (p. 163) to connect book 5 to the overall theme of the five books on the Trinity (if not of the whole of *The Restoration of Christianity*), as stated in the opening paragraph of *Restoration*: "The manifestation of God himself through the Word, and his communication by means of the Spirit, both become substance in Christ alone."

2. Text has also been added to connect book 5 with earlier books. References to the "mystery of the Word" and God's "omniform essence" (p. 164) are reminiscent of books 3 and 4. Book 1 is echoed in a statement like, "The third being could not have said 'this is my son'" (p. 183).

3. Some details have been added to the description of the workings of the brain. The final version specifies that animal spirit is carried by the nerves (p. 172). Different functions are assigned to each of the four ventricles (p. 177).

4. The potential of human beings to share in God's substance is stated more strongly, with the use of the theologically loaded term "hypostatically" (p. 182) and the addition of the word "corporeal" (p. 197).[2]

5. Servetus expands on the idea that "Christ is the source from which the Holy Spirit emanates" (p. 191); that the way the Holy Spirit works in the world now is fundamentally different from what it was before the coming of Christ (pp. 191-192); and

---

[2] The sentence, "With the sublime gift of his [*illegible*] substance, Christ gives us more than was given to the Jews" becomes "With the sublime gift of his substance, <u>both corporeal and spiritual</u>, Christ gives us more than was given to the Jews." Unfortunately the manuscript is somewhat defective at this point, but the missing word is certainly nothing like "corporeal and spiritual." The same theme is expressed by a sentence that has been added on p. 197: "God was manifested in the world in substance, just as he is shared in substance."

that it is through Christ that the Holy Spirit is able to unite with human beings (p. 196).

6. The rejection of original sin has been made more explicit and emphatic. In the final version, Servetus says, "The spirit of the divine was implanted in human beings even after the sin of Adam" (p.168). The manuscript says only that God breathed a soul into Adam.

The first two of these changes are particularly interesting in that they suggest that, when he revised book 5, Servetus was thinking of the books on the Trinity as a single unit, rather than a collection of separate pieces. The five books appear to have been written at different times and for different purposes; we can see this in the close relationship between book 1 of *The Restoration of Christianity* and book 1 of *On the Errors of the Trinity*, and the progressive divergence from *Errors* of the later books of *Restoration*. By the time he was revising book 5, however, Servetus seems to have been trying to shape the five books into a coherent whole. This raises an interesting question for further study. Is *The Restoration of Christianity* best thought of as Servetus's *opera omnia*, a set of independent works united only by being printed in a single volume? Or will closer analysis reveal linkages that justify treating it as a single work?

First page of book 5 in the Paris manuscript

THE PARIS MANUSCRIPT

On the Divine Trinity

Book 5

Concerning the Holy Spirit

[163] <1> We have postponed the discussion of the Holy Spirit until we were familiar with the hypostasis of the Word, revealed by its utterance — because we will here be making frequent reference to the relation [of the Spirit] to the Word. For it is through the Word that we shall come to understand the Spirit.

Just as the original ideal form of the creation of humanity was present in the Word, so too the original ideal form of the creation of the [human] spirit was present in the Spirit. [Word and Spirit are] two different modes and presentations, both subsisting in God from eternity, and both coming forth in creation. In the Word of God was the Spirit. The Spirit proceeded with the Word, since God breathed out as he was speaking. The Word and the Spirit were the same substance, but their modes of activity were different.

[The Word, the Spirit, and the Light]

There are a number of similarities [between the Word and the Spirit]. Our own word and spirit — that is to say, our speech and our breathing — were, from the beginning, an image of the Word and the Spirit of God. In our speech there is breath of spirit, and in itself, except in the manner of its dispensation, it does not differ from the speech of the Spirit in God. If, by God's power, when I speak to you, you could see a human being in my voice; or if you could see what the voice itself signifies, then you would say that, in my visible speech, there is an invisible spirit which is audibly perceptible. You would also say that in my spirit there is a word, located in spiritual substance. In the same way, the Spirit was in the Word of God, **[164]** and the Word was in the Spirit—the visible Word and the perceptible Spirit.

Here is another similarity <u>between created things and</u> the Word and Spirit of God: the image of the heavenly Word, or the cloud of the oracle, is the **<2>** cloud of [earthly] elements. This is the substance of the wind, which goes everywhere in the wind. Thus God is both Word and the Spirit, Word and Spirit being variously distributed into the body and the soul.

A third likeness [to the Word and the Spirit] is the generative seed, which is the substance of the Spirit. For in Christ was both the seed of the Word and the substance of the Spirit from a single deity. Scripture teaches these likenesses; the very nature of things also teaches us, guiding us from created things to the Creator. <u>And so</u> the Word <u>of God</u> brought forth by breath was truly the Word spoken from <u>a dark</u> cloud; it was the seed of the begetting of Christ, containing in itself the Spirit in substantial form.

Light has always been considered to be shared by the Word and the Spirit. The cloud of the Word and the Spirit of God was, in substance, the archetype of this watery and airy cloud. And it was a shining cloud, as if on fire. And all of this is one substance: because there is one primary substance of these three elements, which is corporeal, spiritual, and shining with light. In one mode of divine dispensation, the elementary substance becomes a tangible body; in another it becomes a breath. It is the very same substance, always possessing an innate light. In one mode God appeared as the Word in the cloud. In another he was there sending forth his Spirit. In either mode he was always light—truly without any illusion. In one mode, he is the Word in the flesh; **[165]** in another he is the Spirit in the soul. In either mode he is always light, truly and substantially.

Just as God was the Word, the Spirit, and the light in the cloud, so too are the Word, the Spirit and the light now present in Christ. God united all of these **<3>** hypostatically and substantially, in flesh and in spirit. In Christ God united his own uncreated light with created light, and it was a single form—just as, as I have said, one form is made from combining solar and aqueous light. Also, in the generation of the one Christ, the lower [elements] are united in substance with the higher elements of the archetypal world. Thus, to sum up: the recapitulation of all things is gathered as one in Christ. With the divine Word condensing into the dew of Christ's begetting, and intermingling with the created elements of the earth through the activity of the Spirit of God, the body of Christ came into existence. When both divine and human breath had coalesced and been implanted in his soul, a single hypostasis of his spirit came into existence, which is the hypostasis of the Holy Spirit, revealing [for the first time] the true hypostasis of the sacred Spirit itself, which has always been the divine breath. The same light was shared by both the body and the spirit, and glorified the human elements taken from Mary, shaping everything into one hypostasis with God. Behold, all things are one in Christ.

Note, however, that in archetype, the Word and the Spirit and the light are one and the same; and the same cloud is simultaneously watery, airy and fiery. In the book of Genesis, however, the Word and the Spirit are mentioned before the light, and water and air before fire. God made use of the dispensation of the Word and the Spirit before the light appeared (Genesis 1) — because the light of Christ was to be revealed at a later time. Water and spirit are mentioned in this passage, but not fire, which was subsequently composed of both spirit and light.

The Jews were acquainted with two heavens, the watery one and the airy one, but not the fiery third heaven, as I have shown before.[a] Among the Jews there was no regeneration by water, spirit, and fire. Christ, the Light of the World, <4> revealed to us the true light which was hidden from the Jews. Therefore it is not without mystery that [mention of] fire was omitted by Moses [in chapter 1 of Genesis]. For that fire [in the person of Christ] was sent down to us. **[166]** It is not without mystery that God made use of the dispensation of the Word and the Spirit, before he revealed the light. At that time God bestowed the Word and the Spirit on humankind, but not the light made manifest [in Christ]. In former times God revealed himself to humanity through his word and communicated with humanity through his spirit, as though he were then keeping the light of Christ hidden. *God created all things through Christ*, who — in the Word, the Spirit, and the hidden light — was then with God. It was he who, coming at a later time, gave us a new birth by the Word and the Spirit, revealing the light itself, and illuminating us [with it], in order that the greatness of the glory and

---

[a] *Restoration*, 157 (book 4).

the grace of Christ might be visible to us. In the same way as, in the first generation, God gave the Word and the Spirit to humanity to a greater degree than to other living beings, so too did he in after times give us a new birth in word and spirit by means of the Gospel. Like Christ, we are born by the Holy Spirit through the Word of God.

Making use of these two dispensations from the beginning, God created bodies by the Word and gave them life by the Spirit; just as the heavens were made by his word and all the power in them by <u>the spirit of his mouth</u>. The material of <u>a human being</u> was created by his word, and the soul was put in by the Spirit. In resurrection, the parts of the body were <u>assembled</u> by the Word or voice of God, and the soul was put in by the Spirit (Ezekiel 37).

Thus God distinguishes these things, and so do we. In God, the workings of the Word and the Spirit were once of this kind, these dispensations and modes of activity being identical with God. But later, when God's mysteries were revealed in Christ, a greater distinction [between Word and Spirit] became apparent, because of a more abundant manifestation <u>and utterance</u> of divinity—both of them now appearing joined together in a body made of flesh and born of spirit. <5> Through Christ, the creature is united with the Creator: conformed to him, intermingled and joined with him in the flesh as in the spirit, <u>and</u> made hypostatically one with God. This is the great mystery: our union in substance with the Father through the Son.

The dispensation of the Spirit is the same as God [himself], and not a third metaphysical being. Although I have already demonstrated this, arguing against Peter Lombard towards the end of the first book, I will now show it again. Just as what God made through the Word **[167]** is said to be made by himself, because God was the Word, so too when scripture speaks of things made by his Spirit, it is saying that they are made by God himself, because *God is Spirit*. When the Holy Spirit spoke, it was God who was speaking *through the mouths of* the saints and *prophets* (Acts 3, Hebrews 1).

Thus those things that are done by means of the Holy Spirit, are, in some way, to be attributed to God himself. To receive *the Holy Spirit* means to *receive power from on high* through the arrival of a heavenly messenger (Luke 24 and Acts 1). The Holy Spirit is God's anointing. *God* himself *anoints us* and God *is Spirit* (2 Corinthians 1 and 3). God himself is the Holy Spirit in us, <u>the apostle teaches, saying that</u>

the spirit of God is in us *because God said, I will dwell in them*, and because he said, *you are the temple of God* (1 Corinthians 3 and 6 and 2 Corinthians 6). [Scripture also speaks of] *the dwelling place of God in the Holy Spirit* (Ephesians 2 and Isaiah 57). *Whoever scorns us, scorns God*, because *he gave his Spirit to us* (1 Thessalonians 4). Anyone who lies to the Holy Spirit is lying *not to men but to God* (Acts 5). For the Holy Spirit is a mode of deity, and acts in Christ and through Christ, by [God's] dispensation. This is proven because it is called *the Spirit of Christ* and *the Spirit of the Son* (1 Peter 1 and Galatians 4). Likewise it is written in Romans 8 that *the Spirit of God dwells in you*. <6> But *if anyone does not have the Spirit of Christ, he does not belong to him. And if the spirit of him*—that is, the Father—*who raised Jesus [from the dead dwells in you, he who raised Christ from the dead will also give life to your mortal bodies through his Spirit who dwells in you]*.

On the basis of these words, when Hilary, speaking metaphysically, in his usual way, about a real, invisible Son, says "through the Holy Spirit" in books 2 and 8 of *On The Trinity*, he sometimes means the Father, sometimes the Son, and sometimes a third being. Athanasius says similar things about the spirit of these beings at the beginning of the *Dialogues*. But I think all such things can be easily understood without resorting to metaphysical beings, because the Spirit of God is said [by scripture] to be enlarged or diminished, and divided in some way. For instance, God says to Moses, *I will remove, or cut off, some of your spirit, and give a share to seventy men*. Let me repeat this: in Numbers 11 [God was] removing or taking the spirit that was in Moses and giving it to seventy men. A portion was given to them, without any diminution, through a mode of divine distribution.

The partitioning, enlargement, and diminution of God's spirit **[168]** ought to be understood according to the various modes of divinity. And certainly this is also the case when [spirits] that are truly divided are joined together. The division of ministries and activities [in the early church] was made according to [God's] varied dispensation (1 Corinthians 12). Also, according to [God's] dispensation, *the Spirit* is said to be *greater in Daniel* than in others (Daniel 6), and the apostles were many times *filled with the Holy Spirit* (Acts 2 and 4). To give the Spirit of God means, as [scripture] says, *I will give them heart*, understanding, and intelligence. Wisdom was given to Solomon, which is the Holy Spirit, the spirit of wisdom. *The spirit of wisdom, counsel, knowledge*, piety, and other gifts is given [by God].

[*The Human Body, Soul, and Spirit*]

[*Blood, Breath, and Spirit*]

But God is said to give us his spirit, not only because of gifts like these, but because he alone breathes soul into us (Genesis 2 and 6). Our soul is a lamp of God (Proverbs 20). It is like a spark of the spirit of God, an image of the wisdom of God <7> — created, of course, or produced in the subject, but very similar to [God's] spiritual wisdom — and truly possessing the implanted, innate light of the divine. It is a spark of [God's] primal wisdom, and the very spirit of the divine. As God himself bears witness, through [God's] grace and mercy, the dispensation of our life is given and sustained by his breath (Job 10). God breathed a soul into Adam's nostrils with a breath of air, and [the soul] depends on [the divine breath] (Isaiah 2 and Psalm 103). God himself sustains the breath of life in us by his Spirit, *giving breath to the people who live on earth, and spirit to those who walk upon it*, so that we may *live, move, and have our being* in him (Isaiah 42 and Acts 17).

When God summons wind from the four winds and breath from the four breaths, the bodies of the dead live again (Ezekiel 37). From the breath of the air itself, God brings forth the souls of those [dead] human beings, in whom life is born from the breathing of air. Hence in Hebrew the word for soul is the same as the word for breath. From the air God brings forth the soul. With that very soul he brings forth air, and the spark of that Deity, which fills the air. Hence Orpheus rightly says, "The soul is carried by the winds, and enters [the body] from the universe by means of the breath," **[169]** as quoted by Aristotle. Ezekiel teaches that the soul contains something of the elemental substance [air], and God himself teaches that [the soul is in] the substance of the blood.

I shall now explain this subject at greater length, so that you may understand that the substance of the Holy Spirit itself is, in its essence, united to the substance of the created spirit of Christ. I call the air "spirit," since in the sacred language [Hebrew] there is no other special name for air. This shows that divine breath is in the air, which is filled with the spirit of the Lord.

So that you, Christian reader, may have a complete understanding of how the soul and the spirit function, **<8>** I shall here add divine philosophy, which you will easily understand if you have been trained in anatomy.

[*Blood, Vital Spirit, and Animal Spirit*]

It is said that in us there is a threefold spirit—natural, vital, and animal—formed from the substance of the three higher elements. [Alexander of] Aphrodisias calls them three spirits. But actually they are not distinct spirits. Actually, vital spirit is transmitted through anastomoses from the arteries to the veins, where it is called natural spirit. First, therefore, is the blood, whose seat is in the liver and in the veins of the body. Second is the vital spirit, whose seat is in the heart and in the arteries of the body. And third, like a ray of light, is the animal spirit, whose seat is in the brain and in the nerves of the body. In all of these is the energy of the one spirit and light of God.

Moreover, the development of human beings in the uterus teaches us that so-called natural spirit is transmitted from the heart to the liver. This is because an artery, joined to a vein, passes through the umbilical cord of the fetus. Likewise, after [birth], this artery and vein remain joined together. The soul, having been breathed into Adam by God, is in the heart before it is in the liver, and is transmitted from the heart to the liver. It is by breathing in through the mouth and the nostrils that the soul is brought [into the body]. The breath, however, is directed into the heart. The heart is the first organ to come to life and is the source of heat in the middle of the body. From the liver [the heart] receives the liquid of life [blood] as its matter, and in turn gives life [that is, vital spirit, to the whole body]; just as liquid water supplies matter to the higher elements, and is brought to vigorous life by [these elements], together with light.

[*The Soul Is in the Blood*]

The matter of the soul comes from the blood of the liver by means of a marvelous elaboration, **[170]** of which you will now hear. Hence the soul is said to be in the blood, and the soul itself is blood, or a sanguinary spirit. The soul is not said to be primarily located in the walls of the heart, or in the body of the liver, or in the brain. Rather it is in the blood, as God himself teaches in Genesis 9, Leviticus 17, and Deuteronomy 12.

Appendix A

In this regard, we must first understand the generation, as a substance, of the vital spirit itself. It is composed of, and nourished by, the air that is inhaled, and the most rarefied <9> blood. The vital spirit originates in the left ventricle of the heart, with the lungs greatly assisting in its generation. It is a rarefied spirit, elaborated by the power of heat, of a bright colour and a fiery potency. It is a bright vapour made from very pure blood, containing in itself the substance of water, air, and fire. It is generated in the lungs from a mixture of inhaled air with fine-textured, elaborated blood, which the right ventricle of the heart transmits to the left.

This transmission is not through the middle wall of the heart, as is commonly believed, but, rather, this fine-textured blood is led, by consummate artistry, over a long course through the lungs. It is prepared by the lungs and rendered bright in colour, and then poured from the arterial vein [pulmonary artery] into the venous artery [pulmonary vein]. Next, in the venous artery, [this blood] is mixed with inhaled air, and by exhalation it is cleansed of dark impurities. And, at last, the entire mixture, suitable material for the production of vital spirit, is drawn by diastole into the left ventricle of the heart.

<u>But</u> the communication in the lungs, between the arterial vein [pulmonary artery] and the venous artery [pulmonary vein], [shows that this] is accomplished by the lungs. This is confirmed by the remarkable size of the arterial vein [pulmonary artery], which would neither be made the kind of vessel it is, nor be as large as it is, nor would it drive such a great quantity of the purest blood from the heart to the lungs, merely to nourish them. Nor would the heart serve the lungs in this way — especially since, in the embryo, the lungs received nourishment from another source. For the little membranes or [171] valves of the heart do not open until the moment of birth, as Galen teaches. Therefore, it is for another purpose that blood begins to be poured so copiously from the heart into the lungs at the moment of birth. Likewise, it is not just air, but rather air mixed with blood, that is sent from the lungs to the heart through the venous artery [pulmonary vein].

Therefore, the mixing [of air with blood] takes place in the lungs. The bright colour is given to the to this spiritous blood by the lungs, <10> not by the heart, <u>which gives it a darker colour</u>. <u>Furthermore</u>, the left ventricle is not large enough for such copious mixing, nor is there room to elaborate [the blood] sufficiently to produce its bright colour. Finally, the middle wall [of the heart], being devoid of vessels and any means [of communication between the ventricles], is unsuited for the transmission or elaboration [of blood], although some blood may possibly seep through. By the same artistry by which transmission from the portal vein to the vena cava occurs in the liver for the sake of the blood, so also in the lungs, transmission from the arterial vein [pulmonary artery] into the venous artery [pulmonary vein] occurs for the sake of the spirit. If anyone compares what I have just said with what Galen writes in books 6 and 7 of *On the Usefulness of the Parts [of the Body]*, he will fully understand [that what I am describing is] a truth of which Galen himself was not aware.

[*The Brain*]

[*Animal Spirit*]

Thus the vital spirit is poured from the left ventricle of the heart into the arteries of the entire body in such a way that the part of it which is more rarefied moves toward the upper part [of the body], where it is further elaborated. [It moves] <u>particularly</u> into the retiform plexus, which is located beneath the base of the brain, close to the seat of the rational soul. It is further <u>formed</u>, elaborated and perfected by the fiery power of the mind in the very fine, <u>small</u> vessels, or capillary arteries, which are located in the choroid plexuses. [These plexuses] contain the very mind itself. They penetrate into all the innermost spaces of the brain, and cover the inside of the ventricles of the brain. These vessels, enfolded and interwoven, extend right up to the place of the origin of the nerves, in order to produce in them the power of sensation and movement.

Although these vessels, so finely interwoven in such a wondrous way, are called arteries, they are actually the ends of arteries which, [172] with the assistance of the cerebral membranes [meninges], extend to the place of the origin of the nerves. This is a special kind of vessel. For, just as there is in the lung a special kind of vessel, made from a vein and an artery, for transmitting [blood] from the veins to the arteries, <11> so, too, there is a special kind of vessel for transmitting [spirit] from the arteries to the nerves. It is formed from the outer layer of an artery and the meninges—especially since the meninges themselves maintain their outer layers in the nerves. Nervous sensation is not [located] in the soft matter of the nerves, just as <u>it is not</u> [located in [the soft matter] of the brain. All of the nerves terminate in filaments of membrane which possess the most delicate sensing ability. It is for this reason that spirit is always transmitted in them. From these small vessels of the membranes or choroids, therefore, the luminous animal spirit, like a ray of light, is poured, as from a fountainhead, into the eyes and the other sensory organs. By the same path, but in a reverse direction, the images of the objects of sensation, arriving from without, are sent to the same fountainhead, as if penetrating inwardly through the luminous medium [of spirit].

From all of this, it is evident that it is not correct to say that the soft mass of the brain is the seat of the rational soul, since it is cold and without sensation. Rather it serves as a cushion for the above-mentioned vessels, so that they do not rupture. And it protects the animal spirit, so that it does not blow away when it needs to be transmitted to the nerves. It has to be cold in order to temper the fiery heat contained in these vessels. Hence, also, so that the nerves may act as faithful protectors of the spirit, the previously mentioned vessels maintain a shared outer layer with the membrane in the inner cavity. And [the brain is surrounded] by a thin membrane [pia mater], as also by a thick outer layer [dura mater].

[*The Brain, the Mind, and the Soul*]

Furthermore, those empty spaces <u>or cavities</u> in the ventricles of the brain, which philosophers and physicians regard with wonder, contain nothing less than the soul itself. But the main reason that these ventricles were created is to receive, like sewers, the waste products of the brain, as shown by the passages [from the ventricles] to the palate and the nose, from which unhealthy discharges flow. When <u>those</u> ventricles become so filled with mucus that the arteries of the choroid plexus are immersed in it, **[173]** apoplexy quickly develops. If a noxious humour, whose vapour infects the mind, obstructs a part [of the brain], epilepsy is produced, or some other disease near that part [of the brain], in which the expelled [humour] settles.

Thus we can say that the mind is located in that place, where **<12>** we can clearly observe it being afflicted. Excessive heating of these vessels, or inflammation of the meninges, causes delirium and madness to be produced. Hence we conclude—from the accidents and diseases [that affect them], from their location and substance, and from the actions of the soul that are evident in them—that the small vessels are of the greatest importance, because all the rest [of the vessels] serve them and because the sensory nerves are attached to them, so that they receive their power from them. We can observe the intellect working there, when, deep in thought, we see the pulsing of the arteries that lead to the temples. Anyone who has not observed the place [where this happens], will hardly understand this.

These ventricles were also created for another reason: so that a portion of inhaled air, drawn by diastole into the very vessels of the soul, penetrating the hollow spaces through the ethmoid bones, might renew the animal spirit contained within, and provide ventilation for the soul. In these vessels are the mind, the soul, and the fiery spirit, which require constant fanning. Otherwise, [the mind and spirit] would suffocate, as an ordinary fire does when it is covered up. Like a fire, [the mind] requires fanning and ventilation, not only to obtain fuel from the air, but also to expel its impurities. Just as external elemental fire, having the fluid of a body as fuel, and being ventilated, maintained, and nourished by the air, is bound to a dense earthly body because of shared dryness and a shared form of light; in the same way our fiery spirit and soul, having blood for fuel, and ventilated, maintained, and nourished by an airy spirit through our inhalation and respiration, are bound to our body, forming a unity with it. Thus we have twofold nourishment, spiritual and corporeal.

Here, in the same luminous place where the spiritual [fire] is kindled, just as spirit is drawn to this place when we inhale, it is certainly fitting that the nature of our spirit should be inspired **[174]** by another holy, heavenly, and luminous spirit, exhaled from the mouth of Christ. It is fitting that the place in which our understanding and luminous soul are located should be further illuminated by the light of another, heavenly fire. For God, <13> who lit the first lamp in us, again turns our darkness into light, as it says in Psalm 17 and 2 Samuel 22. And this is what Elihu also teaches in chapters 32 and 33 of Job. Zoroaster, [Hermes] Trismegistus, and Pythagoras, as I will soon show, taught the same thing: that there are two lights within us, one inborn, the other added later.

Appendix A

The formation and tempering of the vessels [where the soul resides], and of their humours, produces a healthy state of mind, because the soul is in a better state when those [vessels] are better arranged. However, just as the light which is implanted in us by a good spirit shines brighter and brighter, it is also darkened by an evil one. If a dark and wicked spirit forces its way into the vessels of the brain that contain the luminous spirit of our soul, you will see demonic madness, just as clear revelations are produced by a good spirit. Those vessels are easily attacked by a wicked spirit, which dwells near the deep watery pits and hollows of the ventricles of the brain. That wicked spirit, whose power is of the air, enters and exits these empty spaces along with the air we breathe, so that, within those vessels, which are like the citadel [of our soul], it is in constant struggle with our spirit. Indeed, it besieges [the soul] from all sides, so that [the soul] is scarcely able to breathe, except when the light of the spirit of God arrives, driving away the evil of the demons.

See how perfectly suited this location is to the workings of the mind, the spirit, revelation, and understanding, whether inborn or acquired — and also for the battle against the greatest temptations, not to mention lesser ones. By means of a similar kind of inhalation, the love of God is kindled in our hearts by the Holy Spirit. The heart, in addition to housing the principle of life, is the seat of the will. Because of the temptations of the intellect and the excitements of the flesh, it is the chief source of sin. This accords with Matthew 15.

But before we move on to the heart, let us first conclude the description the brain. The activities of the mind vary according to the diversity of the brain's vessels, so that [175] there are different organs [of thought] in the various ventricles. These I will now explain.

<14> A small portion of the air we inhale is transmitted, through the ethmoid bones, to the fiery animal spirit contained in the choroid vessels, and from there to the two anterior ventricles of the brain, situated on the right and left sides of the sinciput [upper part of the skull]. Here the capillaries of the choroid artery expand to draw in air to ventilate the soul. There the two optic nerves, having come together, deliver their clear visual images. The auditory and other sensory nerves are covered by a common membrane, providing the safest and most secure protection. For if, in those empty spaces [ventricles], images and spirits were to drift together with the soul itself, everything would be expelled when we blow our noses, or, at any rate, when we sneeze.

If the soul were [in the ventricles] it would no longer be in the blood, since there is no blood outside the vessels. Thus the mind is very securely situated in the choroidal vessels. The membrane is very secure, and the principal sensory nerves extend into the vessels which are located in the anterior ventricles. So this is the beginning of the "common sense," <u>or</u> the common understanding of the external senses, or the imagination: the senses are brought together and begin to be combined. The air that is breathed into the brain is carried from the two anterior ventricles to the middle [ventricle], which is, rather, a common passageway. [The air from the anterior ventricles] comes together beneath the psalloid, where we find the purest and most luminous part of the mind, containing the seeds of ideal forms, which are divinely implanted in us. <u>Once these are grasped, [the mind can] imagine new things, or rather</u>, organize and combine images: to deduce things from other things, to distinguish between things and, illuminated by God, to grasp the pure truth.

The [middle] ventricle is smaller and the reasoning of the intellect is <u>clearer</u>. This is because the choroid arteries, which draw in the fiery spirit by diastole, are more abundant here. And the apprehensions of the common sense lead to more brilliant reasoning, with light penetrating inward through the vessels, and deity **[176]** shining there. There is not as much empty space here as in the other ventricles. Perhaps one ought to call it a passageway <15> rather than a ventricle, or even the long and winding path of rational inquiry. It been fashioned wisely, to suit the difficult task of rational inquiry. This ventricle is smaller [than the anterior ventricles] because this is a purer and clearer part of the mind, so it does not accumulate as much waste material. And what [waste material] is produced here flows easily and directly into the infundibulum underneath, lest it extinguish or impede the light of the mind.

The blood vessels are more numerous around the conarium [pineal body], with more pulsations of the arteries, producing a more powerful activity of the mind and of the fiery spirit here. Also here, near where the pulse pounds more powerfully at the temples, we can detect the working of the intellect, on the outside as well as the inside. This single observation points us directly to the exact location of the mind. In addition, this place is closer <u>than any other</u> to the sense of hearing, which is the sense of learning. The composition of the human body is a tremendous miracle!

Appendix A

Many and long are the winding pathways leading to the cerebellum, so that it requires careful scrutiny to investigate every twist and turn, and to illuminate the darkness. Using the imaginative faculty, what <u>had earlier been</u> stored away in memory can also greatly assist in this task. Here the kindling of the inhaled air is held back <u>for a while</u> by the wormlike doorkeeper [vermis cerebelli] and the sinuous "buttocks" [quadrigeminal bodies], until, fanned and impelled by the pulsation of all the arteries of the mind, a thought is perfected, and everything is illuminated <u>with a clearer light</u>. Thus this fiery place is especially suited for the mind, which is itself fiery and which shares in God's light. And when it conceives an idea, this is likewise a ray of light and a kind of luminous image. Even the external, perceptible likenesses of <u>a [illegible] thing</u> that are sent to the eyes are luminous. Coming from a luminous object, or having the form of light, they are sent through a luminous medium. By this means the mind itself becomes more and more enlightened.

[*The Senses*]

The intellect is not only adorned with the sense of sight, which shows us the many differences among things, but also by the objects perceived by the other senses, <16> which all have an affinity with our luminous spirit. [177] This affinity derives from the substantial form of all things, which is light, as well as from the spiritual component of the action of each [of the senses].

<u>For</u> sound and odor are like spirit. They are perceived as spirit, and act in us the same way that spirit does. Perception of sound occurs at the membrane of the ear, when an external spirit strikes the internal spirit, which contains the light of the soul and the concord of spiritual harmony, regulated by the diastole and systole [of the heart]. <u>Thus the Psalmist expressed the prophetic spirit.</u> The way in which odors are perceived is very similar. Things that are tasted and touched, although they are corporeal, nevertheless have the power, <u>even so</u>, to alter the soul. [The soul is altered] by the common form [of light] <u>and</u> its various effects upon the spirit. By means of light, all substances act upon the soul, <u>and</u> impress upon it the ideal form of all things. The sophists, who once taught that there was nothing to be seen either in God or in us except qualities and masks, now see the substances themselves. But we who see the substantial light in Christ, also look for a vision of the true light in other things.

After all the [sensory images] have been illuminated in the middle ventricle, the doorkeeper [vermis cerebelli] allows the inhaled air to reach the fourth ventricle, located in the parencephalon [cerebellum], and a bright image is kindled in the light of the soul itself. There, in what is actually the base of the brain, the vessels steadfastly stand guard over the treasure trove of memory, and store away the things which have been discovered by the senses and reasoning. These things are not attached to the walls [of the ventricle], but are stored in the very substance of the soul, as if in some material substance where stronger vessels fortify the mind, so that memory does not flow away easily.

Here I briefly mention that it is by this pathway that the faculty of movement of the entire body is transmitted to the muscles, radiating the animal spirit through the large nerves of the spine. So much for the portion of inhaled air drawn into the brain, and the organs of the brain.

[*The Substance of the Soul*]

[178] Most of the other inhaled air is drawn through the trachea into the lungs. It then proceeds into the venous artery [pulmonary vein], in where it is mixed with bright, fine-textured blood and further elaborated. Then the entire mixture is drawn by diastole into the left ventricle of the heart, where it is perfected by the power of the strong life-giving fire <17> contained there. After all the impurities resulting from elaboration are exhaled, it becomes vital spirit.

Besides this mixture [of blood and spirit] described thus far, there are two components of the soul: something created by the breath, or actually produced by its matter; and spirit itself, or divinity instilled by breathing. All of this is one and makes up one soul. What we normally call the soul is breath and spirit, both united in essence with the [Holy] Spirit. It is an ethereal substance, similar to its super-elemental archetype, and also to this world below. It is a single natural soul: vital and at the same time animal.

Behold, then, the whole explanation of [the soul] itself, so that you may understand how *the soul of all flesh is in the blood*, and *the soul itself is blood*. By the breath of God, a gleam of the heavenly spirit, or spark of the ideal, was inhaled through the mouth and nostrils into the hearts and brains of Adam and his progeny. Within them, it joined its essence to the spiritual matter, and made a soul in their innermost

Appendix A

parts (Genesis 2, Isaiah 57, Ezekiel 37, and Zechariah 12). Following the Chaldaeans, the Academics taught that such dissimilar substances could be united in this way. They said that aether was united by God to the elemental air, so that the divine mind could be sent into this solid body. The sacred scriptures teach this very clearly, speaking of the breath of God and the elemental breath.

In *Timaeus*, Plato clearly teaches that the substance of the soul is a mixture of elemental and divine substances. There is [in us] a third, intermediate substance, which shares in in both of these. For the soul bears the signs of deity and of the world of elements. If this were not the case, a soul could not possess the powers of an intelligent mind, and also the life-giving **[179]** faculties of the body.

Hence it happens that when the soul pays heed to the senses, it is seduced by the body, loving its kinship [with the body]. But at other times, it soars on high, more influenced by its kinship with heavenly things, which it had previously neglected. In *Cratylus* the soul, ψυχή (*psyche*), is said to be refreshed by breathing, ἀναψυχή (*anapsyche*). Nevertheless, in a human being, [the soul is said] to be from the divine mind.

Just as the soul gives life to the body, so God breathes life into the soul. Isaiah teaches that spirit, which is from God, **<18>** is wrapped in a breath of air. And so God created passages [in the body] for the breath. Zechariah says that the spirit of the soul is made in a certain fashion in a human being. The words of Genesis confirm this. For it is not simply said that the soul is the breath of God, but rather that a living soul was formed within [the human being] by inhaled breath.

In the elements of the body, just as in a seed, there is a substantial symbol of the soul that is to be brought forth, as we will show further, beyond what has already been shown. There are two things in semen, which are essential for the soul, which cause the soul of a child to be similar to the soul of its father. These are: the formal or formative faculty, and the material of the spirit. The formal and formative faculty is light itself and the ideal form. Souls are brought forth from semen. In human beings, there is the breath of the divine mind, in that ideal form which the nature of the seed requires; and the soul is formed in accordance with this.

The breath of God enters the heart and brain of a human being through the face: the mouth and nostrils. In this way the soul is formed according to the ideal form of humanity. Thus God, like a potter, is called the maker of the soul (Zechariah 12). [God] himself fashions the soul in the heart of each human being (Psalm 32). God is called the maker of light (Isaiah 45). For he actually makes the substantial forms of things in light itself, just as he makes ideal forms in the light of his mind. So God formed and fashioned the soul in light, just as the soul itself later forms and fashions other images in light.

Finally, God is called *the maker of all things* (Jeremiah 10), since he created nothing to which he did not give a definite form. God, the maker, even gave definite forms to angels and souls. Even before we existed, God shaped us both inwardly and outwardly with wondrous artistry and manifold wisdom (Psalm 138). First of all, God, conceiving all things in his mind, shaped them from eternity as patterns based upon the ideal forms in his own [divine] light. Then, bringing each of them out into the world, **[180]** he formed them as he had already pre-formed them [in his mind].

If, by inferior [human] reason, you can understand these actions, you will understand that Christ first had his form in God. From this we have [in turn] received our own [forms], formed in external, created light. In this created light, God gives a real and substantial form to all things, impressing the stamp of his light, or his ideal forms, on all things, and also infusing into humanity the breath of the divine mind. That breath of the soul, sent into us by God, is a kind of lamp or spark of [divine] light. God himself is the fire and God is the spirit, **<19>** who is the source of the fiery and spiritual soul in our fiery and airy vital spirit. The original ideal form of souls and other things is in the light [of the divine mind], and in light is the natural life, as John says. It is the very light of God, *that* naturally *illuminates every human being* born *into the world* (John 1).

The fountain of the soul is in the luminous Word of God, and *in his light we see light* (Psalm 35). According to this understanding, the Holy Spirit given in rebirth is beautifully united with the soul, like light with light and fire with fire. Otherwise we could not speak of the rebirth of the spirit except in the likeness of the first birth and breath. And the new illumination is superior to the old.

Appendix A

Zoroaster the Chaldaean sage taught this in *Oracles of Wisdom*. There [he says that] the soul, which is sent down into us from the light of God, yearns to return to that same light, to be illuminated by it, and to become fire again. He says, "You must ascend to the light itself and to the Father's rays, from which soul, wrapped in the abundant light of the mind, flows into you." And, "[The soul], through the power of the Father, becomes a brilliant flame." In *Pimander* Hermes Trismegistus says, "God the Father, from whom man is born, is light and life. Therefore, if you comprehend that you yourself are made of life and light, you will climb upward again to life and light." In his [*Golden*] *Verses* Pythagoras says, "Take courage, because there exists a divine race of human beings to whom sacred nature reveals all things by bringing them forward into the light."

[*The Spirit of Regeneration*]

There is a hidden light within us, a light that reveals itself in another, greater light by means of God's baptism. By the **[181]** light of Christ's life, the life of our soul goes forth at birth, as does the life of our spirit in rebirth. There is another way [of life for us], just as there was a new and different spirit in Christ himself. [The Holy Spirit] itself, which was once the spirit of Elohim, is now the spirit of the mouth of Christ, generating and regenerating (Psalm 103). However, [it accomplishes these things] in different ways. Regeneration differs from generation, as the Spirit of grace differs from the soul we are born with. This spirit is God. The [human] soul is not God, but through [the Spirit of grace] the soul is made God. The vital spirit of the soul, and the elements which compose it, are subject to corruption. The elements of the new spirit are incorruptible, like the vital spirit that Christ now possesses in heaven. Thus the soul of all flesh is confined within limits ordained by God. The soul originates as a kind of breath of the mind [of God] in the blood. However, the Holy Spirit of regeneration is a new breath of the Deity with the renewed elements of the regeneration of Christ.

<20> Do not be afraid to say that our soul *is* essentially united with such an [incorruptible] elemental substance. The fire of our soul, and the fire of our spirit, are inseparably connected to this [substance]. They are sustained and nourished by it, just as the fires that we can see are sustained and nourished by liquid and air. Just as a fire is extinguished when these [substances] are lacking, so [without

the elemental substance] the soul is extinguished within us, unable to perform its vital activities. Indeed, the substance of the soul, which comes from God—considered by itself, apart from these mundane elements—is like something elemental, as is also <u>angelic</u> substance. For the spirit of God, which is the spirit of the begetting of Christ, from which angels and souls <u>have their being</u>, contained such an elemental substance in the archetypal world. The spirit of Christ now contains [this substance]. The spirit of our regeneration contains this same substance, when we are born [again] by water, spirit, and the fire of heaven. **[182]** And all of these things come together into one <u>system</u> [composed] of soul and spirit.

Consider the kind of substance Christ in heaven contains within himself today, what kind of breath he has, and what kind of vital spirit. For he himself is the Holy Spirit, containing these elements within himself, united hypostatically to himself. By the power of the Resurrection, all the elements of his body and spirit are renewed, glorified, and made incorruptible. And Christ truly shares all these things with us in [the sacraments] of baptism and the Lord's Supper, sharing his whole self with us. The Holy Spirit is the breath of Christ's mouth (John 20). <u>God himself is in us as a spirit distinct from the Father and the Son, the substance of true light.</u> In the same way that God breathes forth the soul together with air, so Christ breathes forth the Holy Spirit together with air.

[*Divinity in Creation*]

In summary, you ought to keep in mind that, just as the soul is understood to be separate and apart from air or fire, but nevertheless the whole is one soul, one idea, and one entity; just so, the Holy Spirit, a mode of the Divine, is understood to be separate and apart from creation, but nevertheless the whole—the Holy Spirit, the vital spirit of Christ—is one Holy Spirit. The addition of Deity to these things, or the addition of these things to God himself, does not change the name [of the things]. Deity in a stone is stone, [deity] in gold is gold, and [deity] in wood is wood. Deity in a human being is a human being, although on a more exalted level, and [deity] in spirit is spirit. So too, the addition of a human being to God is [still] God, and the addition of <u>our</u> spirit to [the Holy Spirit] is the Holy Spirit.

Appendix A

[*The Nature of the Holy Spirit*]

[*The Holy Spirit as an Angel*]

The Holy Spirit is thought of as being present not only in the breath of Christ, but also in angels. Therefore one ought to consider whether an angel is the Holy Spirit, and who is <21> this other [being], the Paraclete. The ministry of an angel is associated with the outpouring of the Holy Spirit, as, for example, when a dove or fiery tongues were seen (Matthew 3 and Acts 2). For the same reason [appearances of God in the Old Testament] are said to be by the ministry of an angel, for events in the Law that happened by the word of God took place through the agency of angels. [For example] an angel in the person of God appeared to Moses in a burning bush (Exodus 3 and Acts 7). The voice of God spoke to Moses through an angel, saying, *I am the God of your fathers*. The substance **[183]** of God in the Word was present there in the manifestation of the angel, just as the substance of God in the [Holy] Spirit was present at the Jordan River, and over the Apostles [at Pentecost]. An angel in the person of God spoke and appeared to Abraham (Genesis 18 and 22), Hagar (Genesis 16 and 21), and Jacob (Genesis 31 and 32). See also Joshua 5 and 6 and Judges 2 and 6.

In Exodus 23 God provides the explanation for this: he was the divinity, or *the name of God*, in the angel, and whoever heard the voice of the angel was hearing the voice of God. Thus, just as [God's] voice from heaven was transmitted through an angel, saying, *I am the God of your fathers*, so too was [God's] voice from heaven transmitted through an angel, when he said, *This is my son*. Indeed, this was the voice of the Holy Spirit (Matthew and Luke 3). Therefore, the Holy Spirit was not a third being, but was a dispensation of the Deity through an angel.

Hence, after the Holy Spirit descended, Christ said, *You will see the angels of God ascending, and descending upon the Son of Man* (John 1). In one [account of Jesus's baptism] it says *angels descending*, in another passage it says *the Spirit descending*, and in a third *the Holy Spirit descending*. In [the story of the conversion of the eunuch] in Acts 8 [the Holy Spirit] is first called an angel, then the Spirit, and finally the Spirit of the Lord. Isidore [of Seville], speaking about the Paraclete, says, "He will announce future events to you." He supposes [the Paraclete] to be an angel, because the word "angel" means "messenger," and the

Holy Spirit delivers many messages through angels. <u>In book 2 of *On the Trinity*, Augustine attributes the name "angel" to the Holy Spirit.</u>[a]

All angels are ministers of the spirit (Psalm 102). And Hebrews 1: God *makes his angels spirits and his ministers fiery flames*. God revealed many things to the good prophets by means of his good angels, just as he chose to deceive the evil prophets by means of evil spirits (3 Kings 22, 2 Chronicles18 and Ezekiel 14). Angels entered the souls of the prophets as spirits, as, for instance, in Ezekiel and Zechariah. Angels are called the spirit of falsehood, the spirit of truth, or the spirit of God. An angel in human form spoke to the centurion, but it spoke to Peter and the others as the Holy Spirit (Acts 10, 11 and 13). The Holy Spirit could not speak to the centurion, **<22>** because he did not know Christ. However, in the human being who is reborn [in Christ] all things are said to be [done] by the Holy Spirit operating within. Hence in Acts, chapter 16, it is called the Spirit and the Holy Spirit, <u>while</u> in [Paul's] dream of the Macedonian man an angel is <u>shown</u>. In the Bible, angels and spirits are spoken of separately. They are really the same, but there is a difference in the manner [in which they appear], just as there is a difference between the Word and the Spirit. **[184]** The Word and angels appear in a human mode, while the Spirit appears in a spiritual mode.

It is not surprising that the words or deeds of an angelic spirit may be said to be [the work of] the Holy Spirit, for the words or deeds of an apostle are [also] <u>said to be</u> the words or deeds of the Holy Spirit. Therefore, an angel is not properly called the Holy Spirit, except in the sense in which, [in Old Testament times], an angel was called Jehovah. What was done by the Word of God under the Law was done by angels. But an angel is not, on that account, said to be the Word of God — except as a kind of semblance and ministry, nor is it said to be God, except as a semblance and ministry. We attribute far less divinity to angels than did the Jews, by whom angels were once worshipped as gods. Hence we conclude that neither in relation to Christ nor with respect to ourselves, can an angel rightly be called the Holy Spirit, but only a minister acting in the service of the Holy Spirit.

---

[a] Augustine, *De trinitate* 2:13 (PL 42 860): "Although I do not recollect that the Holy Spirit is called an angel anywhere else, this may be understood from his work."

Appendix A

[*The Holy Spirit as the Comforter Sent by Christ*]

Thus the Holy Spirit, the Comforter, whom Christ promises will be with the apostles in the future, and who was given to them in Acts 2, is not primarily understood to be an angel, although the angels share in its ministry. But Christ promises them another, internal Comforter in place of this external Comforter, that is, a new spirit of the future, which did not then exist, but which is to be given to them after the Resurrection, and will gloriously participate in an angelic ministry.

The [Holy Spirit], which is truly said for many reasons to be different from the Son, is also separate from the angelic ministry. First of all, the Spirit differs as greatly from the Son as breath does from a human being. Setting aside this created breath, the substance of the Holy Spirit is truly different from the substance of the Son. [The Holy Spirit] is said to be another person [*alius*] and another being [*aliud*] than Christ. But if you take "another being" to denote something discordant, then I will not grant that the Holy Spirit is another being than the Son. Indeed, they are one, just as Christ and the Father are one. For they are in harmony, and they are one and the same Deity. The Deity acts now in one mode, and now in another.

Under the [Old Testament] Law, a sufficient Spirit—with such an essence, distinct and visible, <23> joined together with a human spirit in one everlasting hypostasis—was not given [to humanity]. Therefore it is now more separate [from the former angelic ministry], and is called "another person." Before the Word became a human being, the Holy Spirit, in itself, was actually **[185]** a substantial mode of the Deity, not hypostatically united with the spirit of a human being. Now it has a substantial and everlasting union with the incorruptible human spirit of Christ.

Christ also spoke of the Spirit as another person than himself, since he did not possess the Spirit at the time [of his earthly ministry]. But, as promised by the Father, Christ received at his resurrection a new spirit of glory, which he afterwards transmitted to the apostles. He calls the Holy Spirit another person, because of its surpassing glory, which had never been seen before.

[Christ says:] [The Holy Spirit] will be another person than the spirit which you apostles have already received. It will be a person other than me. Indeed I shall be another person, and a new human being. The quality of glory in [the Holy Spirit] will be very different from what it is now.

This is why [Christ] says, *He* [the Spirit of truth] *will glorify me*. After the Resurrection, so great is the glorified Christ, and the new glory of his Holy Spirit, that the angels, as Peter bears witness, would *desire to look* upon *it*, and would be struck dumb with amazement. This is because the angels, who were themselves gods among the Jews, had never beheld such a dispensation of deity under the Law. Through Christ, a new knowledge of the Holy Spirit was given to the angels, as well as a new knowledge of God given through Christ. The angels learned things about the Kingdom of Christ, which they did not previously know (Ephesians 3). The Kingdom of Christ, which is given to us, is the kingdom of the Spirit. And it is said that in the spirit all things are revealed to us, all things come about, and thus [all things] come about through the Holy Spirit. The Father honoured the Son with such glory, that not only is he God from God, but he also is God, from whom another God proceeds. But if you find the phrase "another God" offensive, then say "another Comforter" and another glory of the Deity. Christ is God, from whom other gods proceed and are born. For we are gods, proceeding from [God] himself and *born of God* (John 1).

But why does Christ say about the Holy Spirit, *He will not speak on his own authority*? Didymus [the Blind] answers [this question] in his book *On the Holy Spirit.* He explains it thus: [Christ says] *He will not speak on his own authority*, that is, not without me, but rather the mode of the divine breath will be from my will and the will of the Father. Here we must ascend gradually to the source from which Christ came, **[186]** so that, through his gift, we may drink from that very source. Keep in mind, reader, that God in himself, considered apart from Christ, is <24> so hidden, and so transcends everything, that he has nothing in common with us—nor with the angelic spirit, which he infinitely exceeds. Remember: the angels themselves do not see God, nor do they have communication with his Spirit, beyond what is given [to them] through Christ. For no one sees the Father, except [the Son] alone and those to whom he wishes to reveal [the Father]. And God communicates to no one by means of the Spirit, except through [the Son].

Appendix A

[*The Holy Spirit as a Mode of the Divine*]

Of course, there are [multiple] divine modes of vision and communication, by which the Father manifests himself to the world, and which he communicates through Jesus Christ alone. And just as he now shows [these divine modes] to us, he preformed them from eternity in accordance with the wisdom of Christ. The Holy Spirit, and its fullness in Christ, is a substantial divine mode, eternal in God. This <u>proves</u> the preformation of the spirit of Christ in God. If that portion, or spark, or measure, or breath, or mode of the spirit, which was in Peter or Paul, was once substantially in God, how much is the fullness [of deity] in Christ himself? <u>For the substance of the spirit that is in Christ, which was substantially in God, is said to be *without measure*.</u>[a] When the Holy Spirit was given to Peter and Paul, no change in God occurred, nor was anything then actually removed from him. But in receiving the [gifts of the Holy Spirit] that had been prepared for them, [Peter and Paul] were changed through union with and reception of [the spirit] that was intended for them. The spirit that was given to them was received from Christ, and prepared for them in Christ.

Certainly the actual substance of the Holy Spirit was in the apostles. It was given to them in a certain measure, which had been prepared for them from eternity. They are said to have been truly filled with the Holy Spirit (Acts 2 and 4). For [the spirit that] was in them so filled them and moved them that they burst into miraculous actions. Yet the Spirit was not in them in its full plenitude and *without measure*. That was reserved for Christ alone (John 3, Romans 12, 2 Corinthians 10, and Ephesians 4). Therefore we speak of a certain measure [of Spirit] as being in this **[187]** spirit, in that one, and in yet another one, and all of them being one spirit. Do not be surprised, then, if Christ said "*another Paraclete*" and "*another spirit*," since even you may speak of one here, another there, and yet another somewhere else. If you take away the sophistical realities, everything will be easy. <u>Just as in God infinite essences are one essence, so infinite spirits [may be] under one spirit.</u>

<25> To sum it all up, the Holy Spirit can be defined in a few [words]. The Holy Spirit is a substantial mode of the divine, adapted to the spirits of angels and human beings. Although the Holy Spirit

---

[a] John 3:34.

forms a substantial unity with the sanctified creation of the Spirit that is in Christ, nevertheless, in itself, <u>the Holy Spirit</u> is understood to be pure deity. In accordance with the mode of [divine] dispensation, deity is from deity, according to the succession of divine distribution; just as in branches, leaves, and flowers there is divinity from the divinity of seeds and roots, and in a sprout there is divinity from the divinity of the vine. Therefore, the Holy Spirit is truly a substantial mode [of the divine], distinct from the Father and the Son: proceeding, subsisting, perceptible by the senses, speaking and acting, now here and now there.

The Holy Spirit is distinct from God the Father, so that we may say that God is in the Holy Spirit, just as God was in the Word and God was in the light. The Holy Spirit is born from God, just as light is born for us from God. God is the father of the Holy Spirit, just as he is *the father of light*, and *the father of glory*. By the same figure of speech God is called the father of wisdom and the father of the Word—as long as you do not understand [his fatherhood] in human terms. God dwells in spirit, and *God is spirit*; God dwells in fire, and God is fire. God <u>is</u> in light, and God is light. God is in the mind; he inhabits the mind; and God is mind itself.

<u>Possibly</u> you will object that God's glory does not seem to be greater now than it was [before the Incarnation]. For the Spirit of God from eternity contained only the divine hypostasis, or the substantial mode of divinity, like the primal ideal form of the elemental breath in God; and now it should [also] have the elements of the human spirit of Christ, united with him in a single essence at the Incarnation. [Furthermore] the glory of God must be greater after the Resurrection than it was when Christ was active on earth. I answer that the glory of God in himself can neither be increased nor diminished. The more he glorifies us, so much greater is the glory in us. In the resurrection of Christ, God showed that his power and glory were so great, that he could create **[188]** incorruptible things from corruptible elements <u>of humanity</u>. And for our glory, <26> he could unite them to his deity with elements like his own, so gloriously that, together with God, they form substantially a single spirit, which is the Holy Spirit. Anything that is in Christ is, in substance, one with God. As [Christ] himself says, *I and the Father are one*.

Just as the body of Christ is so closely joined to God, that it is substantially one with him, so too is his spirit—and <u>our</u> spirit through him—so joined and attached to God, that it is one spirit with him (1 Corinthians 6). But after reading the books on baptism and the Lord's Supper, you will understand these things <u>better</u> than I can possibly [explain them] here. For now it will be enough for you to understand that the substance of the Holy Spirit is divine substance, which can be united to our spirit through Christ, by means of a certain kinship, thereby sanctifying our spirit.

[*The Justice of the Holy Spirit*]

Now that you understand the essence of the Holy Spirit, and the gift of our sanctification, we must also briefly touch on another gift. Accordingly we will now explain what Christ said in John 16: The Paraclete spirit *will convict the world for its sin, according to* my *justice, and pass judgement* on my enemy. Behold the wonderful gift of the Holy Spirit!

[Christ says] *the Spirit will convict the world for its sin, because it does not believe in me.* The Spirit will clearly reveal that it is a manifest sin not to believe in [Christ]—he who was pointed to by the prophets and signs from heaven, who performed so many great miracles for our salvation, suffered so much for our sake, and fulfilled so many divine mysteries.

[Christ says:] [The Holy Spirit] will clearly *convict the world according to* my *justice*, proving that I am just, whom the unjust world falsely accused and called a deceiver. The Spirit will teach that I did everything justly, because I am received by the Father. I would not be received if I were unjust. Not only am I received [in heaven], but I will dwell there forever, so that from now on *you will not see me.* **[189]** Likewise, [the Holy Spirit] will disclose to the world the judgement that was rightly passed against Satan and which [the world] has not understood. He will teach that I have justly overcome and cast out the enemy, who oppressed the world and held it captive in hell.

The judicial power of this judgement is great. For the devil seemed to hold humanity captive by force of law. Having become the slave of sin because they had sinned, humankind was condemned to death by sentence of God. But the Spirit shall teach that the devil <27> acted unjustly in everything, and always acts unjustly, betraying the beloved image of God by so many seductions. For humankind, which was once justly punished by God, is now justly freed by Christ's mercy. We will explain all of this in more detail in the book on original sin, since here, in the section on the Holy Spirit, is not the right place for it.

[*The Holy Spirit Proceeds from the Father through the Son*]

For now, all that needs to be added is that the sophists are tormented needlessly, [asking] whether the Holy Spirit proceeds from the Father [alone], or from the Father and the Son. But I can easily explain this.

The Spirit of truth, which proceeds from the Father, is what the Father gives. For he is the original source, and he gives the good spirit to those who seek him. However, pay careful attention to the sense in which the word "proceed" is to be taken here, lest you become vainly preoccupied with an imaginary meaning.

The word "proceed" in Greek is ἐκπορευομένων (*ekporeuomenon*), that is, set out or go forth. It is not a metaphysical sending forth of beings within [the Deity]. Rather, it is going forth [into the world] to do the work of God. There was not a real intrinsic procession [within God], such as the sophists devise. Rather there was an eternal preformation in the archetypal world, a kind of manifestation.

The first remarkable manifestation of the Word and the Spirit was at the Creation. The substantial modes [of divinity] were directed toward the origin of all substantial things, and the begetting of Christ. In truth, prior to the [*illegible*] Creation there was no motion in God himself, nor was there action or being acted upon. There was no actual begetting, no emanation, no breath of life, no breath of the spirit, no bringing forth [of anything]. There no one [*illegible*]. No one breathed and no one was breathed into. For all of these words indicate kinds of motion, action, and being acted upon.

Therefore, having set aside **[190]** the intrinsic motions of those three invisible beings, we say that [the Holy Spirit] is a dispensation of God, by means of which he unites the spirit of a human being to himself. This is truly what it means to give and to send forth [God's] spirit: when he takes a human being to himself, and unites [a human] spirit to himself. Since God truly does this through Christ, the Spirit truly proceeds from Christ, especially since in [Christ] is all of [God's] original abundance and deity.

We have said that deity proceeds from deity, according to the mode of divine distribution. We grant that these words for the sending forth [of the Holy Spirit] may be attributed to God, [who acts] through the dispensation of a created being and in a particular mode. The Holy Spirit is said **<28>** to proceed visibly, to move, and to descend in the manner of an angel (Matthew 3 and Acts 2). Nevertheless, the substance of God himself, which was in that angel, is not moved. The Spirit of God, which fills all things, illuminates this or that. Thus it moves, while [God] himself does not move. The Holy Spirit proceeds, departs, and goes out from the mouth of Christ, since Christ endows us with this gift by the distribution of his breath.

The Holy Spirit proceeds from the Father and the Son, and it [proceeds] from the Father through the Son. God *poured the Holy Spirit upon us through Jesus Christ* (Titus 3). *And having received from the Father the promise of the Holy Spirit,* Christ *has poured* it upon us (Acts 2). Christ *received gifts* from the Father *when he ascended on high and gave* them to *human beings* (Psalm 67 and Ephesians 4). Christ received these gifts in the Resurrection. He did not have them before, since *he was not yet glorified*. At that time, the *holy spirit* of regeneration, glorifying and restoring humankind, *was not* [*yet*] in existence (John 7).

The spirit that is from the Father is from Christ, having become his own, part of his essence and his nature. Hence Christ said, [*The Comforter*] *whom I shall send to you from the Father* (John 15). When Christ sends [the Spirit] from the Father, he sends it [also] from himself. For the Father is in him. First, Christ gave honour to the Father by saying that the Spirit is given by the Father. Then he added [a reference] to himself, saying that he will be giving [the Spirit]. Although [when he spoke] Christ did not yet have such great [power], nevertheless he said, *I shall send* [the Comforter] and *he* [the Spirit of truth] *will take what is mine and declare it to you. All that the Father has, is* always *mine*. For that reason [Christ] said, [the Spirit of truth] *will take what is mine*, that is, he will take of my substance, **[191]** and of my deity. He will impress upon you the character of my substance, and the ideal form of the Son received by me. And he will now teach you [God's] prescribed order, as he does not speak for himself. I shall communicate [the Holy Spirit] to you from my substance even as *I lay down my life* for you. Therefore the Greeks [in the Eastern church] are wrong when they deny that the Holy Spirit is from the Son. Indeed, the Holy Spirit is in [*illegible*], the soul, and the mind of Christ.

[*The Holy Spirit Is Christ in Us*]

Through the spirit of Christ we possess the very mind of Christ, so that we can live the life of Christ himself. Now we can no longer live, unless Christ lives in us. In us is the spirit of Christ, which comes from his inmost substance and the depths of his heart, and which for this reason is called *the love of God in our hearts* (Romans 5). [The Spirit] is given to us from the depths of his heart, so that, through it, Christ may be truly formed in our hearts, and we may be truly <29> transformed into his image. With powerful reasoning Paul shows the Galatians that, because [the Holy Spirit] is the *Spirit of the Son*, through it we are made *children* [of God]. For it impresses on us the very sonship of the Son of God, so that, as brothers of Christ, we may *cry out* along with him, "*Abba! Father!*"

The Spirit itself contains the ideal form of the Son, just as the soul [is the ideal form] of the body. The Spirit itself contains the form of the Son. It forms him in us according to the model [*illegible*]. In [*illegible*] it forms the pattern of the Son in us, the spirit of υιοθεσίας (*huiothesia*, adoption), which causes us to be born again. In addition [Christ's] very body—blood, flesh, and bones—is afterwards given to us in the Lord's Supper. This was never given to anyone under the Law, nor [was it ever given] prior to the resurrection of Christ. At that time no one was called the brother of Christ, nor a co-*heir* of his kingdom. Such a *spirit* of regeneration and glorification *did not yet* exist *because* Christ *had not yet been glorified* (John 7). Hence, after his resurrection, Christ himself calls us brothers (Matthew 28, John 20).

[*The Holy Spirit and the Spirit of God*]

What I have just said explains why the term "Holy Spirit" is so frequently used in the New Testament but not in the Old. The reason for this difference is that under the Law there were sanctifications of the flesh, but not sanctification of the spirit. No indeed, they did not know the Holy Spirit nor had they *ever even heard that there was a Holy Spirit* (Acts 19).

[192] Although the spirit that was in the prophets was the spirit of Christ, nevertheless the spirt was different in them than it is in us. The dispensation of deity was different, and the spirit acted in a different way. We can say that the Holy Spirit spoke through the prophets, because it is eternal, yet in truth they were actually sanctified in a different way than we are. They imbibed a different spirit, or, rather one that operated in a different way. They *received the spirit of servitude in fear*, but *we receive the spirit* that makes us *children of God* (Romans 8 and Galatians 4). Therefore Christ calls them servants, while he calls us friends and brothers (John 15 and 20). Therefore, in the new

covenant, a new spirit of Christ was given, and this is the reason for the new expression ["Holy Spirit"].

The [ancient] Jews had material sanctifications, which occurred by means of external anointing and touching. Whatever *touched* [*the sacrificial flesh*] *was sanctified* (Exodus 29 and Leviticus 6). By *touching an unclean thing*, a person's sanctity was polluted (Leviticus 5 and 11).

Among the [ancient] Jews the flesh was sanctified, but now the spirit is holy. The anointing which we receive from Christ is of the Spirit (2 Corinthians 1, 1 John 2, and Acts 10). True Christians **<30>** are governed by an internal anointing and sanctification which is done in the Spirit and by the [Holy] Spirit. This is why we call the Spirit holy, and for this reason we are baptized *in the name of the Holy Spirit*, which was unknown to the Jews, so that being *dead to the Law* and buried [with Christ] in the flesh, we should be ever mindful only of the sanctification of the Spirit. No Jew was *born* again by *water and the* Holy *Spirit*. Sometimes we read [in the Old Testament] of the *spirit of holiness*, a special kind of breath from a holy being. But this is a breath of this world, not the Holy Spirit of regeneration, the new Spirit composed of incorruptible elements. If it says in the Law that the spirit of God is in someone, this does not refer to the Holy Spirit of regeneration, as it would among us, but to some kind of understanding, prophetic power, or strength (Exodus 28, 31, and 35; Numbers 24 and 34, and Judges 14).

In the holy scriptures the wind is rightly called the breath of God, because of its **[193]** great power, both literally and spiritually. For there was, in the very breath of the air itself, a life-giving energy, which revealed a mystery: the true substance of the Holy Spirit, and the divine life-giving spirit of Christ. For this reason God is said to bring forth the wind from his storehouses (Psalm 134, Jeremiah 10 and 51). The wind that moved upon the waters, in Genesis 1, is called the Spirit of God. And because it was great and vigorous, it was used to dry up the waters and force them, as it were, into a heap (Psalm 32). By evaporation, this also produced the airy expanse of the heavenly firmament.

[In the account of creation] it is said that the Spirit of God, by some complex mystery, was already present in God himself and in the Christ who was to come. The Hebrews were also aware of this. They knew of the energy of the Spirit of God, which enlivens, stirs up, and fills all things. The Spirit of God enlivened the waters, so that they might, in turn, enliven the earth for the generation of living things. Inquiring further about the Spirit in the *Bereshit Rabbah*, we find that [the rabbis] said that the Spirit that stirred the waters was the spirit of the Messiah himself, which stirred up and enlivened all things from eternity. Thus [the Hebrews] rightly understood [the Spirit of God], without the fantasies of our Trinitarians which were not known by anyone in those days. For being learned in the Law and the Prophets, they knew that in the future the Spirit of God himself would come to rest upon the Messiah, and that this Spirit had existed from the very beginning and had always shaped events.

[*The Spirit and Flesh of Christ*]

<31> Regarding the Holy Spirit of Christ, it remains to be observed that, although in us there is no sanctification of the body, there is, nevertheless, a special sanctification in the body of Christ, as it is said that he was *born of the Holy Spirit* and *by the action of the Holy Spirit* (Matthew 1). [He was born] of the substance of the Holy Spirit, just as [he was born] of the substance of the Word. In the archetypal world, the substance of the spirit of God contained, and even now contains, the same elements of the Word — of which, as we said, there are three higher ones — or the substantial pattern of them. The substance of the Word and the substance of the Spirit were, in God, the same substance.

Now also, although the flesh and the spirit of Christ **[194]** are truly different, nonetheless both have a true participation in the elemental substance — united just like our own flesh and spirit. The flesh of Christ, when it was in the tomb, had its own divine substance, in the heavenly elements and the substantial form of light. The spirit of Christ, which he committed to God as he was dying, contained in itself, and even now contains, the elements of our regeneration, which are the same elements of the Word. And so the three higher elements are common to the body and the spirit. The soul is tied to the earthly body in a common bond, both in Christ and in ourselves. But in us there are only created elements, resulting from the generation of created beings. In Christ there are both created and uncreated [elements], which derive from the propagation of the substances of the Creator and of creation. Thus on account of this common and substantial bond between flesh and spirit, we clearly perceive that the flesh of Christ was begotten in Mary out of the substance of the Holy Spirit.

Whatever is in Christ is holy. In him there is holiness of body and spirit, and immaculate flesh. In Christ alone the sanctification of flesh, and the begetting [of it], takes place by means of the substance of the Spirit of God. And the substance of the Spirit of God is communicated to his flesh in substantial form. Therefore, the body of Christ is not included in the [Platonic] paradox cited previously: that there is no truth in the bodies of this world. On the contrary, the body is actually the food of the spirit. [The body of Christ] is truly united to our spirit as one substance, <32> bound together by the spirit of regeneration. Truly the flesh of Christ is food—much more truly than [ordinary] outward food. There is no truth, as the paradox says, in our ordinary food; rather, the truth is in that [heavenly] food,[a] in which there is unchanging and immaculate purity. This is the true food of the ever-living life that is in us.

The question may arise, if the Holy Spirit was originally in Christ alone, how did it **[195]** descend on him at the Jordan River? I reply that before the Resurrection Christ had not yet acquired the full glory and power of God. By a special dispensation of God, this was reserved until the Resurrection. At the Jordan, the new power and glory of the regeneration of baptism was revealed, just as Christ in his regeneration [at the Resurrection] received a new spirit of glory. By the Incarnation, the divine form was cast into a servile condition; by the Resurrection it was glorified. Therefore, now Christ alone hypostatically contains [within himself] the entire glory of the Word and the Spirit.

[*As He Is, So We Are*]

[*Union with Christ*]

The Holy Spirit is truly and substantially implanted in [Christ] alone. And by his gift, it comes to us from him alone. Thus we are [one with him] in substance, just as he is one with the Father.

At this point, one might ask, if the substance of the Holy Spirit unites with our soul to form one thing, what is that one thing? I reply that it is the soul, and it is the Holy Spirit. Where the deity is located

---

[a] The manuscript acutally says "rather, the truth is not in that [heavenly] food" (*sed in illo cibo non est veritas*). This must be a copying error.

does not change the name of either the species or the individual. The soul is in the Holy Spirit and the Holy Spirit is in the soul. Just as God is in Christ, Christ is in God, and Christ is God while remaining a human being, so the soul, by its rebirth, becomes the Holy Spirit through hypostatic union, yet remains the soul. In this way a human being becomes one with God. You will clearly understand that this whole is a single substance—just as fire combines with fire and light with light, as we said earlier—if you remember that Christ's entire vital spirit, in which there is both soul and the Holy Spirit, is a single entity. Moreover, the very air that we breathe is made one substance with our soul, after it has been joined to our vital spirit, deep inside our hearts.

We have shown that supervening forms are one with the form of light already in us. We have also said that supervening ideas are one in essence with the soul, <33> like light with light and spirit with spirit. [196] Just as Christ is one with God, as he himself says, so we are made one with him by the Holy Spirit. Indeed, we become part of a greater unity. There is born within us a new, substantial, and immortal human being, made from blood and bone, who is in substance one with the soul. You will see this happen in baptism and the Lord's Supper. It is no trifling thing to take communion with Christ and eat his flesh. The rebirth of the spirit is not trifling, but sublime. Christ shares his eternal vital spirit with us in substance, just as he does his flesh. He truly shares his whole self with us.

Now we know the reason why Christ said that the new spirit, and *eternal life* itself, will *remain* in *us forever.* For the spirit was at one time given to the Jews, in corruptible elements of the soul, when those elements had not yet been made incorruptible through Christ. After our regeneration, however, the spirit of Christ remains in us forever, with its eternal elements as they are in the resurrected [Christ], just as his eternal flesh remains in us. Thus, before the Incarnation, God was not united with a human being, as the spirit of the human Christ is now united [with us]. True incorruptibility enters our soul at regeneration, and the Holy Spirit remains with the incorruptible *human being within us*, inseparably and forever.

The seed of Christ is said to be incorruptible, and the *human being within us* is incorruptible (1 Peter 1 and 3). That human being is *born not of blood, nor of* the pleasure of *the flesh, but of God* (John 1 and 3, and 1 John 3). From this John concludes that *in this world we are as Christ is in heaven* (1 John 4). As Peter says, by sharing in the deity of Christ, we truly become gods, true *partakers of the divine nature*. In a foreshadowing of this truth, [God] once said, *I said you are gods.* The *human being within us* is God, from heaven, and of the **[197]** substance of God.

When you understand divine regeneration—heavenly regeneration—all this will be better understood. Then [as Virgil prophesied] "a new generation will be sent down from heaven on high." A divine generation of Christians will be born, which Isaiah regards with wonder. Human beings will be born, and *will never die*.

[*The Spirit and the Word*]

Before we end this book, let us once more compare the Spirit with the Word, <34> as it once was and as it now is, by recapitulating what has already been said.

Just as God is the Logos, so too is he the Spirit. By means of the Word he commands something to be; by means of the Spirit he gives it life. By means of the Word, material bodies are created in heaven and on earth; then by means of the Spirit they are given life; and at the same time, the form of light is introduced into these things. Just as nothing is made without the Word, so nothing has any power without the energy of the Spirit and of light. In the Word itself there is spirit and light. The Spirit comes forth with the Word, and God breathes it out in speaking, just we ourselves are unable to speak without breathing. Therefore it is called the spirit of [Christ's] mouth, the spirit of [his] lips. Just as the substance of the Word was visibly manifest in the corporeal elements of Christ, and substantially contained in his natural body, so also the spirit of God is seen in Christ's spiritual elements, and is substantially contained in his natural spirit.[a]

---

[a] At this point in the manuscript some text is duplicated, so that it reads, "...substantially contained in his natural body, so also the spirit of God is seen in Christ's spiritual elements, and is substantially contained in his natural **body, so also the spirit of God is seen in Christ's spiritual elements, and is substantially contained in his natural** spirit" — a common form of copying error known as dittography.

Just as, in Christ, the Word of God is *one body* in substance with the substance of humanity, (Ephesians 2), so the spirit of God and the spirit of humanity are *one spirit* (1 Corinthians 6). God dwells in the Son, and the Son is God. God dwells in the Holy Spirit, and the Holy Spirit is God. Our very own spirit is God, proceeding and being born from God, just as Christ is God, having proceeded and been born from God. He was the first born, and through him we are the second. The spirit of regeneration comes to us from the very mouth of Christ. With the sublime gift of his [*illegible*] substance, Christ gives us more than was given to the Jews.

Before the coming of Christ, no hypostasis of the spirit was visible. **[198]** But Christ wished this [hypostasis] to be shown to the apostles, first at his baptism, then after the glory of his resurrection, so that we might thus be better able to evaluate the effect, and grace, of his coming. Once Christ had been seen and heard, the Holy Spirit was seen and heard, and we became aware of the Comforter within us. Not only did we see the Spirit <35> as a dove and as fire, but we heard it (John 3) and felt it within ourselves (John 14). Thus in Acts 2 *tongues of fire* were seen, and the inward power [of the Spirit] was felt.

In addition, the incarnation of the Word bears a resemblance to the sending forth of the Spirit, through which we become like the Son of God. The Word descending makes Christ descend from heaven, just as, through Christ's descent, we ourselves descend from heaven. We also ascend with Christ. For Christ himself is now called the Word of God, as if the [divine] oracle departed from God and came into a human being, when the Word was made flesh. But it did not really depart. Rather, Christ ascended to God. In the same way, the Spirit seemed to depart from Christ when it was sent to the apostles (Acts 2). But it did not really depart. Rather we climb up to Christ himself, and begin to take our places in heaven with him. There we already reign with him. Would that we might reign [there with him] forever! Amen.

Appendix B

The Galenic Physiological System

The Circulatory System

Nowadays, certain basic ideas about the body and its systems are so commonplace that they are known even by young children.[1] For example, most people know that the heart is a pump, sending blood containing nutrients and oxygen to every part of the body via the arteries. Deoxygenated blood, containing carbon dioxide and other waste products, returns to the heart via the veins. The heart then pumps it to the lungs to be recharged with oxygen before it is returned to the arterial system. Oxygen from the air is taken into the body when we inhale; carbon dioxide is expelled from the body when we exhale.

Figure 1 shows a simplified schematic diagram of the circulatory system, as it is understood today.

1. The left ventricle of the heart pumps oxygenated blood throughout the body, through progressively smaller arteries. (Note: in this model the designation of "step 1" is arbitrary; since the process is cyclical, there is no actual starting or ending point.)

---

[1] This is literally true. All of the information in this paragraph can be found in a 40-page picture book aimed at children aged 4 to 8. Samuel John, *Human Body Systems for Kids* (Independently published, 2022).

Appendix B

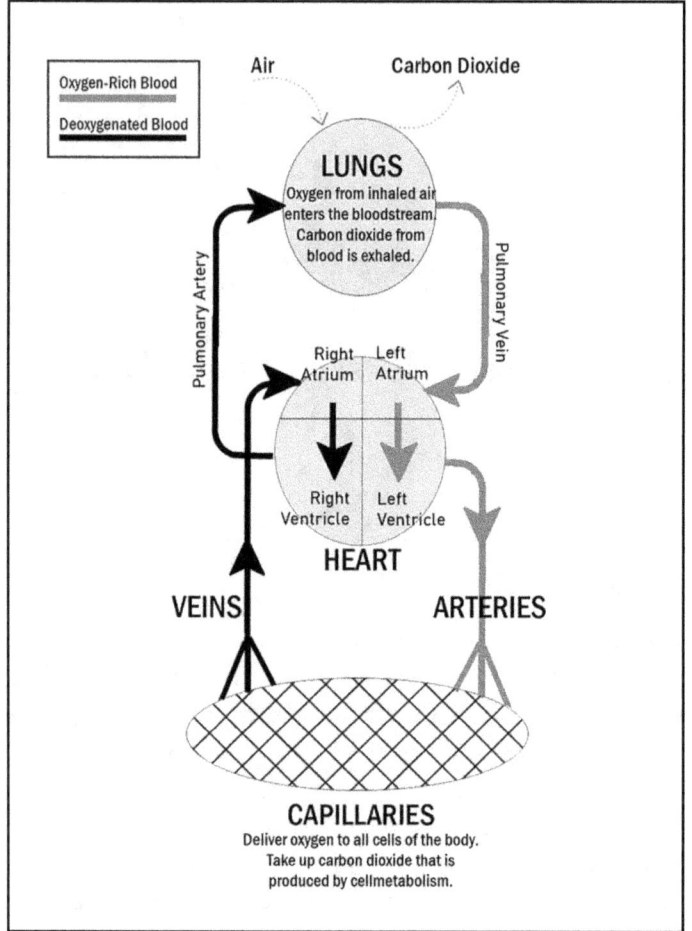

Figure 1. A schematic diagram of the circulatory system

2. The smallest blood vessels, the capillaries, supply oxygen and nutrients to the tissues of the body, and pick up carbon dioxide and waste products.

3. The capillaries join to form progressively larger veins, returning deoxygenated blood to the right atrium of the heart. The tricuspid valve controls the flow of blood from the right atrium to the right ventricle.

4. The right ventricle pumps blood to the lungs through the pulmonary artery.

5. The lungs are the interface between the circulatory system and the respiratory system. Oxygen from inhaled air enters the bloodstream, and carbon dioxide returns to the lungs to be exhaled.

6. Oxygenated blood flows from the lungs through the pulmonary vein to the left atrium of the heart. The mitral valve controls the flow of blood from the left atrium to the left ventricle.

7. The blood has now returned to the starting point, ready to be pumped throughout the body.

The Galenic System

Before the pioneering work of William Harvey in the seventeenth century, the prevailing model of the body and its workings was very different, since there was no concept of the circulation of the blood. Sixteenth-century anatomists knew that blood flowed in the arteries and veins, but they did not think that the primary purpose of the veins and arteries was to transport blood—and they certainly did not think it was to transport oxygen, which was not discovered until the eighteenth century. Instead, the purpose of the arteries, veins, and nerves was to collect, transform, and transport spirit, or *pneuma*.

The Greek word *pneuma* has a range of meanings, including wind, breath, and spirit. In ancient Greek philosophy and physiology, pneuma is the life force—the quality that distinguishes living things from non-living matter. In the second century CE, the flow of pneuma through the body was described in detail by the physician and philosopher Galen. Galen's system, with some later modifications and elaborations, was medical orthodoxy from the time of Galen to the time of Harvey.

There were held to be three types of pneuma (in Latin, *spiritus*). In increasing order of refinement, these are:

1. Natural spirit—produced in the liver, responsible for nutrition and the growth and maintenance of body tissues.

2. Vital spirit—produced in the heart, responsible for blood flow and the regulation of body temperature.

3. Animal spirit—produced in the brain, responsible for sensation and movement.

Appendix B

In the Galenic model, there was no conception that any of these substances circulated in the body. Each system was considered to flow one way: a substance was created at one point, and consumed as it travelled from the starting point to all parts of the body, through progressively smaller branchings. An analogy would be the way water travels through a tree, from the roots through the main trunk, smaller branches, twigs, and finally to each leaf, from which any excess water evaporates.

Figure 2 illustrates the Galenic physiological system.

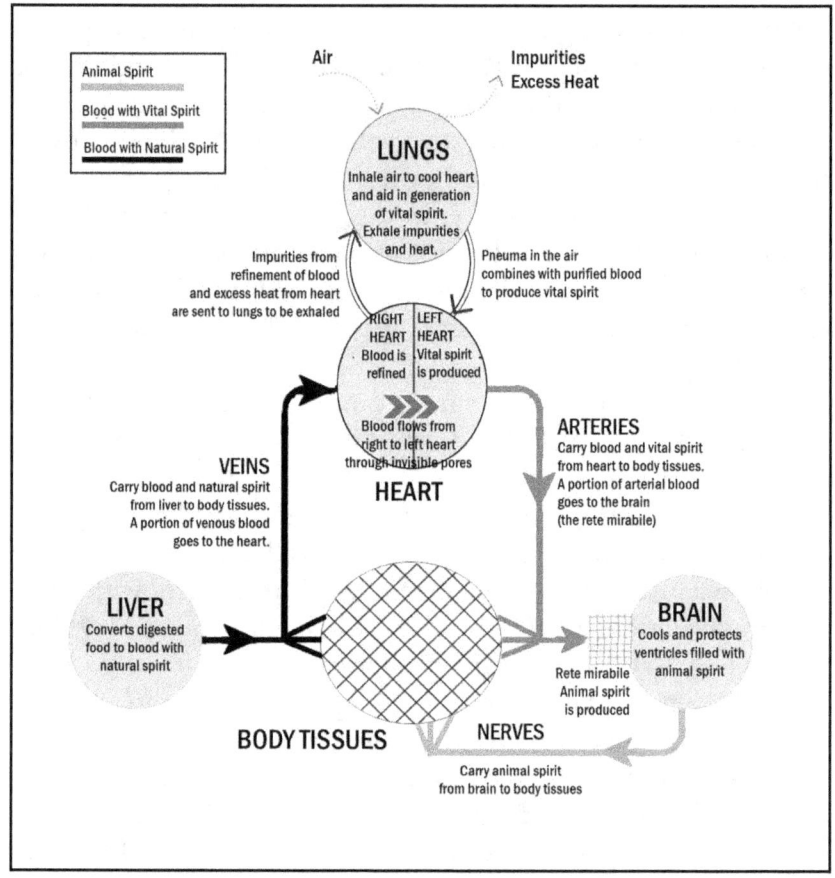

Figure 2. A diagram of the Galenic physiological system

The Galenic Physiological System

1. Food is absorbed by the digestive tract and brought to the liver, where it is transformed into the least refined type of blood, imbued with natural spirit.

2. The network of veins, which has its point of origin in the liver, carries this blood, with its nutriment and natural spirit, to all parts of the body, where it is used to restore and replenish the tissues of the body.

3. A small portion of venous blood, with its associated natural spirit, is sent to the right side of the heart. There it is refined, with impurities being exhaled through the lungs.

4. The purified blood is sent to the left side of the heart. It was not entirely clear how this happened, but it was conjectured that there must be invisible pores in the septum separating the right and left sides of the heart. (Some blood does flow from the heart to the lungs in this model, but this is just to nourish the lungs.)

5. In the left side of the heart, the purified blood is mixed with air inhaled through the lungs. The heart was pictured as something like a furnace, where pneuma from the air is forged into vital spirit. Excess heat is expelled from the body through the lungs, which also act as a kind of bellows to fan the flame in the heart.

6. The arteries carry the blood and vital spirit to all parts of the body.

7. A small portion of arterial blood is sent to the *rete mirabile* or retiform plexus, a fine network of arteries at the base of the brain. There it is further refined to create the highest form of pneuma, psychic or animal spirit.

8. Animal spirit is stored in ventricles in the brain. From there, the nerves — conceived as hollow tubes, like the veins and arteries — carry the animal spirit to all parts of the body, where it is responsible for sensation and movement.

Note that Figure 2 includes the brain, nerves, and liver, which were not shown in Figure 1. Nowadays we think of the bodily functions as being divided into separate systems — the circulatory system, nervous system, digestive system, and so on — and can illustrate each system independently for purposes of study, although we know that they all interact in the living body. However, these additional organs must be included in Figure 2 because they are integral parts of the Galenic system. In fact, the entire system can be seen as an extension of the process of digestion, by which ingested food is progressively refined into purer and purer products until finally it leaves its material part behind and becomes pure spirit.

The Galenic model was accepted for some 1500 years because it is logical and internally consistent, and agrees reasonably well with the observed functioning of the body. Nevertheless, it is based on many assumptions that are now known to be incorrect. Blood is not produced in the liver, and the veins do not originate in the liver. The direction of flow in the veins is from the tissues of the body to the heart, not from the liver to the tissues. The septum dividing the heart is not permeable. There is no *rete mirabile* in the human brain; this structure is found in some herbivorous mammals such as sheep and cattle, but does not exist in primates. The nerves are not hollow tubes, and do not carry a substance derived from the blood. Instead, they carry impulses from the brain, which control the entire process (and all other body systems).

Servetus's Modification of the Galenic System

When Servetus studied medicine in Paris from 1536 to 1538, the curriculum consisted largely of study of the Galenic system. Servetus's teacher, Johann Winter von Andernach, praised him as a particularly proficient Galenist.

Servetus did not question most of Galen's ideas. What he proposed was a refinement to the Galenic system, which included a solution to the problem of how blood passes from the right side of the heart to the left, when there are no visible openings in the septum dividing the sides of the heart. He proposed that blood was transmitted from the right side of the heart to the left by passing through the lungs rather than by seeping through the septum, so that the mixing of refined blood with pneuma from

The Galenic Physiological System

the air takes place in the lungs instead of in the heart. He also believed (as did some of his contemporaries) that there was no such thing as natural spirit; instead, blood produced by the liver was infused with vital spirit produced by the heart.

Figure 3 shows Servetus's version of the Galenic system.

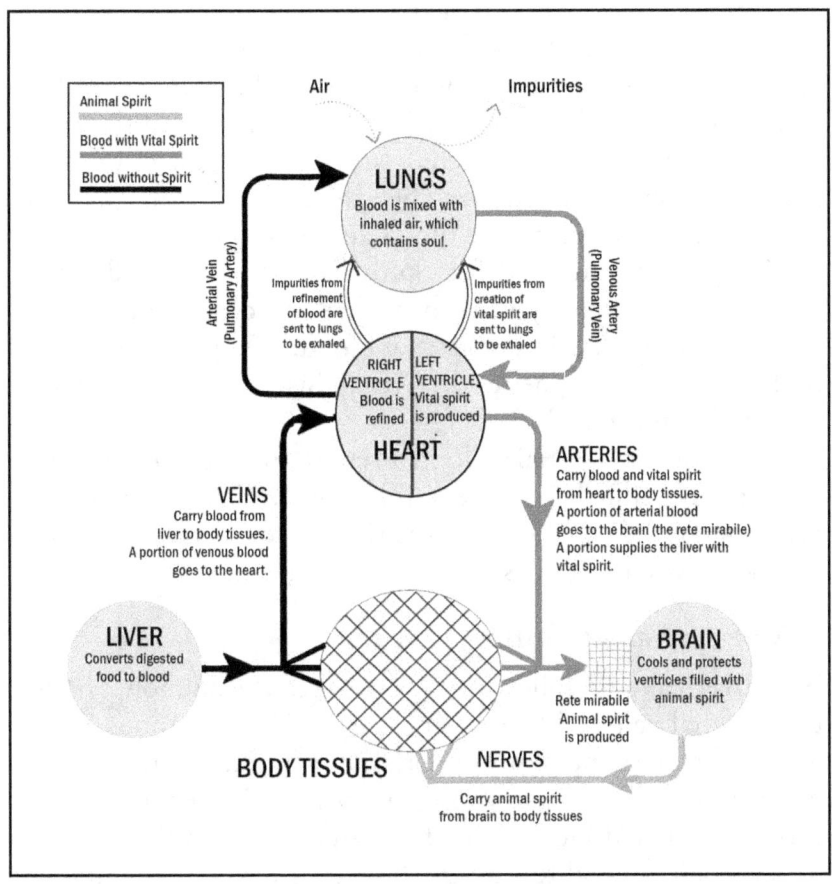

Figure 3. A diagram of Servetus's modification of the Galenic physiological system

1. As in the standard Galenic model, blood is created in the liver, but at this point it contains physical nutriment only—it does not contain any spirit.

2. The veins carry blood from the liver to nourish all parts of the body.

3. A portion of venous blood is sent to the right ventricle of the heart. There it is refined, with impurities being exhaled through the lungs.

4. The purified blood flows from the right ventricle to the lungs through the arterial vein (pulmonary artery). In the lungs, the blood is mixed with inhaled air.

5. The mixture of blood and air flows from the lungs to the left ventricle through the venous artery (pulmonary vein). Vital spirit is created in the left ventricle "by the power of the strong life-giving fire contained there." Impurities resulting from this process are sent to the lungs to be exhaled.

6. The arteries carry the blood and vital spirit to all parts of the body, including the liver. Spirit here may be called natural spirit, but it is actually vital spirit that was created in the heart and sent to the liver in the arterial blood. (Only a small portion of the arterial blood goes to the liver — just enough to supply the liver with vital spirit.)

7. A portion of arterial blood is sent to the *rete mirabile*, where it is further refined to create animal spirit. This is stored in the ventricles of the brain and and distributed to all parts of the body via the nerves, just as described by Galen.

A Note on Nomenclature

Note that Servetus, following Galen, called the pulmonary artery the "arterial vein" and the pulmonary vein the "venous artery." This difference in nomenclature reflects a difference in the underlying model of the cardiovascular system. In general, arteries carry oxygenated blood away from the heart, while veins carry deoxygenated blood toward the heart. However, the pulmonary vessels are an exception to this rule: deoxygenated blood moves away from the heart (to the lungs, to be supplied with oxygen), while oxygenated blood moves from the lungs toward the heart. So, which of these vessels is an artery, and which is a vein?

In modern nomenclature, any vessel that carries blood away from the heart is an artery, and any vessel that carries blood toward the heart is a vein. Thus, the vessel that carries blood from the heart to the lungs is the pulmonary artery, even though it carries deoxygenated blood; and the vessel that carries blood from the lungs to the heart is the pulmonary vein, even though it carries oxygen-rich blood. In the Galenic system, however, the arteries and the veins were believed to be largely separate systems, for the transmission of different substances. Any vessel that carries bright-coloured blood (i.e. blood imbued with vital spirit) was considered an artery; this includes the vessel that we call the pulmonary vein. And any vessel, including the one we call the pulmonary artery, that carries dark-coloured blood was considered a vein.

A Note on Sources

Basic information about the modern understanding of the respiratory and cardiovascular systems is readily available at every level, from picture books to textbooks for nursing and medical students. One source we found useful is *Knowledge Encyclopedia: Human Body* (Wonder House Books, 2024), aimed at children aged 9 and up.

Concerning the Galenic system, the primary source is Galen, *On the Usefulness of the Parts of the Body*, chapters 6 and 7. The secondary sources consulted are: Singer and Rabin, *Prelude to Modern Science*, xxxviii-xxxix; Pagel, *William Harvey's Biological Ideas*, 127-136; Aird, "Discovery of the cardiovascular system"; and Harris, *Heart and Vascular System*, 267-396. For Servetus's modification of Galen's system, the primary source is *Restoration*, 169-171.

The diagrams in this appendix were produced by Lynn Gordon Hughes, based on these sources.

Appendix C

Servetus's Place in Medical History

This appendix is adapted from two articles by Justo Hernández and Peter Hughes, which were unfinished at the time of Peter's death.

Part 1: The Credit That Is Due

The question of the scientific credit due to Servetus has been raised so many times without resolution, that some feel it is pointless, even counterproductive, to continue asking it. José Pardo-Tomás, in his recent article, "Servetus as an Anatomist," contends that "the historical evidence seems to be truly exhausted," so that further debate along this line is unfruitful and distracts us from considering "the exact historical and cultural setting of anatomical knowledge and practice during the first half of the sixteenth century."[1]

While sympathizing with the frustration expressed by Pardo-Tomás, we believe that there is actually more to be discovered, especially through a careful reading of Servetus's works. We think that further discussion of the question of the assignment of credit for the discovery of the pulmonary transit, if conducted with a mind open to a variety of conclusions, can lead us in the same general direction that Pardo-Tomás advocates, based on modern understanding of collaborative breakthroughs in the history of science.

---

[1] José Pardo-Tomás, "Servet, Anatomista," *Revista de historia Jerónimo Zurita* 92 (2017), 29.

Circulation, Lesser Circulation, and Pulmonary Transit

Before discussing how Servetus came to know about the pulmonary transit and what credit he may or may not deserve for this important medical discovery, it is necessary to clarify the scope and extent of his possible contribution, especially when it is compared with the later work of William Harvey.

Before Harvey there was no concept of blood circulation. In *On the Motion of the Heart and Blood* (1628), Harvey was aware of having made a great and new discovery, for with justice he claimed that "this is the only book that states that blood flows out and returns by a new path."[2] He specified that this new path was a closed circuit and that blood was in continuous motion.[3]

The pulmonary transit described by Servetus has sometimes been called "the pulmonary circulation" or "the lesser circulation," but these terms are misleading. The journey taken by the blood, from the right ventricle of the heart through the lungs to the left ventricle, does not show blood completing a circuit. One could attempt to describe it as a loop by saying it starts in the heart, goes through the lungs, and returns to the heart. But it actually starts in the right ventricle of the heart and returns to the left ventricle. Despite the fact that these two ventricles are both in the organ we call the heart, they are, in fact, two quite different places. As Servetus and a number of his contemporaries point out, there is no passage of blood through the middle wall of the heart. The two ventricles are isolated from one another. Harvey introduced the idea that the heart is a pump. It is actually two pumps working together. It is effectively two organs in one compact space.

Servetus clearly did not know of the heart's function as a pump, which is essential to any theory of circulation. Moreover, Servetus accepted the traditional Galenic view that blood was consumed during its passage through the body and had to be continuously replenished by blood newly formed in the liver.[4] And he did not

---

[2] William Harvey, *Exercitatio Anatomica de Motu Cordis in Sanguinis in Animalibus* (Frankfurt, 1628), 6.

[3] Harvey, *Exercitatio Anatomica*, 58.

[4] *Restoration*, 169.

grasp many details, including auricles, valves, and capillaries, that describe and explain the flow of blood through the heart and lungs as modern medicine understands it.

Nevertheless, Servetus did know something that Galen did not know; he was a good enough scholar of Galen to be aware of that and to state it confidently in *The Restoration of Christianity*.[5] He did outline a pulmonary transit of some kind: that blood was sent from the right ventricle of the heart to the left through the lungs, and in the process was changed. This had not been mentioned in any printed literature prior to the publication and intended dissemination of his book.

With this in mind, let us turn to the question of how Servetus knew what he knew.

Biblical Inspiration

In book 5 of *The Restoration of Christianity*, Servetus introduces his discussion of the pulmonary transit by saying, "So that you, reader, may have a complete understanding of how the soul and spirit function, I shall here add divine philosophy, which you will easily understand if you have been trained in anatomy."[6] Here, at the outset, he makes two important points. First, he is writing as someone "trained in anatomy," and expects that a certain amount of technical medical knowledge will be required to fully understand his argument. Second, and more important, his purpose in writing is to explain the functioning of the soul and spirit; the functioning of the heart and lungs is incidental.

Until this point, on page 169 of *The Restoration of Christianity*, almost everything that Servetus wrote in book 5 has been based on the Bible.[7] The citations range over passages from the Pentateuch, history, wisdom literature, the prophets, the Gospels, Acts of the

---

[5] *Restoration*, 171.

[6] *Restoration*, 169.

[7] There are three non-biblical references in pp. 163-169. In dismissing the idea that the Holy Spirit is part of the Trinity, Servetus alludes briefly to the Church Fathers, citing a work by Hilary and one that was thought to be by Athanasius. He also mentions approvingly an "Orphic" saying quoted by Aristotle, to the effect that the soul enters the body through the breath.

Apostles, and the epistles of the New Testament. Because of Servetus's theological preoccupations, Andrew Cunningham, historian of medicine at Cambridge University, reasoned that the Bible must have been the principal inspiration and source of Servetus's pioneering description of the pulmonary transit:

> All that Servetus says, both about the Trinity and about the blood, is based and built on the literal text of the Bible. In particular, his belief that the blood has to pass to the lung (to be mixed and imbued with the Holy Spirit) is based on a literal reading of the biblical words that "the soul is in the blood" (Leviticus 17, verses 11, 14). For, given this, Servetus found it necessary to be able to specify precisely where and how the soul or spirit came into the blood.[8]

While this claim may be a bit strong, it seems, at the very least, that Servetus's theology, and his reading of the Bible, provided a strong predisposition and motivation for him to pay particular attention to the heart and lungs and the associated blood vessels. His belief that the Holy Spirit was an activity of God, rather than a "person," may have disposed him to be receptive to critical pieces of physiological information, drawn from his reading of ancient and modern medical researchers, that were required to generate an account of the nourishing transit of the blood that was consistent with his reading of the Bible.

Reading Galen

It is a common speculation that Servetus's physiological insights may have been based upon original discoveries made in the dissection theatre. But his practical experience in dissection may actually have been quite limited. This is hinted by the recollection of the University of Paris anatomy professor Johann Winter von Andernach,[9]

---

[8] Andrew Cunningham, *The Anatomical Renaissance: The Resurrection of the Anatomical Projects of the Ancients* (Aldershot: Scholar Press, 1997), 255.

[9] There is much confusion about the name of Johann Winter von Andernach. His original name was Johann Winter (Andernach is his birthplace). In Italian and Latin, the "W" in his name was replaced by "Gu," so that "Winter" became "Guinter," "Guinther," "Guenther," and other variants. This was then confused with the common German name Guenther or Günther.

who wrote in the "Dedicatory Epistle" to the 1539 edition of his *Principles of Anatomy*:

> I had assistants: first, Andreas Vesalius, a young man indeed greatly devoted to anatomy ... After him, Michael Villanovanus worked closely with me in dissections, a man quite distinguished in the study of all branches of the literature, and second to none in knowledge of the teachings of Galen.[10]

Although this shows that, during a brief period of his life, Servetus did engage in dissection, it also appears from this that he may have acquired most of his anatomical knowledge by studying canonical medical literature, rather than through direct observation. Servetus's familiarity with the works of Galen is shown in his little book on syrups, in which he cited thirty-seven of them. He mentioned a few more in his discourse on astrology and nine in *The Restoration of Christianity*.[11]

Around forty of Galen's works had been translated into Latin by Johann Winter von Andernach. Presumably, in the course of his studies, Servetus read or consulted many of these, including *Anatomical Procedures*, a practical guide to dissection. Charles Donald O'Malley, in his commentary on Servetus's scientific writings, reminds us "that to a considerable degree [Servetus] was what might be termed a medical philologist and that his formal medical training in Paris was of brief duration. It is true that he had been praised by Guinther von Andernach [*sic*] as his assistant in anatomy, but the kindly professor was himself more philologist than anatomist."[12]

In *The Restoration of Christianity* there is evidence to suggest that Servetus may have deduced the idea of the pulmonary transit of

---

[10] Winter von Andernach, Dedicatory Epistle to *Institutionum anatomicarum*. "Michael Villanovanus" is the Latin form of Michel de Villeneuve, the name that Servetus used when living in France.

[11] The nine works of Galen referenced in *Restoration* are: *De usu partium, De placitis Hippocratis et Platonis, De facultatibus naturalibus, De substantia facultatum naturalium, De causis pulsuum, De semine, Quod animi mores corporis temperatura sequantur, De simplicium medicamentorum facultatibus*, and *De methodo medendi*. See *Restoration*, 214-215, 251, 302, 563.

[12] O'Malley, *Servetus's Geographical, Medical and Astrological Writings*, 199-200.

the blood by closely and selectively reading Galen. The cardiologist and medical historian Rudolf E. Siegel, who made a special study of the physiology of Galen, became convinced that Galen, when read correctly, ought to be understood as the first to discover and describe the transit of the blood through the lungs. He thought that during the intervening centuries, up to the time of Harvey, Galen's description of the pulmonary blood-flow, particularly in *On the Usefulness of the Parts of the Body*, was neglected and misunderstood. Here is Siegel's paraphrase of what he considered a key passage in *On the Usefulness of the Parts*:

> Galen explained how the pumping mechanism of the chest wall propels the blood from the branches of the pulmonary artery into those of the pulmonary vein. He assumed the existence of anastomoses between these two large vessels in order to explain the functional connection of the arterial and the venous system of the lungs. These anastomoses correspond to our alveolar capillaries. Galen stated that during the respiratory movement of the lungs, the blood becomes intimately mixed with the air entering through the pores of the finest ramification of the bronchial tree.[13]

This interpretation of Galen implies a major flow of blood from the pulmonary artery to the pulmonary vein through the branches and capillaries in the lung. Siegel translates a key passage from *On the Usefulness of the Parts* as:

> The contracting thorax compresses the pulmonary veins in the lungs from all sides; therefore they push the air which they contain forcefully forward. These veins also take up from the minute anastomoses (i.e. between the pulmonary artery and vein) ... Thus, the blood is squeezed in one forward direction, and is flowing drop by drop, into the pulmonary veins.[14]

But another translation of the same passage reads:

> When the thorax contracts, the venous arteries, pushed inwards and compressed from all sides, instantly force out the pneuma they

---

[13] Siegel, "Influence of Galen's Doctrine," 311.

[14] Galen, UP 6.10, translated by Rudolf E. Siegel. Siegel, "Influence of Galen's Doctrine," 312.

contain and receive in exchange a portion of blood through those fine openings ... when the blood is compressed and cut off from returning through the large orifice, some of it trickles through those fine openings into the arteries.[15]

Reading Galen in this latter way, the passage of all the blood, and its freshening with air, does not seem to be implied. The air (*pneuma* or spirit) in the pulmonary veins is sent to the heart to be mixed there with blood, while a portion — possibly quite a small portion — of the blood in the pulmonary artery comes through the tiny openings (*anastomoses* or capillaries) "in exchange" for air. Later in this passage, Galen mentions that the blood under discussion is only for the nourishment of the vein itself.

It thus seems that Galen can be read as providing both a summa of ancient Graeco-Roman physiology and hints of proto-Harveyan circulatory ideas. For, while Siegel did not actually prove that the pulmonary transit was known by Galen, he did demonstrate that a few of Galen's observations on the lungs were amenable to suggesting the idea of the pulmonary transit — especially if one were already disposed to believe that Galen meant to indicate such a transit. Could it be that Servetus, mentally prepared by ideas drawn from the Bible, interpreted Galen in much the same way as Siegel did?

In *The Restoration of Christianity*, however, Servetus makes it clear that, on the subject of the pulmonary transit, he thought that Galen was wrong: "If anyone compares what I have just said with what Galen writes in books 6 and 7 of *On the Usefulness of the Parts*, he will fully understand [that what I am describing is] a truth of which Galen himself was not aware."[16]

Siegel, because he believed that everything that Servetus needed for his own description of the pulmonary transit was readily available to any sufficiently discerning reader of Galen, was not inclined to award much credit for its discovery to Servetus.[17] But it could

---

[15] Galen, UP 6.10, translated by Margaret Tallmadge May. *Galen on the Usefulness of the Parts of the Body*, 303-304.

[16] *Restoration*, 171.

[17] Siegel, "Influence of Galen's Doctrine," 322.

equally be argued that Servetus's assemblage of ideas drawn from the vast Galenic corpus was itself a creative distillation not far removed in spirit from the discoveries being made at the same time through observation by masters of the art of dissection.

As Siegel admits, this Galenic information had been misread throughout the Middle Ages. If William Harvey is to be awarded great credit for deducing the entire circulatory system by correctly reading the dissected body, might not Servetus be allowed some credit for being, perhaps, the first to have interpreted some of Galen's intriguing observations more correctly than even Galen himself had understood them? All the more so, because Servetus may have combined hints drawn from Galen with critical corrections resulting from his and others' experience at the dissection table.

Servetus and Vesalius

Concerning the septum, or middle wall, of the heart, Andreas Vesalius wrote, in *On the Fabric of the Human Body* (1543), "We are forced to admire the care of the Creator whereby blood sweats through passages which escape visual detection, from the right ventricle into the left."[18] Interestingly, Servetus used the same verb (*resudare*, to sweat) to describe the presumed passage of a small amount of blood through the septum: "Finally, the middle wall [of the heart], being devoid of vessels and any means [of communication between the ventricles], is unsuited for the transmission or elaboration [of blood], although some blood may possibly sweat through."[19] It thus appears not unlikely that Servetus read Vesalius. If so, he was selective in his adoption of the many new anatomical insights provided by Vesalius, since, for the most part, he adhered to more traditional Galenic depictions of bodily function.

For instance, Servetus followed traditional teaching about the location of the mental faculties: "There are four ventricles in the brain and three internal senses. For the first two ventricles together produce one common sense, which is the receiver of images. The

---

[18] Vesalius, *Fabrica* (1543), 589.

[19] *Restoration*, 171.

middle one is for thinking and the last is for memory."[20] But this idea had already been challenged. Jacopo Berengario da Carpi, anatomist and professor of medicine in Bologna, in *Brief Introductions* (1530), reallocated all of these faculties to the lateral ventricles.[21] Vesalius, taking a relatively agnostic point of view, said that the only thing he could say about the ventricles was that they were where vital spirit was transformed into animal spirit. He thought it impossible to determine the locations in the brain of the specific operations of the soul.[22]

Another organ that Servetus worked into his description of the journey of the inhaled spirit into the mind and soul is the retiform plexus (*rete mirabile*, or amazing net), which was thought to be an important network of arteries at the base of the skull. He wrote:

> Thus the vital spirit is poured from the left ventricle of the heart into the arteries of the entire body in such a way that the part of it which is more rarefied moves toward the upper part [of the body], where it is further elaborated. [It moves] especially into the retiform plexus, which is located beneath the base of the brain, close to the seat of the rational soul.[23]

The existence of the retiform plexus in human beings, its appearance, and its function were for a long time controversial subjects. Its Galenic interpretation as a vital organ, which extracted the animal spirit from the blood, was first questioned by Berengario da Carpi, who claimed that he could not find such a structure when he dissected human corpses.[24] A few decades later, Vesalius dismissed the existence of the retiform plexus in human beings, explaining

---

[20] *Restoration*, 177.

[21] Jacopo Berengario da Carpi, *Isagogae breves et exactissimae in anatomiam humani corporis* (Strasbourg, 1530), O 2.

[22] Vesalius, *Fabrica* (1543), 636. Vesalius also pointed out that the brains of quadrupedal mammals so closely resemble human brains that we must wonder at the church teaching which denies that these animals have reasoning and rational souls [*Fabrica* (1543), 624]. Yet, unlike Servetus, Vesalius had no desire to challenge ecclesiastical authority. "I shall, from now on, keep far away from debate about the kinds of soul and their locations, lest I bump up against some censor of heresy" [*Fabrica* (1543), 594].

[23] *Restoration*, 171.

[24] Berengario da Carpi, *Isagogae breves*, O 5.

that Galen incorrectly supposed that the retiform plexus existed in human beings based on his dissection of the brains of cows.[25] Nevertheless, the idea that the retiform plexus existed in humans did not disappear after Vesalius, but remained part of anatomical and physiological discourse.[26] Servetus was one of the many who chose to continue to follow Galen rather than Vesalius in this respect. Servetus found it useful, in the physiological depiction of his theological system, to locate the rational soul under the base of the brain and to have its spirit refined in the retiform plexus.

We also see Servetus choosing Galen over Vesalius when he mentions "passages [from the ventricles] to the palate and the nose, from which unhealthy discharges flow."[27] Here he was following Galen, who said that mucus is excreted into the nose through the cribriform plate of the ethmoid bone.[28] Vesalius disagreed, saying, "Galen described this bone incorrectly, as perforated like a sieve or a sponge, and used for conveying mucus out of the brain. For the bone is in no way penetrated by tiny holes of that kind, and one can see that its surface is everywhere continuous and unbroken."[29]

Even as Servetus generally sided with the wisdom of the ancients, Vesalius's flair in dissection and persistent questioning spirit may have sown sufficient doubt that Servetus was prepared to accept the idea that Galen might occasionally be wrong.

The Question of Priority

Realdo Colombo's claim

Realdo Colombo (c.1515-1559), who studied and worked at the universities in Padua and Pisa in the 1540s, was at first a friend and

---

[25] Vesalius, *Fabrica* (1543), 310.

[26] Sebastian Pranghofer, " 'It Could Be Seen More Clearly in Unreasonable Animals than in Humans': The Representation of the *Rete Mirabile* in Early Modern Anatomy," *Medical History* 53 (2009), 561-586.

[27] *Restoration*, 172.

[28] Galen, UP 8.7, 9.3. Both "ethmoid" and "cribriform" mean "sieve-like," from the words for "sieve" in Greek and Latin.

[29] Vesalius, *Fabrica* (1543), 32.

colleague of Vesalius, and later a rival. He performed dissection and animal vivisection, and gave well-attended public lectures on his findings. Among the discoveries that he claimed was the pulmonary transit of the blood. The results of his work were not published in his lifetime, but came out in *On the Subject of Anatomy* in 1559. In this he wrote:

> Between the ventricles [of the heart] there is a septum, through which nearly everyone supposes an entrance is opened for blood to go from the right to the left ventricle ... but they erred by a long shot; for the blood is carried through the pulmonary artery to the lung, and is there attenuated. Next, combined with air, it is conveyed through the pulmonary vein to the left ventricle of the heart.[30]

Observing that the pulmonary artery was too large to have as its sole use provision of nourishment to the lungs, Colombo concluded that it must have another use as well:

> Blood of this sort is stirred up on account of the constant motion of the lung, made thinner, and mixed together with air, which itself is also prepared in this refraction and collision, so that at the same time blood is mixed, air also is received through the branches of pulmonary vein, and finally it is conveyed through its trunk to the left ventricle of the heart. It is conveyed, so well mixed, and also so attenuated, that very little work remains for the heart to do afterwards.[31]

Although Colombo's anatomical and physiological discussion is fuller and more complete than Servetus's, his description of the pulmonary passage of the blood and the main function of the lungs is notably similar. However, Colombo does not seem to have believed that he was in debt to anyone else for this new information. In fact he made several claims for priority of discovery: "No one, until now, has either noticed or written about this, although certainly it ought to have been noticed by everybody."[32] And, "no anatomist has, so far, ever dreamed of this new use of the lung."[33]

---

[30] Colombo, *De re anatomica*, 177.

[31] Colombo, *De re anatomica*, 223.

[32] Colombo, *De re anatomica*, 177.

[33] Colombo, *De re anatomica*, 223.

Appendix C

Dating Servetus's description

Did Servetus deduce the pulmonary transit from his biblically-inspired reading of Galen, supplemented by his own anatomical experience and the doubts of Vesalius, or did he receive his information principally from Colombo? Alternatively, were Colombo's dissections guided by his knowledge of what Servetus had already proposed? In deciding priority, chronology gives us less help than we would like.

The Restoration of Christianity came out in 1553, making Servetus undeniably the first to publish the result; Colombo's *On the Subject of Anatomy* was not in print until fully six years later. However, both books had likely been in the works for many years. We can only venture an educated guess at the timing of the research that led to the information about the pulmonary transit that is disclosed in these publications.

To begin with, based on the similarity in wording to Vesalius's description of the inter-ventricular septum, we can surmise that Servetus composed the passage about the heart and lungs no earlier than 1543, the date of the first edition of Vesalius's *On the Fabric of the Human Body*.[34] And it was obviously written no later than the autumn of 1552, when the text was submitted to the printer.

It has been suggested that we can date the writing more precisely by referring to a manuscript, now in the Bibliothèque Nationale in Paris, which contains a draft of part of *The Restoration of Christianity*, including book 5 (see appendix A, "The Paris Manuscript"). As this manuscript is missing a number of late additions present in the printed version of *Restoration*, it must have been written earlier than the autumn of 1552. But how much earlier?

It was once hypothesized that the Paris manuscript was a copy of the draft that Servetus sent to Calvin in 1546, and that therefore we could date Servetus's description of the pulmonary transit to

---

[34] Vesalius's stronger statements about the impermeability of the septum did not appear until the 1555 edition, so that is no help. Vesalius, *Fabrica* (1555), 734, 746.

1545 at the latest.[35] We now know that this is not the case, since the manuscript refers to a collection of works attributed to Athanasius, which was not issued until 1548.[36] And, as it turns out, the new material must have been added very late in the composition of *Restoration*, for it makes use of a 1551 edition of the works of Clement of Alexandria.[37] The most we can conclude is that the original of the Paris manuscript was probably written between 1549 and 1551. Combining this with the *terminus a quo* based on the date of Vesalius's *On the Fabric of the Human Body*, we get a window of about 1544-1551 for Servetus to have developed his description of the pulmonary transit. Thus, the Paris manuscript does little to narrow down the date range.

Of course Servetus may have had all the essential elements of his description of the pulmonary transit in mind years before the publication of Vesalius's *magnum opus*. If it was in any way based upon his own participation in anatomical procedures (dissection or animal vivisection), then he may have arrived at his new ideas about the heart and lungs as early as the late 1530s, the period of his experience in Paris as a dissector.

Dating Colombo's discovery

Colombo's writing is also hard to date. After training as a surgeon, he began his studies under Vesalius in 1540, soon becoming his mentor's principal dissection assistant. When Vesalius left Padua in 1542, Colombo took over the anatomical procedures and teaching.

---

[35] Mackall, "A Manuscript of the Christianismi Restitutio," 35-38. Bainton, "The Smaller Circulation," 371-374. Alcalá, introduction to *Obras Completas* vol. 3, xxvi.

[36] In book 5, and in the version of book 5 in the Paris manuscript, Servetus cited a work attributed to Athanasius, *De unitate sanctissimae trinitatis* (*Restoration*, 167; manuscript, 6). This work is also cited, along with several other Athanasius and pseudo-Athanasius works, in book 1 (*Restoration*, 38-43). Based on the specific set of works that Servetus mentioned in book 1, the titles he used for them, and his references to the placement of the individual works within the volume, it can be shown that he was using *D. Athanasii ... Opera omnia* (Cologne, 1548). A detailed discussion of this is found in A.R1.96 (*On the Trinity and the Bible*, 371-372).

[37] *Restoration*, 140, citing Clement of Alexandria, *Omnia opera* (1551), 168, 232.

Appendix C

When in 1543 Vesalius made a temporary return, he discovered that his pupil had been criticizing him. Vesalius wrote in 1546: "During the time I was away from Padua, having dissected a body, he boasted that he found a vein that I didn't know about."[38] Given two years of study directed by Vesalius, and, after that, a little time to pursue his own investigations, Colombo may have come to his new conclusion about the pulmonary transit as early as 1544. Since, on the opening page of *On the Subject of Anatomy* he wrote, "I commenced [this work] many years ago," it would seem that he may have been in full possession of the material required for his 1559 publication for a decade or more. And it must have been substantially complete by 1548, when he moved to Rome, because for a time he had hopes of producing it as a work with illustrations by Michelangelo.[39] Thus, it seems reasonable to push back the date of Colombo's knowledge of the pulmonary transit of the blood to the period 1544-1548.

In 1556, three years before *On the Subject of Anatomy* was published, Colombo's student Juan de Valverde (c.1525-c.1587) published a description of the pulmonary transit, mentioning his teacher. He wrote:

> Since there is blood in [the pulmonary] vein, and blood cannot enter it from the left ventricle, as is shown by the placement of the valves that we indicated are in the mouth of this vein, I believe that it is certain that the blood oozes from the pulmonary artery into the substance of the lung, where it is thinned out and is readied to be converted into spirit. Afterwards it is mixed with the air, which has entered through the branches of the trachea, and goes together with the blood into the pulmonary vein and goes from there to the left ventricle of the heart. It mixes there with the thicker blood, which passes from the right to the left ventricle of the heart — if any does pass, because until now I have not been able to see where it can pass.[40]

---

[38] Andreas Vesalius, *Epistola, rationem modumque propinandi radicis Chynae decocti* (Basel, 1546), 136.

[39] Coppola, "Discovery of the Pulmonary Circulation," 55-56.

[40] Juan de Valverde, *Historia de la composición del cuerpo humano* (Rome, 1556), 97v.

The date of Valverde's book does not do much to shrink the *terminus ad quem* for the discovery.[41] Nevertheless there is a way that Valverde can help guide us to an approximate date. He could have learned about the pulmonary transit from Colombo late in the period 1542-1545, after his initial medical studies under Colombo in Padua, where he eventually became Colombo's principal dissection assistant; or possibly during the years 1545-1548, when he worked with his supervisor at a new post at the university at Pisa.[42] This roughly corroborates our previous estimate.

The possibility of influence

The approximate dates for Colombo's and Servetus's conjectured discovery are so close that at first it seems that there could have been some avenue of communication between them. There is, however, no record indicating any such thing. We can only make guesses based upon plausible possibilities.

For instance, if Servetus was indebted to Colombo, he might have learned about the pulmonary transit by hearing a report made by someone who had attended one of Colombo's public lectures or demonstrations. One such candidate is Pierre Palmier, Servetus's archbishop patron and employer, who travelled widely, including to Italy, during the time that Servetus lived in Vienne. It is well-known that Palmier was an enthusiastic auditor of scientific lectures, and he was largely absent from his diocese between 1541 and 1546.[43] It is also possible that there were other travellers who could have brought or sent Servetus reports from Italy mentioning new medical discoveries. Nevertheless, if Servetus learned about Colombo's results before he wrote about the pulmonary transit in book 5 of *The Restoration of Christianity*, this may only have confirmed what he was already thinking in his physiological-theological model of the Holy Spirit.

---

[41] Bainton, "The Smaller Circulation," 372-373.

[42] José Miguel Hernández Mansilla, *Juan Valverde de Amusco y la Anatomía del Renacimiento Hispanoitaliano* (Madrid: San Gregorio, 2020), 36-37.

[43] Cavard, *Le procès de Michel Servet*, 101.

It is more difficult to imagine how Colombo might have learned about the pulmonary transit from Servetus.[44] *The Restoration of Christianity* was printed in 1553, but not made available to the public. Even if a copy had been available, there would have been no reason for a purely medical researcher such as Colombo to consult such a theological work. In any case, as we have seen, the printing was almost certainly far too late to have influenced Colombo or directed his anatomical procedures. In spite of his being a physician, there is no evidence that Dr. Michel de Villeneuve felt called upon to present his description of the pulmonary blood flow as new medical knowledge. Unlike Colombo, he never claimed to have anatomical information that no one else possessed. He merely said that he knew something that Galen did not know. On this basis, it is more likely that Colombo influenced Servetus than *vice versa*. But, unless new information comes to light, we cannot know for sure.

What the world was ready to learn

We must also consider the possibility of independent simultaneous discovery. When the time is ripe, that is, when the underlying ideas have arisen and the necessary technologies have been developed, a major breakthrough in knowledge may be made by several, or even many, people at almost the same time. That happened, for example, in 1858, when Alfred Russel Wallace and Charles Darwin both proposed a theory of evolution by natural selection. In the late seventeenth century, calculus was independently developed

---

[44] The nineteenth-century Servetus enthusiast Henri Tollin claimed that the Paris manuscript was sent to Dr. Horatio Curione in Padua in 1546 and that others in the Padua medical community also received copies of a draft of *Christianismi restitutio* [Henri Tollin, *Michel Servet, Portrait-Charactère* (Paris, 1879), 64-65]. This claim has no foundation except wishful thinking. Moreover, it is implausible that Servetus would spend time making many manuscript copies of his incomplete work to send abroad. The association with Curione is entirely based on the fact that the Paris manuscript is signed on its cover by Horatio Curione and was thus, at some time, in his possession. In 1546 Horatio Curione was twelve years old and not yet a doctor, nor yet in Padua. He likely obtained the manuscript from his father, the antitrinitarian humanist scholar, Celio Secondo Curione. Almost certainly the Curiones treasured the book for its theological import rather than its medical news.

by Isaac Newton and Gottfried Wilhelm Leibniz. And oxygen, the crucial element in enriching the blood in the pulmonary transit, was identified in the late eighteenth century by Joseph Priestley, Antoine Lavoisier, and Carl Scheele. This phenomenon is not uncommon. Indeed some have contended that it is the rule rather than the exception.[45]

In the case of the pulmonary transit, the prerequisites for discovery included the widespread adoption of the printing press, providing ready availability of all of the writings of Galen and a means for rapidly distributing newly acquired medical information; the proliferation of universities with medical schools; and an increase in the frequency of the practice of human dissection and animal vivisection.[46] Dissection led many in the early sixteenth century to question received knowledge. For example, the anatomist Niccolò Massa (1489-1569) was yet another who remarked on the thick hardness of the heart's middle wall.[47] Under these conditions, with the discovery of the pulmonary transit of the blood nearly inevitable, it would not be at all surprising if it happened more than once and independently.

Another way of looking at this phenomenon is as a paradigm shift, as described by Thomas Kuhn in *The Structure of Scientific Revolutions* (1962). The impermeability of the septum dividing the left from the right ventricle of the heart was one among several anomalies that challenged the prevailing Galenic picture of the origin and operation of the blood within the body. These anomalies, as we have seen, posed a challenge to such investigators as Massa, Vesalius, Colombo, Valverde, and Servetus. Vesalius, when confronted with the apparent thickness and solidity of the septum, at first proposed that there were "passages which escape visual detection." But once

---

[45] William Ogburn and Dorothy Thomas, "Are Inventions Inevitable? A Note on Social Evolution," *Political Science Quarterly* 37:1 (1922), 83-98. Robert Merton, "Singletons and Multiples in Scientific Discovery: A Chapter in the Sociology of Science," *Proceedings of the American Philosophical Society* 105:5 (1961), 470-486.

[46] Allen Shotwell, "The Revival of Vivisection in the Sixteenth Century," *Journal of the History of Biology* 46:2 (2013), 171-197. Pardo-Tomás, "Servet, Anatomista," 41.

[47] Niccolò Massa, *Introductorius Anatomiae* (Venice, 1536), 56r.

it became clear that no significant amount of blood could seep through the middle wall of the heart, the whole map of the blood flow, and the purpose of the major internal organs, was up for rethinking. The part of the map which concerned the heart and lungs was the first to be reconfigured. The entire paradigm shift would not be complete until the idea of the circulatory system, as we know it, was proposed by William Harvey some two generations later.

Non-European honours: Ibn al-Nafis

Some three hundred years before Servetus and Colombo, the Arab physician Ibn al-Nafis (1213-1288), in *Commentary on the Anatomy of the Canon* (c.1242), gave a description of the pulmonary transit of the blood:

> When blood is refined in this [right] ventricle it must be transported to the left ventricle where the spirit is generated. However, there is no passage between the two ventricles, for there the body of the heart is solid and there are no visible passages, as believed by the majority, nor an invisible passage appropriate for transporting the blood, as believed by Galen ... Hence, once the blood is refined, it is transported by the artery-like vein [pulmonary artery] to the lungs in order to disperse in the body of the lung and mix with the air, so that its finer parts are purified. Then it is carried to the vein-like artery [pulmonary vein], and from there to the left of the two ventricles of the heart.[48]

This manuscript work, written in Arabic, remained untranslated and unavailable to European readers for centuries. It has been speculated that the Italian physician Andrea Alpago (c.1450-1521), who lived in Damascus between 1487 and 1517, may have brought knowledge of al-Nafis's discovery back with him to Venice in the form of a manuscript and that his nephew Paolo might have communicated this knowledge to one or more of his contemporaries

---

[48] Ibn al-Nafis, *Commentary on the Anatomy of the Canon*, translated in Nahyan Fancy, *Science and Religion in Mamluk Egypt: Ibn al-Nafis, Pulmonary Transit and Bodily Resurrection* (London: Routledge, 2013), 102. See also John B. West, "Ibn al-Nafis, the Pulmonary Circulation, and the Islamic Golden Age," *Journal of Applied Physiology* (2008), 10.1152/japplphysiol.91171.2008

in Padua: Niccolò Massa, Andreas Vesalius, or Realdo Colombo. There is, however, no known manuscript containing a Latin translation of *Commentary on the Anatomy*, nor is there any evidence that Paolo Alpago was acquainted with al-Nafis's views on the pulmonary transit.[49]

Interestingly, it turns out that al-Nafis, like Servetus, was primarily interested in diagramming the pulmonary transit for theological reasons. As none of his many later medical writings further explore this particular corner of physiology, it appears that he did not consider it a stepping stone to a new overall understanding of the body. According to Nahyan Fancy, al-Nafis's description was merely "an anatomical corollary to his new understanding of the soul-spirit-body relationship."[50] Fascinating though it is, al-Nafis's book, like Servetus's, may represent another dead end in the transmission-history of the emerging physiological idea of the circulation of the blood.

Conclusion: The Credit That Is Due

Michael Servetus was undoubtedly the first European to publish an account of the pulmonary transit of the blood. Although it is highly doubtful that he was the first European to know about it, he was, in any case, among the first in his time to entertain and accept the novel idea that blood was in some way nourished by being passed through the lungs. Discovery and acceptance are both essential elements in the story of any intellectual advance.

Since very few copies of *The Restoration of Christianity* survived, it is unlikely that this work had any influence on the growth of medical knowledge between the date of Servetus's death and the time of Harvey. For our modern interpretation of the history of medicine, the importance of the passage about anatomy and physiology in Servetus's book 5, in combination with results reported by Colombo and Valverde and the doubts expressed by Vesalius, is that it demonstrates that the idea of the pulmonary transit was quietly

---

[49] Coppola, "Discovery of the Pulmonary Circulation," 67-74.
[50] Fancy, *Science and Religion in Mamluk Egypt*, 109.

becoming widespread and was on the verge of being influential enough to overturn long-accepted ideas. This passage also shows that, in a last fling, a careful study of the ancient Galenic writings could help usher the way to new results — though the future of medicine belonged primarily to those who, moving past Galen, trusted more in the evidence provided by their own experiments. As far as the biography of Servetus is concerned, at the very least, this passage illuminates the portrait of a man who, though he was devoted to and honoured the wisdom of the ancients, thought for himself and was open to new and ground-breaking ideas.

A nod to Michael Servetus, in the history of the development of modern ideas about the heart, lungs, and flow of blood, should not be taken as detracting in any way from the genius and reputation of either Realdo Colombo or William Harvey. The story of medicine runs directly through them and can effectively be told without the need to mention Servetus. But consideration of the case of Servetus does provide us with a set of interesting sidelights, demonstrating that Galenism could act as a spur as well as an obstacle to scientific progress, showing the connections between medical science and other fields of study, and enriching our appreciation of the collective nature of the discovery process.

Part 2: *The Credit That Is Given*

During the more than three centuries since Servetus's description of the pulmonary transit came to light, there have been many claims for his priority as the discoverer, not only of the pulmonary transit, but also of the whole idea of blood circulation. In a sample of over 200 writers from the eighteenth to the twenty-first century, more than a third credit Servetus with knowledge (however imperfect) of the entire circulatory system. And three-quarters of the rest claim that he knew of the "pulmonary" or "lesser" circulation. Some have claimed that Servetus's description of the pulmonary transit implies that he must have possessed an understanding of the entire circulatory system, even if he did not describe it as such. Or that he was on the verge of discovering circulation when his life was cut short. At the opposite extreme, some recent experts on the anatomy and physiology of the circulatory system conclude that not only did

Servetus not describe circulation, but that his description was hardly an advance over Galen, and does not merit being called a discovery at all.[51] Here we survey the history of ideas about Servetus and circulation, and explore the reasons for the persistence of ideas that have been revealed as fallacies.

The Initial Announcement of Servetus as a Medical Pioneer

The news that the sixteenth-century heretic Michael Servetus had made a pioneering discovery in the field of anatomy and physiology originated in England in 1686. The *Journal of the Royal Society* records that, at the April 7 session, "Mr. [Abraham] Hill read a paper about the circulation of the blood taken out of a book written by one Servetus & printed in the year 1553."[52] Hill had recently found a manuscript copy of *Christianismi restitutio* in the library of John Moore, the bishop of Norwich. This copy had been taken from one of the three surviving specimens of the original print run, which was, until 1720, in the Hesse-Cassel Landgrave library.[53]

Charles Bernard, a surgeon who was present at Hill's talk, passed the news on to William Wotton, an Anglican minister, who mentioned it in the chapter "Of the circulation of the Blood," in *Reflections upon Ancient and Modern Learning* (1694). Wotton wrote that "the first that I could ever find who had a distinct *Idea* of this Matter was *Michael Servetus*."[54] Only in his second edition (1697) did he make the qualification that Servetus "had imperfect

---

[51] Alfred E. Cohn, *The Development of the Harveian Circulation* (New York, 1928). Willem van Hoorn, "Servet and the Non-Discovery of the Lesser Circulation," in Juan Naya and Marian Hillar, eds., *Michael Servetus: Heartfelt* (Lanham, MD: University Press of America, 2011). Justo Hernández, "Miguel Serveto (1511-1553): una nueva perspectiva," *Dendra Médica Revista de Humanidades* 10:2 (2011).

[52] Journal Book Original (minutes of meetings of the Royal Society) 8 (1685-90), 51. https://www.allabouthistory.co.uk/History/Books/Thing/Journal-Book-Original-Minutes-of-the-Ordinary-Meetings-of-the-Royal-Society.html?nNqEHHdS

[53] Geoffrey M. Sill, "The Authorship of *An Impartial History of Michael Servetus*," *Papers of the Bibliographical Society of America* 87 (1993), 306-307.

[54] William Wotton, *Reflections upon Ancient and Modern Learning* (London, 1694), 211.

Glimmerings of that Light which afterwards Dr. Harvey communicated."[55] James Douglas, a fellow of the Royal Society, further spread the news about Servetus's discovery: "In this work ... there are passages that appear to be about the circulation of the blood, which show that [this idea] was well-known to the author."[56] Michel de La Roche, in *Bibliothèque angloise* (1717), passed this along: "Mr. Douglas comments that Servetus knew about the circulation of the blood."[57]

These early announcements, coupling Servetus's name with "the circulation of the blood," introduced confusion, misunderstanding, and endless debate about Servetus's place in medical history. Those who, in the late seventeenth century, rediscovered Servetus's description of the pulmonary transit could see at a glance that he was in advance of his time in some of the anatomical and physiological information that he commanded. It seemed to them a small jump from his unexpected exposition of the pulmonary transit to the conclusion that he knew about the circulatory system as a whole. And since he was a physician who had studied anatomy under the professor who had trained the great Vesalius, they jumped to the further conclusion that he must have been able to make the discovery himself.[58] After Hill's paper, Servetus was often credited as being the first discoverer of circulation, anticipating Harvey by three-quarters of a century.

The majority of those who drew back from suggesting that Servetus discovered, or knew about, circulation as Harvey knew it,

---

[55] Wotton, *Reflections upon Ancient and Modern Learning*, second edition (London, 1697), xxxiii.

[56] James Douglas, *Bibliographia anatomicae specimen* (London, 1715), 84-85. Nevertheless, he maintained that Harvey was the one who really introduced the idea of circulation to the world. *Bibliographia*, 202-203.

[57] Michel de La Roche, *Bibliothèque angloise, ou, Histoire littéraire de la Grande Bretagne*, vol. 1, part 1 (Amsterdam, 1717).

[58] As noted earlier, Servetus's practice of dissection was actually quite limited. While studying at the University of Paris in the 1530s, he assisted his teacher, Johann Winter von Andernach, who praised him more for his Galenic scholarship than for dissection. Afterwards, as a practicing physician in the provinces, he did not have time or opportunity to engage in anatomical procedures.

still retained the word "circulation" in the more limited, or qualified, claim that was made for him. They wrote that Servetus discovered the "lesser circulation" or the "minor circulation" or the "pulmonary circulation." This claim is more defensible, since it limits Servetus's new anatomical and physiological knowledge to the area of the heart and the lungs, but it is still misleading, as it encourages the idea that Servetus had some hint of the modern conception of blood circulating throughout the body. These misconceptions spread quickly among both medical practitioners and scholars in general.

Many have since tried to rebut or correct those who put Servetus forward as the discoverer of the circulatory system. It is not the case that fairly correct evaluations of Servetus's knowledge of blood flow have existed only in recent years; there have been voices of caution in all eras since the time of Abraham Hill, advising us not to oversell Servetus as a medical pioneer. Nevertheless, the claim that Servetus discovered the circulation of the blood persists and is to be found in works of scholarship to this day.

Eighteenth-Century Schools of Thought on Servetus and Circulation

From statements about Servetus and circulation made in the eighteenth century, we can discern most of the principal variants of the emerging legend.

Variant 1: Servetus knew about the circulation of the blood.

In 1714, in the first doctoral thesis to mention Servetus and circulation, the physician Paul Gottfried Sievert called Servetus "the first one to publish a notice about the circuit of the blood."[59] Among other medical practitioners who passed along this claim for Servetus were the Genevan physician Jean-Jacques Manget.[60] In 1763 Jean Astruc, a noted specialist in women's diseases, wrote: "I do not think

---

[59] Paul G. Sievert, *Dissertatio inauguralis physico-medica de Morbis a motu Humorum circulatio aucto oriundis...* (Basel, 1714), 26.

[60] Jean-Jacques Manget, *Bibliotheca scriptorum medicorum*, vol. 2, part 2 (Geneva, 1731), 258.

that anyone could doubt that Servetus and Colombo knew about the circulation of blood."[61]

Samuel Crellius, a theologian of the Polish Brethren, who held Servetus in high honour, credited theological study for having inspired Servetus's discovery.[62] Servetus's early and influential biographer, Henrik van Allwoerden, claimed that Servetus taught the circulation of the blood.[63] A number of historians, including some clergymen especially critical of Calvin, were also quick to recognize Servetus as a landmark scientist.[64] The most widely-read of Calvin's critics was Voltaire. In his *Essai sur les moeurs et l'esprit des nations* (1756), he claimed that Servetus "has earned untroubled glory for having discovered the circulation of the blood long before Harvey."[65] These words were soon incorporated in the French *Encyclopédie* (1765).[66]

Spanish historians were also quick to promote their countryman's claim to fame. Among these were the bibliographer Felix de Latassa y Ortin and the Benedictine monk Benito Jerónimo Feijoo, who, while claiming distinction for Servetus, thought that circulation had been discovered even earlier by other Spaniards.[67] The Jesuit scholar, Francisco Xavier Lampillas, made his claim quite unequivocally: "Indeed, if we speak of the first who has clearly

---

[61] Jean Astruc, *Traité des maladies des femmes, avec un catalogue chronologique des médecins qui ont écrit sur ces maladies* (Avignon, 1763), 3:390-394.

[62] Samuel Crellius, "Annotationes quaedam de Michaele Serveto," *Bibliotheca historico-philologico-theologica* 1 (1719), 758.

[63] Henrik van Allwoerden, *Historia Michaelis Serveti* (Helmstadt, 1727), 230.

[64] Among these are: Gilbert Charles Legendre, *Traité historique et critique de l'opinion* (Paris, 1735), 544. George Benson, *A Collection of Tracts* (London, 1748), xvii. Erasmus Middleton, *Biographia Evangelica*, vol. 2 (London, 1780), 47. George Thomson, *The Spirit of General History* (London-Carlisle, 1791), 341.

[65] Voltaire, *Essai sur les moeurs* (Geneva, 1756), 4:113.

[66] *Encyclopédie, ou dictionnaire raisonné des Sciences, des arts et des métiers*, vol. 17 (Neufchastel, 1765), 274.

[67] Felix de Latassa y Ortin, "Miguel Serveto," *Biblioteca nueva de los escritores aragoneses* (Pamplona, 1798), 153. Benito Jerónimo Feijoo, *Cartas eruditas y curiosas* (Madrid, 1765), 371-372.

affirmed the circulation of the blood, no one can dispute that this honour goes to Servetus."[68]

Variant 2: Servetus knew about the circulation of the blood. Or so they say.

A few writers, such as the lexicographer Jean Pierre Niceron and the bibliographer Christian Wilhelm Kestner, having taken their information at second hand, merely reported that some other writers had made the claim that Servetus knew about blood circulation.[69] The French priest Antoine d'Artigny, whose account of Servetus's life preserves the content of the no longer extant records of Servetus's interrogation by the Inquisition, pointed out that *The Restoration of Christianity* contains "a remarkable passage on the circulation of the blood, which many people claim that Servetus was the first to recognize."[70]

Variant 3: Servetus came close to knowing about the circulation of the blood.

Some writers, while they acknowledged that Servetus did not understand circulation in the way that Harvey did, claimed that Servetus could nevertheless, after a fashion, be said to have known about it. In 1706 Gottfried Leibniz, having consulted the copy of *Christianismi restitutio* in the Hesse-Cassel Landgrave library, wrote that "[Servetus] better understood the circulation of the blood than all those who preceded him."[71]

The celebrated Edinburgh anatomist Alexander Monro at first lectured, in the 1720s and 1730s, that claims for Servetus were an effort to diminish Harvey. In his lectures from the 1740s, however, there was a change in Monro's tone toward Servetus. He then wrote,

---

[68] Xavier Lampillas, *Ensayo histórico-apologético de la literatura española* (Zaragoza, 1784), 235.

[69] Jean Pierre Niceron, *Mémoires pour servir à l'histoire des hommes illustres* (Paris, 1730), 11:244. Christian Wilhelm Kestner, *Medizinisches Gelehrten-Lexicon* (Jena, 1740), 784.

[70] Antoine Gachet d'Artigny, "Mémoires pour servir à l'histoire de Michel Servet," in *Nouveaux mémoires d'histoire, de critique et de littérature* (Paris, 1749), 2:77.

[71] Letter to Mathurin La Croze, 2 Dec 1706, Lettre 3 in Gottfried Leibniz, *Opera omnia* vol. 5 (Geneva, 1768), 479.

"The first of the Moderns, that is, opposed to Harvey, as having any Idea of the Circulation is Michale Servetus, a Spanish physician, who in 1553 wrote a book called *Christianismi Restitutio*."[72]

The great taxonomist Carl Linnaeus qualified Servetus's contribution in this way: "Servetus, Aquapendens and Caesalpinus looked closely at the circulation of blood; Harvey, who exposed this same matter to the public light, took the honour."[73] The anatomist and medical historian, Antoine Portal, also allowed that Servetus understood the circulation of the blood, albeit in a way that was somehow less than that of Harvey.[74] Interestingly, he added the claim that "the communication of the arteries and the veins has been discovered by Servetus."[75]

Variant 4: Since he described the pulmonary transit, Servetus must have known about the circulation of the blood.

Pierre Bayle, the Huguenot philosopher and proto-encyclopedist, decided that the knowledge about the pulmonary transit that Servetus demonstrated indicated that he must also have known about blood circulation in general.[76] James Douglas, already mentioned, falls into the same category. William Hunter, in his medical lectures, claimed that Servetus's and Colombo's descriptions of "the circulation of the blood through the lungs" were "at least, three quarters of the discovery."[77]

Variant 5: Had he lived longer, Servetus would have worked out a fuller or more perfect picture of the circulatory system.

The anonymous 1723 book, *An Impartial History of Michael Servetus*, after claiming that "[Servetus] is the first who mentioned

---

[72] Alexander Monro, *The History of Anatomy*, c. 1725 (British Library Manuscript Collection, Add. Mss. 4376) ff. 104-105; cited in Geoffrey Sill, *The Cure of the Passions and the Origins of the English Novel* (Cambridge University Press, 2001), 60.

[73] Carolus Linnaeus, *Amoenitates academicae*, vol. 7 (Erlangen, 1789), 398.

[74] Antoine Portal, *Histoire de l'anatomie et de la chirurgie* (Paris, 1770), 1:300, 2:467.

[75] Portal, *Histoire de l'anatomie*, 2:23.

[76] Pierre Bayle, *Nouvelles de la République des lettres* (Apr 1707), 457.

[77] William Hunter, *Two Introductory Lectures* (London, 1784), 44.

the circulation of the blood," went on to say that "Servetus was a great observer of nature, and no doubt would have improved those notions, and carried them much further, had he not been prevented by an untimely death."[78]

Variant 6: Servetus had a general picture of circulation, but his ideas were imperfect.

The celebrated Dutch physician, Hermann Boerhaave, said that Servetus and others "seem to have had a distant view of the blood's true course, but in part only" and that "they did not understand or explain the whole, and confirm it by sufficient proofs."[79] In John Noorthouck's *An Historical and Classical Dictionary*, it was merely allowed that Servetus "appears to have had some obscure conception of the circulation of the blood."[80]

Variant 7: Servetus discovered only a part of the circulation of the blood: the "lesser" or "pulmonary" circulation.

The clear statement that Servetus's knowledge of circulation was limited to pulmonary circulation is to be found in a number of eighteenth-century authors, but by no means a majority of them. Among these are the Italian anatomist Giambattista Morgagni,[81] the English physician Robert Colborne,[82] the Scottish physiologist Malcolm Flemyng,[83] Boerhaave's Swiss pupil Albrecht von Haller,[84] the physician and medical historian Nicolas Eloy,[85] and Bartolomeo Castelli, the compiler of an influential medical dictionary.[86] The great English historian Edward Gibbon, who

---

[78] *An Impartial History of Michael Servetus, Burnt Alive at Geneva for Heresie*, (London, 1723), 65, 70.

[79] Hermann Boerhaave, *Academical Lectures on the Theory of Physic*, vol. 2 (London, 1743), 38-39.

[80] John Noorthouck, *An Historical and Classical Dictionary* (London, 1776).

[81] Giambattista Morgagni, *Epistolae anatomicae duae* (Leiden, 1728), 95.

[82] Robert Colborne, *The Plain English Dispensary* (London, 1753), xiii.

[83] Malcolm Flemyng, *Introduction to Physiology* (London, 1759), 46-47.

[84] Albrecht von Haller, *Bibliotheca anatomica* (Zurich, 1774), 193.

[85] Nicolas Eloy, *Dictionnaire Historique de la Médecine*, vol. 4 (Mons, 1778), 257.

[86] Bartolomeo Castelli, *Lexicon medicum graeco-latinum*, vol. 2 (Leipzig, 1762), 10.

found himself "more deeply scandalised at the single execution of Servetus than at the hecatombs which have blazed on the Auto da Fés of Spain and Portugal,"[87] was careful to limit his claim for Servetus's advanced physiological knowledge. In his memoirs Gibbon remarked that "the merit of... Servetus is now reduced to a single passage, which indicates the smaller circulation of the blood through the lungs, from and to the lungs, from and to the heart."[88]

Variant 8: Servetus knew nothing about circulation.

A solitary commentator, the English physician John Freind, was not, in any degree, sympathetic to the idea of presenting Servetus as a medical pioneer. In *The History of Physic*, the first English history of medicine, he dismissed Servetus as one "who is said to have known the circulation of the blood, but did not."[89]

Servetus's Evolving Medical Reputation in the Nineteenth Century

All of these lines of thinking about Servetus and circulation, along with a few others, can be found, in various proportions, down to the present.

In the early eighteenth century, immediately after the discovery of Servetus's description of the pulmonary transit, the overwhelming majority of the writers who mentioned the subject credited Servetus with at least some knowledge of circulation. Later in the century the number who specified that Servetus knew only the "pulmonary," or "lesser," circulation grew, but almost half of the writers still claimed, without any qualification, that Servetus knew about the circulatory system.

Opinion shifted noticeably in the nineteenth century. Only about ten percent of the writers asserted that Servetus knew about

---

[87] Edward Gibbon, *The Decline and Fall of the Roman Empire* (London, 1776-1788), ch. 54, n. 36.

[88] Edward Gibbon, *The Miscellaneous Works: with memoirs of his life and writings* (London, 1837), 98.

[89] John Freind, *The History of Physic* (London, 1725-26), 320.

circulation in general,[90] and another twenty percent believed that he knew it incompletely[91] or else mentioned that others had alleged that Servetus knew it.[92] A majority now carefully pointed out that Servetus knew only about the "pulmonary circulation," and that it looked as though he had no conception of general circulation.[93] One such was the English historian Henry Hallam, who wrote, "That Servetus had a just idea of the pulmonary circulation and the aeration of the blood in the lungs, is manifest by this passage, and denied by no one; but it has been the opinion of anatomists that he did not apprehend the return of the mass of the blood through the veins to the right auricle of the heart."[94] Some gave Servetus limited credit, but avoided using the term "circulation."[95] A few,

---

[90] For example: George Sigmond, *The Unnoticed Theories of Servetus* (London, 1826), 33. Henri Martin, *Histoire de France* (Paris, 1857), 484. "Michael Servetus: Discovery of the Circulation of the Blood," *The Book-Worm* (Oct 1866), 152.

[91] Richard Dugard Grainger, *Elements of General Anatomy* (London, 1829), 243. Sir William Hamilton, *The History of Medicine, Surgery, and Anatomy* (London, 1831), 63. Philippe André Grandidier, *Fragments d'une Alsatia litterata* (Comar, 1898), 501-502.

[92] John Watson, "Practical Education in Medicine," *The New York Journal of Medicine* (Jan 1847), 14. "The Antitrinitarians," *The London Encyclopedia* (1845), 411. Antonius van der Linde, *Michel Servet, Een Brandoffer der Gereformeerde Inquisite* (Groningen, 1891), 123.

[93] A few examples, from many: Antonio Hernández Morejón, *Historia Bibliográfica de la Medicina Española* (Madrid, 1843), 49. Cesare Cantù, *Histoire universelle* (Turin, 1848), 662. Gustav Valentin, *Versuch einer Physiologischen Pathologie des Blutes* (Leipzig-Heidelberg, 1866), 472. Charles Daremburg, *Histoire des sciences médicales* (Paris, 1870), 593-594. Marcelino Menéndez y Pelayo, *Historia de los Heterodoxos Españoles*, vol. 3 (Madrid, 1880), 271-273. Robert Willis, *Servetus and Calvin* (London, 1877), viii, 212. Charles Dardier, "Michel Servet d'après ses plus récents biographes," *Revue historique* 10 (May-June 1879), 33. Henry C. Chapman, *History of the Discovery of the Circulation of the Blood* (Philadelphia, 1884), 26.

[94] Henry Hallam, *Introduction to the Literature of Europe in the Fifteenth, Sixteenth, and Seventeenth Centuries* (London, 1839), 437.

[95] Robert Hooper, *The Anatomist's Vade-mecum* (London, 1805), xiii. William Paley, *The Works of William Paley*, vol. 1 (London, 1838), 73-81. Thomas Lamb Eliot, "The Martyrdom of Servetus," *The Unitarian Review and Religious Magazine* 19 (1883), 60.

like Giulio Ceradini, went so far as to deny Servetus any credit, saying that others had preceded him[96] or that his knowledge was mere guesswork and not science.[97]

Some writers seemed to want to have it both ways, stating that Servetus knew about the "pulmonary circulation," but implying that he had also grasped the concept of general circulation. The eminent physiologist Jean Pierre Flourens wrote, "Servetus discovered the pulmonary circulation. That fact is clear."[98] But he also thought that the fact that "the blood left the heart and returned to the heart" indicated "a circuit, circulation" — despite the fact that the two ventricles of the heart are actually very different places. Accordingly he concluded that "this idea of the circulation, so grand and so new, was first formed by Servetus."[99] Another such is Servetus biographer Henri Tollin: he claimed only that Servetus knew about the pulmonary circulation, but his title, *The Discovery of the Circulatory System by Michael Servetus*, says otherwise.[100]

The romantic idea that Servetus only failed to gain an understanding of the circulatory system as a whole because of his early death due to religious persecution attracted some adherents during

---

[96] Making the case for Realdo Colombo: Achille Chéreau, *Histoire d'un livre: Michel Servet et la circulation pulmonaire* (Paris, 1879), 32-33. Giulio Ceradini, *Qualche appunto storico-crítico intorno alla scoperta della circolazione del sangue* (Genoa, 1875) and *La scoperta della circolazione del sangue* (Milan, 1876). Claiming the priority of other Spaniards: Anastasio Chinchilla, *Triunfo de la medicina española* (Seville, 1861), 30.

[97] Émile Saisset, "Michael Servetus," *The Christian Reformer* (May 1848), 268. Edward Meryon, *History of Medicine*, vol. 1 (London, 1861), 295-296.

[98] Pierre Flourens, *History of the Discovery of the Circulation of the Blood* (Cincinnati, 1859), 122; translated by J. C. Reeve from Flourens, *Histoire de la découverte de la circulation du sang* (1854). See also a translation from Flourens in Charles Dickens's magazine, *Household Words* (13 June 1857), 562.

[99] Flourens, *History*, 21.

[100] Henri Tollin, *Der Entdeckung des Blutkreislaufs durch Michael Servet* (Jena, 1877), 77. Sampson Gamgee wrote, "Tollin's claim that [Servetus] was the discoverer of the circulation of the blood is inadmissible." "Harvey and Cesalpinus," *The Lancet* (20 Jan 1877), 81.

this period.[101] The Unitarian clergyman Andrews Norton speculated that "if his life had not been prematurely cut off, he might have passed on to higher attainments, and anticipated the honor of that complete discovery of the circulation of the blood, which has immortalized the name of Harvey."[102]

Another new way of formulating Servetus's contribution got its start in the nineteenth century. This was the idea that, whatever he understood about circulation, Servetus had in some way provided the beginning of a new line of physiological thinking that ultimately led Harvey to propose the circulatory system.[103] The historian of medicine Claude-François Michéa predicted that "this unfortunate thinker will be forever known as the point of departure in the chain, in which Cesalpino and Harvey are the last links."[104] The American physiologist John Call Dalton said that Servetus was an "instance of a remarkable physiological truth first stated by an author who afterward remained unknown until the doctrine of circulation had advanced far beyond its condition as understood by him."[105]

Servetus's Medical Reputation in the Twentieth Century and Beyond

In the twentieth century a greater proportion of writers confined Servetus's apparent knowledge to what was usually termed "pulmonary circulation,"[106] with still only a very few carefully labeling the

---

[101] Richard Wright, *An Apology for Dr. Michael Servetus* (Wisbech, 1806), 317. Erastus Edgerton Marcy, *The Homeopathic Theory and Practice of Medicine* (New York, 1868), 1:48.

[102] Andrews Norton, "Life of Michael Servetus," *General Repository and Review* 4 (1813), 41.

[103] Kurt Sprengel, *Histoire de la médecine* (Paris, 1815), 257. William Hamilton Drummond, *The Life of Michael Servetus* (London, 1848), v. Eusèbe Henri Alban Gaullieur, *Genève depuis la constitution* (Geneva, 1856), 51.

[104] Claude-François Michéa, "Galerie des célébrités médicales de la renaissance," *Gazette Médicale de Paris* 12 (1844), 569.

[105] John Call Dalton, *Doctrines of the Circulation* (Philadelphia, 1884), 122.

[106] For example: Auguste Dide, *Michel Servet et Calvin* (Paris, 1907), 71. Ephraim Emerton, "Calvin and Servetus," *Harvard Theological Review* 2 (1909), 154. Carl

latter "the pulmonary transit."[107] Among these is Roland Bainton, whose 1953 book *Hunted Heretic* has long been considered the most authoritative biography of Servetus. He wrote that Servetus "was the first in the West to grasp the pulmonary circulation of the blood — or more accurately, the transit or circuit of the blood in the lungs, since no return occurs to the point of departure."[108] Sir William Osler, the Canadian physician and educator known as "The Father of Internal Medicine," employed the words "pulmonary circulation," but was careful to say precisely what he meant: "The discovery was nothing less than that of the passage of the blood from the right side of the heart to the left through the lungs, what is known as the pulmonary, or lesser circulation."[109]

Remaining very much a minority opinion, even among medical writers, was the idea that Servetus did nothing to advance scientific knowledge. The Mexican physiologist and medical historian José Joaquín Izquierdo complained that "On the whole Servetus's work appears rather as a product of imagination and fantasy, than as a conquest by scientific methods which were introduced a century

---

Theophilus Odhner, *Michael Servetus: His Life and Teachings* (Philadelphia, 1910), 45. Stefan Zweig, *The Right to Heresy* (New York, 1936), 95. Earl Morse Wilbur, *A History of Unitarianism* (Cambridge, MA, 1945), 1:148-149. John F. Fulton, "Michael Servetus and the Lesser Circulation of the Blood through the Lungs," in Bruno Becker, ed., *Autour de Michel Servet et de Sébastien Castellion* (Haarlem, 1953), 62. O'Malley, *Servetus's Geographical, Medical and Astrological Writings*, 197. José Barón Fernández, *Miguel Servet: Su vida y su obra* (Madrid: Espasa-Calpe, 1970), 293-294. Charles Howe, *For Faith and Freedom* (Boston: Skinner House, 1977), 27. Fernando Solsona, *Miguel Servet* (Zaragoza: Dis putación General de Aragón, 1988), 80. Fernando Martínez Laínez, *Miguel Servet: Historia de un fugitivo* (Barcelona: Rueda J. M., 1991), 132. George Huntston Williams, *The Radical Reformation*, 3rd ed. (Kirksville, MO: Truman State University Press 2000), 500.

[107] Roland Bainton, "Michael Servetus and the Pulmonary Transit," *Bulletin of the History of Medicine* 25 (1951), 2. Walter Pagel, "Vesalius and the Pulmonary Transit of Venous Blood," *Journal of the History of Medicine* 19 (1964), 327. Alfred P. Fishman and Dickinson W. Richards, *Circulation of the Blood: Men and Ideas* (New York: Oxford University Press, 1982), 21.

[108] Bainton, *Hunted Heretic*, 78.

[109] William Osler, *Michael Servetus* (London, 1909), 24.

later by Harvey."[110] The eminent American cardiologist Alfred Cohn said that "neither Columbus [Colombo] nor Servetus did the Galenic system any real damage. In reality they strengthened it, for the systems of both continued to imply that a small portion only of the venous blood passed the tricuspid valve, and moved onward to the left ventricle."[111]

Meanwhile, about five percent of writers on the subject still claimed unqualified knowledge of blood circulation for Servetus.[112] One of these, the Spanish doctor Pompeyo Gener, went so far as to say that "Today's premier scientific authorities have established that Servetus was the first person to record this phenomenon, basic to life: the circulation of the blood through the veins and arteries."[113] And the Spanish historian Nicasio Mariscal y Garcia de Rello explained that "Servetus discovered the two circulations, pulmonary and general. If he did not detail a description of the general one, it was because he did not need it for his [theological] argument, and also because he found it simpler and easier [to understand] than the pulmonary one."[114]

Some decided to sit on the fence. The Unitarian minister and historian Alexander Gordon wrote that "Whether [Servetus] had grasped the larger truth of the general circulation of the blood may be left in doubt, for while there are indications that fit in with this,

---

[110] José Joaquín Izquierdo, "A New and More Correct Version of the Views of Servetus on the Circulation of the Blood," *Bulletin of the Institute of the History of Medicine* 5 (1937), 931.

[111] Cohn, *Development of the Harveian Circulation*, 16.

[112] For example: John Sistaire Caulkins, "What Harvey Owes to Servetus," *Physician and Surgeon* (Dec 1910), 441-446. Eleanor Gertrude Brown, *Milton's Blindness* (Columbia University Press, 1934), 4. Juan Manuel Palacios Sánchez, *El ilustre aragonés Miguel Servet: breve biografía del sabio español, descubridor de la circulación de la sangre* (Huesca, 1956), 21. José Roca Cuxart, *Glorias de Cataluña y del México primitivo* (Mexico City, 1962), 67, 69. David Lawton, *Blasphemy* (New York: Harvester Wheatsheaf, 1993), 58.

[113] Pompeyo Gener, *Servet* (Barcelona-Buenos Aires, 1911), 133-134.

[114] Nicasio Mariscal y Garcia de Rello, *La participación que tuvieron los médicos españoles en el descubrimiento de la circulación de la sangre* (Madrid, 1931), 77-78.

they should not be pressed too far."[115] After quoting Gordon, and several others, Edinburgh University librarian and researcher David Cuthbertson concluded the subject of Servetus and circulation by saying, "Here, then, we leave the various opinions about Servetus and the discovery of circulation as problematic only."[116]

Interestingly, in the twenty-first century, the number of writers reporting that Servetus knew about circulation has gone up, both in absolute numbers and as a proportion of the whole. These still represent a minority, but no longer a tiny and diminishing one. Some of these appear to be lightweight scholars and popularizers, whose knowledge both of Servetus and of medical history is superficial.[117] Among the more well-known of the popularizers is the husband-and-wife team of Lawrence and Nancy Goldstone, book collectors interested in tracing the history of "one of the rarest books in the world." The Goldstones claim only that Servetus knew about the pulmonary circulation, but make the manifestly incorrect statement that he understood the true function of the heart.[118] On the other hand, Marian Hillar and Ángel Alcalá — two recent and significant Servetus biographers, familiar with a great deal of literature on the subject — follow in the footsteps of Mariscal y Garcia, and claim that Servetus knew about the circulatory system as whole, but failed to mention it because describing it would not have added anything to his discussion of the soul.[119]

In 2008, the Dutch cardiologist Chris van Tellingen published an article in the *Netherlands Heart Journal* entitled "Scientific

---

[115] Alexander Gordon, *The Personality of Michael Servetus* (Manchester, 1910), 24.

[116] David Cuthbertson, *A Tragedy of the Reformation* (Edinburgh, 1912), 59.

[117] For example: Bill Missett, *Awakening the Soul, Book 2* (AuthorHouse, 2005), 277. E. Michael Jones, *The Jewish Revolutionary Spirit* (South Bend, IN: Fidelity Press, 2008), 342. William Stacy Johnson, *John Calvin: Reformer for the 21st Century* (Louisville, KY: Westminster John Knox Press, 2009), 113.

[118] Lawrence and Nancy Goldstone, *Out of the Flames* (New York: Broadway Books, 2002), 198.

[119] Hillar, *Michael Servetus*, 117. Alcalá, introduction to *Obras Completas* vol. 1, xcix.

progress — or just another day at the office," in which he characterized knowledge of the circulation of the blood as a progressive discovery that started with Hippocrates and Galen, was continued by Servetus, and finished by Harvey.[120] This elicited a letter to the editor entitled "Michael Servetus (1511-1553) did not discover the lesser circulation," by H. H. Kruyswijk and W. van Hoorn. In the letter the authors listed the reasons why Servetus's description of the pulmonary transit could in no way be described as circulation: 1) he "held that the blood is prepared in the liver and transported to the other organs for food by the veins"; 2) "There is no mention of the motive function of the heart"; and 3) he "did not give any indication of return of blood to the heart."[121]

How Could So Many People Be So Wrong?

Servetus plainly did not know about the circulation of the blood. What he described is an essential part of the circulatory system, but he presented it as merely a modest modification of the old Galenic system. His idea of the function of the lungs, which we look upon as quite advanced, did not imply the more modern view of the heart as a pump or our picture of the arteries and veins as parts of the same system. His physiological ideas did not include the return of blood to its starting place. These facts are plain to see in *The Restoration of Christianity*. So why did almost everyone get it wrong for over three hundred years?

Reason 1: Confusion of a part with the whole

There is a Greek-derived word, *synecdoche*, which means a figure of speech that allows one to talk of part of something as if it were the whole (or vice-versa). For example, using synecdoche one can refer to an automobile as "wheels." For people who know what both automobiles and wheels are, there is no confusion here: people generally

---

[120] Chris van Tellingen, "Scientific progress — or just another day at the office," *Netherlands Heart Journal* 16:4 (2008), 143-146.

[121] H. H. Keuyswijk and W. Van Hoorn, "Michael Servetus (1511-1553) did not discover the lesser circulation," *Netherlands Heart Journal* 16:7/8 (2008), 284.

understand that while wheels are an essential component of these vehicles, the existence of wheels does not imply automobiles. The ancient Sumerians knew a lot about wheels but had no conception of the motor, another essential component of the automobile. Thus, it would be ridiculous to say that the Sumerians understood automotive engineering.

Although the pulmonary transit is part of the circulatory system, it is a false and confusing use of synecdoche to refer to this as "circulation." In the case of Servetus, it seems evident that many of the writers who used this kind of synecdoche fully understood what they meant when they said that Servetus had a partial understanding of circulation: they took it to mean that Servetus had described an essential component of what later came to be viewed as the circulatory system. But their figure-of-speech shorthand has clearly led others astray.

Reason 2: Making one circulatory system into two

Servetus's connection with circulation is often qualified by the idea that his contribution is confined to the "lesser," "minor," or "pulmonary" circulation. This preserves for Servetus (or Colombo) a pioneering role in the discovery of circulation, while reserving the glory of the "greater" or "major" circulation for Harvey. But this implies that there are two circulations, when there is actually only one. As we have seen, the "lesser circulation" is actually no circulation at all — it is not a closed loop. With no circuit, there can be no claim for the discovery any kind of circulation.

Again, many writers well understood that the "pulmonary circulation," by itself, was no circulation, and some of these even took it for granted that knowledge of the "lesser" circulation did not imply, or even intimate, any understanding of a "greater." But it is easy to see how the casual employment of this kind of makeshift, and, from a modern viewpoint, careless, nomenclature could give rise to much misunderstanding.

Reason 3: Not reading the source document thoroughly

Most writers who have expressed themselves on the subject of Servetus's place in the history of medicine have been handicapped by the difficulty of becoming acquainted with *Christianismi restitutio*. In the first century following Abraham Hill's announcement, the book was only available in a very few collections, and could not easily be consulted. A transcription of one of the three surviving copies was published in Nuremburg in 1790. But this, issued in a very short print run, made it only somewhat easier to find the text.[122] Furthermore, as the book constitutes more than 700 pages of mostly theological Latin, medical historians and non-specialists have had to resort to taking the word of earlier authorities or else have fallen back on studying short excerpts translated by others.

A problem with this latter strategy is that the quoted passages are often only brief excerpts cherry-picked from the pages of Servetus's physiological description. These quotations naturally highlight the places where Servetus's description appears to be consistent with a modern view of circulation, and downplay those that demonstrate his more traditional Galenic thinking. Only by reading the physiological material in full could one grasp that Servetus could not possibly have had an overall view that could remotely be classified as blood circulation.

Reason 4: Unwarranted speculation

A few writers have employed guesswork and speculation in order to fill in the places that Servetus left blank. This is particularly true of those who have claimed that Servetus actually knew about the entire circulatory system, but did not feel the need to write about it.[123] Well, Servetus might have known a lot of things that he did not write down, but unless some particular bit of knowledge is preserved for us in his works, we are not justified in assuming that he knew it. Nor can we make meaningful guesses about what he would have learned, had he lived long enough.

---

[122] See Madeline E. Stanton, "Bibliography of Servetus," in John F. Fulton, *Michael Servetus* (New York, 1953), 84-90. See also Goldstone, *Out of the Flames*, 274-275.

[123] For example: Seth Beach Curtis, "Michael Servetus," *Unitarian Review* 22 (1884), 437. Mariscal y Garcia, *La participación*, 77-78. Alcalá, introduction to *Obras Completas* vol. 3, xcix.

Reason 5: Partisan bias

Wishful thinking may be a factor in the way Servetus is presented by partisans. Among these are the Spanish, who are naturally proud of the many achievements of their countryman. Over the years Spanish-speaking scholars have credited Servetus with knowledge of general circulation at a rate twice as high as writers in general. Interestingly, two voices among these, Benito Jerónimo Feijoo and Anastasio Chinchilla, give absolute priority to other Spaniards.[124] On the other hand, the Mexican, José Izquierdo, is among the writers, worldwide, most skeptical about Servetus's role in the history of circulation.[125]

Some have overrated Servetus's contribution to medicine for religious reasons. Servetus was unquestionably a religious innovator. Some of those who admired his religious ideas, or who were shocked by the intolerance that led to his execution, succumbed to the temptation to add one more leaf to his laurel wreath. Surprisingly, although many Unitarians see Servetus as a spiritual ancestor, Unitarians, as a group, are not much more prone to this kind of over-admiration than the average writer. However, biographers of Servetus, especially those writing before 1900, are more likely than most to make exaggerated claims for their subject.

Other attitudes that may have affected writers on this subject are negative biases: amongst medical writers, towards Harvey, and amongst others, towards Calvin.

Reason 6: Uncritical scholarship

There are so many writers whose claims about the place of Servetus in medical history are not backed up by any scholarly apparatus, that one suspects that their sources are not supported either. In recent years too many appear to have gathered their information about Servetus almost entirely from popular and uncritical histories and websites. Those claiming that Servetus knew about blood circulation are guilty of not checking a sufficient number of sources back up

---

[124] Feijoo, *Cartas eruditas*, 371-372. Chinchilla, *Triunfo de la medicina*, 30.
[125] Izquierdo, "A New and More Correct Version," 931.

their statements, and of not taking pains to find out which among the many voices are the most reliable ones.

The most unreliable scholarship is done by those who have strayed too far beyond their own area of expertise. In works of popular nonfiction, information about Servetus — and not just about circulation — is often wildly inaccurate. For example, in one recently published book we find multiple errors on the subject in one short paragraph:

> But the worst was yet to come, in the horrible treatment accorded to Michael Servetus (1511-1553), a Spanish physician and theologian, who the Church declared a heretic after he became the first medical scientist to accurately describe the human body's blood circulation system. In 1553, Servetus published *Christianismi restitutio*, which challenged the Church on numerous points of theology, contained his theories of blood circulation, and also contained his theory that the Soul is contained in the blood. For this, he was arrested and tried by the Catholic Church's Inquisition in Lyon, France, found guilty of heresy and sentenced to death.[126]

If Servetus had been a much more famous figure, on the level with Martin Luther, John Calvin, Napoleon, or Abraham Lincoln, his doings would have been much more widely and critically discussed. But outside of a handful of "cottage industries" turning out information for a few clusters of scholars and enthusiasts, Servetus generally receives only passing, and often not very critical, attention.

Reason 7: An error of the Enlightenment

The original announcement in 1686 was that there was something in a book by Servetus "about the circulation of the blood." This, and the respectful discussion that immediately followed, unfortunately gave the high ground to those who promoted the idea that Servetus had anticipated Harvey in discovering circulation. Thus it then seemed incumbent upon those who would say otherwise to prove that Servetus did not know about the circulatory system. However, it is generally a more difficult task to prove that someone does not

---

[126] Missett, *Awakening the Soul*, 277.

know something than to prove what they do know. By the time that a more accurate point of view had begun to be well and precisely articulated, the Servetus-circulation meme had spread so far and so widely, that it was almost impossible to contain it.

What was the cause of this error of the Enlightenment? One might speculate that, since Harvey's circulatory system was only gradually accepted by Galenic physicians,[127] there remained some residual anti-Harvey animus that sought expression. Or, more likely, it may be that late seventeenth-century physicians still regarded Harvey as an empiric (or, in common parlance, a quack) because he trusted in experience and experiment more than theory. In 1636, when challenged by Caspar Hofmann at the Altdorf demonstration, Harvey, who did not take note of the difference between venous and arterial blood, could not come up with a rationale for circulating the blood.[128] No doubt Servetus's presentation had a certain appeal. Servetus did not overturn Galenism — in fact he was known to be a great Galenist — and he did provide a plausible rationale for the pulmonary transit: the enrichment of the blood as it traveled through the lungs. Of course his explanation did not involve enrichment by oxygen — this was a chemical substance only discovered in the eighteenth century — but an alteration brought about by an intangible substance known as spirit or pneuma. And, of course, Servetus provided no theory to explain general circulation, for he did not know of its existence.

Reason 8: The legend of the medical martyr

Servetus was demonstrably executed for what he wrote in *The Restoration of Christianity*. One small part of this massive religious tome contains a description of the pulmonary transit, which was included in order to make a theological point. The fact that Servetus appears to be a medical and scientific pioneer in addition to being the formulator of highly original (and heretical) theological ideas

---

[127] Pagel, *William Harvey's Biological Ideas*, 349-350. Thomas Wright, *Circulation: William Harvey's Revolutionary Idea* (London: Vintage, 2012), 195-203.

[128] Wright, *Harvey's Revolutionary Idea*, 200-202.

makes his death by burning at the stake seem doubly poignant and twice as unjust.

In 1860, an article in a magazine edited by Charles Dickens erroneously proclaimed that "poor Servetus was burned, partly for disproving the theory then existing that the veins carried the blood to the various parts of the body."[129] The characterization of Servetus as a "medical martyr" or a "martyr to science" became increasingly frequent in the late nineteenth and early twentieth centuries.[130] Among the more specific claims were: Servetus was "condemned to death for writing the book that contained the most momentous physiological discovery of the time,"[131] and Servetus "was condemned to death by the Protestant leader John Calvin for proposing (correctly as it turned out) the theory of the lesser or pulmonary circulation of the blood, contradicting the teaching of Galen."[132]

Using legendary or mythical thinking, Servetus may be made to fall into a category with scientists who were victims of religious persecution, such as Galileo. Servetus has more in common with Giordano Bruno, who, although he held some cosmological views which were in advance of his time, was, like Servetus, condemned and executed for non-scientific heresies only. This particular trinity —Servetus, Bruno, and Galileo — is often found, grouped together, in scientific apologetic literature.[133] The ubiquity of this popular

---

[129] Charles Dickens, ed., *All the Year Round* (4 Feb 1860), 355.

[130] For example: James Bell Pettigrew, "On the Physiology of the Circulation, in Plants, in the Lower Animals, and in Man," *Edinburgh Medical and Surgical Journal* (July 1872), 5. J. M. Ball, Jr., "The Story of Michael Servetus, Being a Contribution to the History of Medicine," *The Iowa State Medical Reporter* (Sep 1886), 141. Robert Oswald Moon, *The Relation of Medicine to Philosophy* (London, 1909), 122. Joseph Needham (ed.), *Science, Religion and Reality* (London, 1925), 122.

[131] Victor Robinson, *Pathfinders in Medicine* (New York, 1912), 76.

[132] *Oxford Illustrated Companion to Medicine* (1986), 484.

[133] This is a major theme of John William Draper, *History of the Conflict between Religion and Science* (London, 1875). Another example, among many: DeWitt Stettin, Jr., "Research and Regulation," in Aubrey Milunsky and George Annas, eds., *Genetics and the Law II* (New York: Plenum Press, 1979), 9.

classification encourages acceptance of the misleading idea that Servetus was killed on account of his scientific beliefs.

Whether or not Servetus is considered a martyr for science, his death and the suppression of his work appear to many to have been a setback for the progress of science, engineered by the forces of retrograde thinking and intolerance. The greater his contribution to medicine is held to be, the greater the injustice, and the more interesting his story seems to be. The idea that Servetus discovered the circulation of the blood only feeds this myth. As a newspaper reporter cynically pronounces at the end of John Ford's 1962 film, *The Man Who Shot Liberty Valance*, "When the legend becomes fact, print the legend."

Conclusion: Servetus's Place in History

Servetus had a way of casting his net widely and learning things in many different fields. He knew medical literature, ancient and modern. He was enough of an expert on geography, and the literature of geography, to edit a new edition of Ptolemy. He delivered lectures on astrology and mathematics. He made a study of the Bible in its original languages. He was well-read in the Church Fathers and Neoplatonic literature. He was conversant in medieval scholastic literature, rabbinic literature, and ancient Greek philosophy. He had bits and pieces of legal knowledge and could cite the Quran (albeit in Latin translation).

In the field of religion, which he understood to be a pursuit that gathered together the fruits of his endeavours in every subject area, Servetus was a brilliant pioneer. Although he did not succeed in attracting converts and founding a church, he was, in himself, a one-man Spanish reformation. His theological works, including *The Restoration of Christianity*, advocate a broader, more inclusive form of Christianity. Servetus should be greatly honoured for this, if for nothing else.

Servetus has deservedly secured a prominent place in the history of toleration and freedom of thought. He is remembered as one who suffered for his religious ideas, and he has inspired many others, down through the ages, to strive for the individual's right to liberty of conscience.

Servetus's Place in Medical History

Thus, even if we conclude that Servetus was not an outstanding pioneer in medicine, but merely an early adopter of new ideas that came his way and, almost by accident, the first to record in print a description of the pulmonary transit, we have not done much damage to the reputation of this remarkable and versatile man. We have but helped to refocus attention on his overwhelming and vital interests, his theology and spirituality — the only things for which he would have cared to be long remembered.

ANNOTATIONS

Annotations
Book 5

1. The Greek word *hypostasis*, like the Latin word *substantia*, is formed from roots meaning "under" and "stand," and means something that stands under or underlies. But the word *hypostasis* has come to have a specialized meaning when applied to the Trinity. The trinitarian formula is three *hypostases* (persons) in one *ousia* (substance or essence).

Servetus rejected the formula of three persons in one substance — this was, in his view, the principal "error of the Trinity." According to him there was just one hypostasis, God, and Christ was its presentation to humankind.

2. The word translated here as "shining with light" is *splendens*. By using this word, Servetus probably intended to suggest the related word *splendor* — a connection that is lost in translation. ("Splendid" or "resplendent" would have preserved the etymology, but obscured the meaning.) *Splendor* occupies an important place in Servetus's view of the structure of the world. As he explained in book 4, Servetus subscribed to the Neoplatonist view that all physical things (animate and inanimate) are composed of matter and form, and that forms are made of light.[1] Furthermore, he explained, there are

---

[1] *Restoration*, 146-147, 151-152.

two kinds of light: the warm light of the sun, and the cool light of water, which is called *splendor*. As such, *splendor* is one of the four sources of all natural things.[2]

3. Historically, the phrase "truly and substantially" (*vere et substantialiter*) has been used to refer to the presence of the body and blood of Christ in the Eucharist. For example, the Wittenberg Concord of 1536 — an attempt by Reformed and Lutheran theologians to resolve their theological differences, later repudiated by the Reformed — affirmed that "with the bread and wine the body and blood of Christ are truly and substantially present, offered, and received."[3]

4. Recapitulation, in the theological sense, refers to the idea that Christ is the second Adam, able to repair the damage done by the first Adam. The doctrine was developed by Irenaeus, who wrote:

> When [Christ] was incarnated as a human being, he recapitulated in himself the long line of human beings, providing salvation for us; so that we would receive in Christ Jesus what we had lost in Adam, that is, to be in accordance with the image and likeness of God.[4]

5. The Hebrew word *ruach*, like the Greek word *pneuma*, can mean spirit, breath, or wind. Servetus goes beyond this, asserting that one Hebrew word — presumably, he was thinking of *ruach* — means both soul and breath[5] and both air and spirit.[6] However, Hebrew has other, more specific words for soul (*nephesh*) and for air (*avir*).

6. In Ezekiel 37:9, God instructs Ezekiel to prophesy to the breath, saying, "Come from the four winds, O breath, and breathe on these

---

[2] The sources of matter are earth and water; the sources of form are the light of the sun and the *splendor* of water. *Restoration*, 161.

[3] The Latin text of the Wittenberg Concord is in *Corpus Reformatorum*, vol. 3 (Halle, 1836), 75–77. An English translation by Amy Nelson Burnett is found in "The Wittenberg Concord 1536," *Reformation and Renaissance Review* 18:1 (March 2016), 25-27.

[4] Irenaeus, *Adversus haereses* 3.18.1 (PG 7 932B).

[5] *Restoration*, 168. The Latin words are *anima* (soul) and *spiratio* (breath).

[6] *Restoration*, 169. The Latin words are *aer* (air) and *spiritus* (spirit).

slain, that they may live." Equating wind with air and breath with soul (see A.R5.5), this implies that the soul contains the elemental substance, air.

7. In his influential work *On the Teachings of Hippocrates and Plato*, Galen credited Plato with the idea that there are three parts of the soul, and that these are located in different parts of the body: reason in the head, anger in the heart, and desire in the liver.[7] Galen himself was reluctant to name or describe the substance of the soul, though he accepted the idea, originated by Alexandrian physicians several centuries earlier, that movement and sensation were caused by the flow of "soul spirit" (*pneuma psychikon* in Greek, or *spiritus animalis* in Latin) to and from the brain, via the nerves. Extending this model to the other body parts discussed by Plato, Galen speculated that it was "not unlikely" that there might be a similar flow of "vital spirit" to and from the heart via the arteries. He was much more skeptical about the existence of a third spirit, but said that if such a spirit existed, it would flow to and from the liver via the veins.[8] Later Galenists developed the fully elaborated "Galenic" system, in which spirit is progressively purified and refined — from natural spirit to vital spirit to animal spirit — as it flows from liver to heart to brain. See appendix B, "The Galenic Physiological System."

8. Alexander of Aphrodisias (fl. c.200 CE) was a prolific commentator on the works of Aristotle. A Latin translation of his commentary on Aristotle's *On the Soul* was published in 1495. In his commentary, Alexander closely follows Aristotle in describing the three faculties of the soul as nutrition (the vegetative soul), perception (the sensitive soul), and intellect (the rational soul).[9] The

---

[7] Galen, PHP 9.9. This is based on the passage in *Timaeus* where Plato describes how the Creator designed the human body so as to avoid polluting the seat of the immortal soul (the head) with the irrational emotions of fear, rashness, and anger, which would be confined to the thorax; and the still lower appetites for food, drink, and sex, which would be sequestered below the diaphragm. Plato, *Timaeus* (69b-72d).

[8] Owsei Temkin, "On Galen's Pneumatology," *Gesnerus* (1951), 8:182-184.

[9] Alexander of Aphrodisas, *De anima ex Aristotelis institutione*, trans. Hieronymus Donatus (Brescia, 1495).

word "spirit" does not appear in this section of the commentary; nor is it likely that Alexander would use the word, since he believed that the soul was the form of the body, inseparable from the body, and not immortal. If Servetus was asserting here that Alexander called the parts of the soul "spirits," he must have read this in a secondary source. However, since this sentence appears immediately before the discussion of whether there are two or three distinct spirits, it is possible that Servetus meant only that Alexander identified three, rather than two, parts or faculties in the soul.

9. An anastomosis is a connection between two channels (anatomical or otherwise) that do not normally connect. In the Galenic physiological system, the arterial and venous systems are taken to be almost entirely separate, so that any connection between the two would be considered an anastomosis. Anastomoses between the arteries and veins were needed, Galen thought, in order to supply the arteries with the nourishment carried by the veins, and to supply the veins with the vital spirit carried by the arteries. Galen's description of these anastomoses — "invisible and extremely narrow passages" connecting arteries and veins — sounds intriguingly like what we now call capillaries. However, whereas we think of capillaries as a vital link in the circulatory system, Galen saw these "anastomoses" as a minor phenomenon, needed only for the nourishment of the blood vessels themselves.[10]

10. By the time of Servetus, medical orthodoxy had embraced the idea of three parallel, symmetrical flows: natural spirit to and from the liver via the veins; vital spirit to and from the heart via the arteries; and animal spirit to and from the brain via the nerves (see appendix B, "The Galenic Physiological System"). However, there were some, including Servetus's old nemesis Leonhart Fuchs,[11] who

---

[10] Galen, UP 6.10.

[11] In 1536 Servetus published a pamphlet entitled *In Leonardum Fuchsium apologia*, in which he waded into a controversy between the physician and botanist Leonhart Fuchs and Servetus's friend and patron, Symphorien Champier. In it Servetus attacked Fuchs on a variety of matters including justification by faith, the origin of syphilis, and Fuchs's publishing practices.

argued for only two kinds of spirit. Fuchs pointed out that Galen doubted the existence of "natural spirit," and that it did not appear to contribute anything essential to the functioning of the body.[12] Servetus agreed that there are only two kinds of spirit: vital spirit, which is created in the left ventricle of the heart and transmitted throughout the body by the arteries; and animal spirit, which is created in the brain and transmitted by the nerves. He thought that what was called natural spirit was actually vital spirit that entered the veins — as it entered all other parts of the body — via the arteries.

11. This is part of Servetus's argument that there is really no such thing as natural spirit — that the spirit contained in the venous blood is actually vital spirit formed in the heart, and transmitted from the arteries to the veins via anastomoses (see A.R5.9 and A.R5.10). The fetal circulatory system includes three shunts, or anastomoses, which close after birth. Two of them carry blood from the veins directly to the arteries, bypassing the lungs, which do not begin to function until the newborn begins to breathe air. These two were known to Galen. The third, which was first described by Vesalius in 1543, carries oxygenated blood from the placenta to the inferior vena cava (one of the large veins that returns blood to the heart), bypassing the liver. Thus, this third shunt is an example of bright red, oxygen-rich blood (in sixteenth-century terms, blood imbued with vital spirit) entering the venous system.[13]

12. This is the crucial point at which Servetus parts company from Galen and Vesalius. Galen believed that blood passed from the right to the left ventricle of the heart through imperceptibly small perforations in the septum that separates the two ventricles. Vesalius admitted that the openings could not be seen, but at first accepted that they existed.[14] In the second edition of *On the Fabric*

---

[12] Fuchs, *Methodus seu ratio*, 24v-25r.

[13] Fabio Zampieri et al., "The three fetal shunts: A story of wrong eponyms," *Journal of Anatomy* (Apr 2021), 1028-1035.

[14] Vesalius, *Fabrica* (1543) 6.11.

of the Human Body (1555), Vesalius noted that he had established by dissection that there are no pores in the cardiac septum, but was unable to provide an alternative explanation of how the blood went from the right to the left side of the heart.[15]

13. It was known in ancient times that the ventricles of the heart pulsate, alternately filling (diastole) and emptying (systole). It is now commonplace to compare the heart to a pump. In Galen's time the usual model was a forge or furnace. Diastole, or dilation, was considered the active phase of the cycle, during which a chamber of the heart would expand to draw in blood, as a bellows expands to draw in air.[16]

14. The retiform plexus, also known as the *rete mirabile* ("amazing net") is a complex of small arteries arising from the internal carotid artery in the brains of many mammals, including the sheep, cows, and other domestic animals that Galen used in his anatomical studies. It does not exist in primates, including human beings. However, Galen not only included it in his description of the human brain, but assigned it a key role, as the site of the transformation of vital spirit to animal spirit.[17] In *On the Fabric of the Human Body*, Vesalius categorically denied that the *rete mirabile* exists in human beings, and used this example to illustrate how readily anatomists (including his own younger self) continued to repeat misinformation based on Galen, instead of checking it by performing their own independent dissections.[18] Nevertheless, the *rete mirabile* continued to be pictured and discussed as a structure in the human brain until at least the eighteenth century.[19]

---

[15] Justin Barr, "The Anatomist Andreas Vesalius at 500 Years Old," *Journal of Vascular Surgery* 61:5 (May 2015). C. D. O'Malley, *Andreas Vesalius of Brussels* (University of California Press, 1964), 280-281. Vesalius, *Fabrica* (1555) 6.11, 6.15. See esp. pp. 734 and 746, and illustration on pp. 703-704.

[16] Galen, UP, 6.15. Aird, "Discovery of the cardiovascular system," 121.

[17] Galen, UP 9.4.

[18] Vesalius, *Fabrica* (1543) 7.12.

[19] Sebastian Pranghofer, " 'It could be Seen more Clearly in Unreasonable Animals than in Humans': The Representation of the Rete Mirabile in Early Modern Anatomy," *Medical History* 53:4 (2009), 561-586.

15. The word translated here as "outer layer" is *tunica*, which literally means a garment such as a shirt or coat. The word was used to describe the close connections formed by the meninges (membranes that surround the brain and spinal cord) with nerves[20] and blood vessels.[21]

16. As discussed in book 4, in the ancient world there were two primary theories about the nature of vision. "Extramission," the theory associated with Pythagoras and Plato, is the idea that the eyes emit some kind of rays or beams. Seeing takes place when an object is encountered by this visual stream in the presence of light.[22] The alternative theory, "intromission," held that objects emit forms or images that are detected by the eye. Aristotle favoured a more sophisticated version of intromission, in which images are not directly produced by objects, but instead are assembled in the mind or soul based on a pattern of vibrations perceived by the eye. These vibrations are produced by light acting on the surface of an object — specifically, its colour — and are transmitted from the object to the eye by a transparent medium such as air or water.[23]

Servetus might have been expected to favour extramission, since that was the theory taught by Galen.[24] But this passage shows that he subscribed to the theory of intromission. The reference to transmission through a luminous medium echoes Aristotle's concept of the transparent medium, which transmits visual information only

---

[20] "The outermost connective tissue of peripheral nerve, the epineurium, is continuous with the outermost meningeal covering, the dura mater." Ananda Weerasuriya and Andrew Mizisin, "The Blood-Nerve Barrier: Structure and Functional Significance," *Methods in Molecular Biology* (Jan 2011), 149-173.

[21] "The cerebral pia mater [innermost layer of the meninges] forms sheaths around the blood vessels that enter and exit the brain perpendicular to the meninges." National Institutes of Health, National Library of Medicine, "Neuroanatomy, Cranial Meninges," https://www.ncbi.nlm.nih.gov/books/NBK539882/

[22] Plato, *Timaeus* (45a-b).

[23] Aristotle, *On the Soul* 2.7 (419a). "Colour sets in motion not the sense organ but what is transparent, e.g. the air, and that, extending continuously from the object to the organ, sets the latter in movement." Translated by J. A. Smith.

[24] Galen, PHP 7.5.

when illuminated.[25] Servetus may have found this model more congenial than Galen's because it is consistent with his belief that light is the form of all things, and that objects are able to emit and transmit light because their very nature is light.

17. Aristotle taught that the heart was the hottest part of the body, the source of vital heat and the centre of activity and sensation. The brain, being cold and dry, served to balance the heat of the heart.[26] Galen agreed with Aristotle that the heart was the source of heat, but strenuously denied that the brain was cold or that its purpose was to cool the heart (that, he thought, was the function of the lungs).[27] By Servetus's time it was well established that the brain was the source of the nerves, the seat of sensation, motion, and intellect. However, although Servetus followed Galen's teaching as to the function of the specific structures in the brain (the ventricles, plexuses, meninges, blood vessels, etc.), he also agreed with Aristotle about the brain's cooling function. Outside of the specific structures with their specialized uses, he thought of brain tissue as an undifferentiated "soft mass," serving only to cushion and cool the rest of the brain.

18. The ethmoid bone separates the nasal cavity from the cranial cavity. Galen believed that mucus is discharged from the ventricles of the brain through sieve-like perforations in the ethmoid bone — hence the name, from a Greek word meaning "sieve." Vesalius denied that such perforations exist (although the bone is pierced by openings through which fibres of the olfactory nerve pass.)[28]

19. In medical writing of this era, the expression "common sense" refers to the belief that information from the various sense organs is combined in the anterior ventricles of the brain. Servetus returns to this topic on p. 177: "There are four ventricles in the brain and three internal senses. For the first two ventricles together produce

---

[25] Aristotle, *On the Soul* 2.7 (418a-b).
[26] Aristotle, *On the Parts of Animals* 2.1 (647a), 2.7 (652a-b).
[27] Galen, UP 8.2-3.
[28] Galen, UP 8.7, 9.3. Vesalius, *Fabrica* (1543), 32.

one common sense, which is the receiver of images. The middle one is for thinking and the last is for memory." This was a late addition to book 5; it does not appear in the Paris manuscript.

20. The psalloid, or fornix, is a C-shaped bundle of densely packed nerve fibres in the brain. It was named "psalloid" from the Greek word meaning to play a stringed instrument, because its shape reminded early anatomists of a lyre. Galen called the fornix the "vault-shaped body" and assigned it a structural role.[29] The structure that Servetus calls "the area beneath the psalloid" is probably the hippocampus. The hippocampus and the fornix play an essential part in the formation of long-term memories.

21. The floor of the third ventricle is formed by the infundibulum (literally, "funnel"), a tubelike structure that connects the hypothalamus and the posterior pituitary. It provides a passage for the release of hormones synthesized in the hypothalamus. Its purpose could not have been guessed in Servetus's time, since hormones were not discovered until the twentieth century. Here Servetus follows Galen's teaching that it was a channel to collect "watery and slimy" waste products from the brain and convey them to the nasal passages for elimination.[30]

22. The conarium is what we now call the pineal gland (both names mean "pine cone"). It was described by Galen, but — like other components of the endocrine system — its purpose was not understood until the twentieth century. Galen guessed that the function of the glands was to provide structural reinforcement for the blood vessels at the points where they branch.[31]

23. The *vermis cerebelli* ("worm of the cerebellum") is a structure located between the two hemispheres of the cerebellum. It is involved in the sensing of bodily position and the control of movement. Because of its position, Galen saw it as the "doorkeeper" between the third and fourth ventricle. Vesalius, however, disputed

---

[29] Galen, UP 8.11.
[30] Galen, UP 9.3.
[31] Galen, UP 5.2.

the need for a "doorkeeper," because he could see no reason why the "door" should ever be closed.[32]

24. The quadrigeminal bodies are four rounded clusters of nerve cells located on the posterior surface of the midbrain. The upper two are involved in the processing of visual stimuli, while the lower two process auditory stimuli. They are now known as the inferior and superior colliculi, or "little hills." Galen called them by the more colourful names of "little buttocks" and "little testicles."[33]

25. Servetus cites the Chaldaeans and the Academics as authorities on aether. Although he sometimes used the word "Chaldaean" to mean the Targums (the Aramaic version of the Hebrew scriptures) here he is referring to the Chaldaean Oracles, a collection of fragments, sometimes attributed to Zoroaster, much used by the Neoplatonists of the third to sixth century CE.[34] In the Chaldaean Oracles, the aether is the zone of the fixed stars and the planets, located between the zone of God (the "First Principle") and the terrestrial world. The Academics are Plato and later members of Plato's Academy. Plato used the word "aether" for the brightest or most transparent part of the air.[35] Aristotle described it as the unchangeable and incorruptible "fifth element" that makes up the celestial spheres.[36]

26. The Greek word ἀναψυχή (*anapsyche*) means refreshment or relaxation. The word is used once in the New Testament, in 2 Timothy 1:16: "The Lord grant mercy to the household of

---

[32] Vesalius, *Fabrica* (1543) 7.10.208. "The channel that extends from the third cerebral ventricle ... must always stand open so that animal spirit may flow continuously into the spinal marrow."

[33] Galen, UP 8.14.

[34] The editor of a recent book on the Chaldaean Oracles describes them as "incoherent and only partly intelligible fragments of a collection of Greek magico-mystical poems of later antiquity which, by a strange conversion, was elevated by the Neoplatonists to the rank of a scripture or holy revelation." Introduction to Hans Lewy, *Chaldaean Oracles and Theurgy*, third edition, ed. Michel Tardieu (Paris: Institut d'Etudes Augustiniennes, 2011), xiii.

[35] Plato, *Timaeus* (58d).

[36] Aristotle, *On the Heavens* 1.3 (270b).

Onesiphorus, for he often refreshed me." In *Cratylus*, Socrates suggests that the word ψυχή (*psyche*, soul) is derived from ἀναψυχή, because "the soul when in the body is the source of life, and gives the power of breath and revival."[37]

27. Παράκλητος (*Paráklētos*, often anglicized as Paraclete) is a Greek word meaning advocate, counsellor, or helper. It occurs four times in the Gospel of John and once in the first Epistle of John.[38] It is often (as in this book) translated as "Comforter."

28. The word translated here as "another person" is *alius*; the word translated as "another being" is *aliud*. *Alius* and *aliud* are forms of the same word: *alius* is the masculine form; *aliud* is neuter. Thus *alius* carries the sense of "another man" or "someone else," while *aliud* carries the sense of "something else."[39]

Here Servetus seems to think that *aliud* will be perceived as a stronger kind of "otherness" than *alius*, and may even suggest discord between Christ and the Holy Spirit. Although he has just been arguing that the Holy Spirit is truly different from the Son, he is willing to concede that they are one, if that is what it takes to avoid the suggestion of disharmony. Because of the harmony between them, the Son and the Holy Spirit are one "just as Christ and the Father are one." This recalls what Servetus said about Christ and the Father in book 1: that they are one "because there is one divinity, one power, one harmony of thought, and one will."[40]

29. Jesus certainly does not speak of being "one" with the Holy Spirit, in the way he speaks of being one with the Father (especially in the Gospel of John). Instead, he speaks of the Holy Spirit as

---

[37] Plato, *Cratylus* (399d-e). Translated by B. Jowett (1892). This is one of two etymologies for *psyche* proposed (perhaps ironically) by Socrates in this section of *Cratylus*. See A.R4.19 (*On the Mysteries of the Word*, 227-228).

[38] John 14:16, 26; 15:26; 16:7; 1 John 2:1.

[39] The difference between *alius* and *aliud*, when applied to the Trinity, is discussed in Peter Lombard's *Sentences*. There the argument is even more subtle, since it involves a second grammatical distinction: that between *eiusdem* ("the same" in the genitive case) and *eadem* ("the same" in the nominative case). See Peter Lombard, *Sententiae* 1.25.4 (PL 192 588-589).

[40] *Restoration*, 24.

something separate from himself. He makes a distinction between the Son of Man and the Holy Spirit: "If anyone speaks a word against the Son of Man, it will be forgiven him; but if anyone speaks against the Holy Spirit, it will not be forgiven him."[41] Perhaps the clearest distinction is in the discussions of the Comforter who will come after Jesus's death: "But the Comforter, the Holy Spirit, whom the Father will send in my name, will teach you all things, and bring to your remembrance all things that I said to you ... if I do not go away, the Comforter will not come to you; but if I depart, I will send him to you."[42]

30. The instruction to "take away sophistical realities" comes after a series of discussions in which the Holy Spirit is referred to as "another": another person, another Comforter, another God, another spirit, another Paraclete. Here Servetus seems to be warning against a too literal understanding of "another." Only a sophist, he says, would think that this "other" had a reality of its own, separate from the Holy Spirit. This is more explicit in the Paris manuscript, where the warning against "sophistical realities" is followed by, "Just as in God infinite essences are one essence, so infinite spirits [may be] under one spirit."

31. "Four Books on Heavenly Regeneration and the Kingdom of the Antichrist" is one of the major components of *The Restoration of Christianity*. The four books are:

    1. On the destruction of the world, and its restoration by Christ (pp. 357-409)
    2. On true circumcision, and the other mysteries of Christ and Antichrist (pp. 410-469)
    3. On the services of the church of Christ, and their efficacy (pp. 470-524)
    4. On the mysteries of regeneration (pp. 525-575)

The "books on baptism and the Lord's Supper" are two sections within book 3. Book 3 also includes a section on preaching.

---

[41] Matt 12:32; similar passage in Luke 12:10.

[42] John 14:26; 16:7. The word translated here as "Comforter" is Paraclete (see A.R5.27).

32. The "book on original sin" is the first of the "Four Books on Heavenly Regeneration and the Kingdom of the Antichrist" (see A.R5.31). It begins with a denial of the doctrine of original sin.

33. Ephesians 4:8 quotes Psalm 68:18, but appears to have reversed the meaning of one of the phrases: in the psalm the Lord "received gifts from" human beings, whereas in Ephesians, Christ "gave gifts to" human beings. But Psalm 68 is a notoriously difficult text; it exists in several different forms in Hebrew, and may not be a single poem at all, but a collection of fragments of other poems.[43] Therefore it is not clear whether the quotation in Ephesians is purposely altering the sense of the psalm, or whether it is based on a variant form of Psalm 68 in which the Lord is the giver of the gifts.

34. In the Hebrew Bible, wind is not commonly called the breath of God. There is one place where the expression "breath of God" could be construed as referring to wind, or at least to weather: "By the breath of God ice is given, and the broad waters are frozen" (Job 37:10). More often, "breath of God" or "breath of the Lord" is used as a metaphor for the awesome power of God: it is the power that gives life or takes it away, or that creates or destroys the world and the things in it.[44] Breath as power and breath as wind are combined in Ezekiel 37:9, where the breath that restores life to the dry bones is summoned from the four winds.

35. The concept of the "three higher elements" was introduced in book 4, and forms a recurring motif throughout book 5. Of the four classical elements — earth, water, air, and fire — Servetus tells us in book 4 that only earth is thoroughly and irredeemably material, perishable, and corruptible. Water, air, and fire, the "three higher elements," belong to both the earthly and the heavenly realm.[45] In book 5 Servetus elaborates on the heavenly role of the three higher

---

[43] The twentieth-century Hebrew scholar W. F. Albright believed Psalm 68 to be a list of the first lines of thirty or so different poems. "A Catalogue of Early Hebrew Lyric Poems," *Hebrew Union College Annual* (1 Jan 1950).

[44] For example: Gen 2:7, Job 33:4 (gives life); Job 4:9, Isa 40:7 (takes away life); Ps 33:6 (creates); 2 Sam 22:16 (destroys).

[45] *Restoration*, 159.

elements. Earlier in book 5 we were told that the three elements form "one primary substance ... which is corporeal, spiritual, and shining with light,"[46] and that this substance is the stuff of the human spirit.[47] Now we find out that these elements are also divine: the higher elements are contained in the spirit of God and are "the elements of the Word." The idea that the same elements are found in the corporeal and spiritual realms underlies Servetus's belief that, as he said at the Geneva trial, "This is my fundamental principle: that all things are a part and portion of God, and the nature of things is the substantial spirit of God."[48]

36. In philosophy, entity A is said to supervene entity B if no change in A is possible without a change in B. In modern philosophy, the "higher," or supervening, entity is understood to be dependent on the lower. For example, a change in the body reflects a change in the cells making up the body; a change in society reflects a change in the people making up the society. In Neoplatonic philosophy, however, the dependency runs the other way: a change in the supervening form causes, rather than reflects, a change in the entity that it supervenes. In this sense, the soul is the supervening form of the body.

---

[46] *Restoration*, 164. See A.R5.2.
[47] *Restoration*, 169. "It is said that in us there is a threefold spirit — natural, vital, and animal — formed from the substance of the three higher elements."
[48] *Calvini opera* 8:496. Translated by Roland H. Bainton in *Hunted Heretic*, 127.

Bibliography

Abbreviations

The following abbreviations are used in the Bibliography.

Ante-Nicene Fathers	*Ante-Nicene Fathers: The Writings of the Fathers down to A.D. 325.* New York: Christian Literature Company, 1885-1896. Online edition: Christian Classics Ethereal Library, https://www.ccel.org/fathers2
Calvini opera	*Ioannis Calvini opera quae supersunt omnia* (vol. 29-87 of *Corpus Reformatorum*, 1863-1900)
Nicene and Post-Nicene Fathers	*Nicene and Post-Nicene Fathers, Series I and II.* New York: Christian Literature Company, 1886-1900. Online edition: Christian Classics Ethereal Library, https://www.ccel.org/fathers2
Obras Completas	*Miguel Servet: Obras Completas.* Edited by Ángel Alcalá. Zaragoza: Larumbe, 2003-2006.
On the Mysteries of the Word	*Michael Servetus: On the Mysteries of the Word* (volume 2 of *An Annotated Translation of* The Restoration of Christianity). Toronto: Blackstone Editions, 2024.
On the Trinity and the Bible	*Michael Servetus: On the Trinity and the Bible* (volume 1 of *An Annotated Translation of* The Restoration of Christianity). Toronto: Blackstone Editions, 2023.
Servetus Writings (trans. O'Malley)	*Michael Servetus: A Translation of his Geographical, Medical and Astrological Writings.* Translated by Charles Donald O'Malley. Philadelphia: American Philosophical Society, 1953.

Bibliography

Works by Servetus

Apologetica disceptatio pro astrologia. Paris, 1538. Republished, Berlin, 1880.

[English translation] In Servetus Writings (trans. O'Malley).

Christianismi restitutio. Vienne, 1553. Republished, Nuremberg, 1790; reprint of 1790 edition, Frankfurt: Minerva, 1966.

There are three surviving copies of the 1553 edition: in the Österreichische Nationalbibliothek in Vienna, the Bibliothèque Nationale in Paris, and the University of Edinburgh Library. A facsimile of the first 576 pages of the Vienna copy is included in volumes 5 and 6 of *Obras Completas.* The Paris copy is available online on BnF Gallica, the web site of the Bibliothèque Nationale.

[English translation] *The Restoration of Christianity: An English Translation of Christianismi Restitutio, 1553 by Michael Servetus (1511-1553).* Translated by Christopher A. Hoffman and Marian Hillar. Lewiston, NY: Mellen Press, 2007-2010. 4 volumes.

[English translation, books 1 and 2] *On the Trinity and the Bible.*

[English translation, books 3 and 4] *On the Mysteries of the Word.*

Christianismi restitutio [Paris manuscript]. Unpublished manuscript in the Bibliothèque Nationale, containing variant versions of book 3, 4, 5, and dialogue 1. It is available online on BnF Gallica, as Latin manuscript 18212.

[English translation, books 3 and 4] In *On the Mysteries of the Word.*

De Trinitatis erroribus libri septem. Hagenau, 1531. Facsimile reprint, Frankfurt: Minerva, 1965.

[English translation] In *The Two Treatises of Servetus on the Trinity.* Translated by Earl Morse Wilbur. Cambridge, MA: Harvard University Press, 1932. Reprint, New York: Kraus Reprint Company, 1969.

In Leonardum Fuchsium apologia. Lyons, 1536.

[English translation] In Servetus Writings (trans. O'Malley).

Syruporum universa ratio. Paris, 1537.

[English translation] In Servetus Writings (trans. O'Malley).

Scriptures

Biblia sacra vulgata [The Vulgate].
  Many editions in the late fifteenth and early sixteenth century.

Biblia sacra. Translated by Santes Pagnini.
  First edition: Lyons, 1527-28.
  Unauthorized second edition: *Biblia sacra iuxta germanam Hebraici.* Edited by Melchior von Neuss. Cologne, 1541.
  Second edition: *Biblia sacra ex Santis Pagnini tralatione.* Edited by Servetus. Lyons, 1542.

Novum Testamentum. Translated by Erasmus.
  First edition: *Novum Instrumentum.* Basel, 1516.
  Second through fifth editions: *Novum Testamentum.* Basel, 1519, 1522, 1527, 1535.

Servetus's Sources

The following list represents our best estimate of the non-Biblical sources that Servetus used in writing book 5 of *The Restoration of Christianity*. The list includes works that are explicitly mentioned in the text of *Restoration*, as well as others that have been identified, with varying degrees of certainty, as sources of information used by Servetus. All of these works were available in Servetus's day, some of them in multiple editions. The editions listed are ones that Servetus could have used, but not necessarily those that he did use.

Alexander of Aphrodisias. *Alexandri aphrodisei enarratio de anima ex Aristotelis institutione.* Translated by Hieronymus Donatus (Girolamo Donato). Brescia, 1495.

[Athanasius]. *De unitate sanctissimae trinitatis, ad Theophilum.* In *D. Athanasii ... Opera Omnia.* Cologne, 1548.

Augustine. *De trinitate.* In *Operum divi Aurelii Augustini*, vol. 3. Basel, 1528-29.
  [English translation]
    (1) In *Nicene and Post-Nicene Fathers*, series 1, vol. 3.
    (2) *The Trinity.* Translated by Edmund Hill, O.P. Hyde Park, NY: New City Press, 1991.

Didymus of Alexandria (Didymus the Blind). *De spiritu sancto*. Translated by Jerome. Cologne, 1531.

[English translation] In *Works on the Spirit: Athanasius the Great and Didymus the Blind*. Translated by Mark DelCogliano, Andrew Radde-Gallwitz, and Lewis Ayres. St. Vladimir's Seminary Press, 2012.

Ficino, Marsilio. *Theologia Platonica*. Venice, 1525.

[English translation] *Platonic Theology*. Translated by Michael J. B. Allen. Harvard University Press, 2001-2006. 6 volumes.

———, trans. [Hermes Trismegistus]. *Corpus Hermeticum*. In *Mercurii Trismegesti Pymander de potestate et sapientia Dei…* Basel, 1532.

[English translation]

(1) *Marsilio Ficino, Corpus Hermeticum*. Translated by Maxwell Lewis Latham. London: Falcon Books Publishing Ltd., 2019.

(2) *Hermetica*. Translated by Brian P. Copenhaver. Cambridge University Press, 1992.

———, trans. *Omnia divini Platonis opera tralatione Marsilii Ficini*. Basel, 1539.

Includes Ficino's translations, commentaries, and epitomes of Plato's dialogues

[Partial English translation] *Gardens of Philosophy: Ficino on Plato*. Translated by Arthur Farndell. London: Shepheard-Walwyn Publishers Ltd, 2006.

Galen. *De facultatibus naturalibus* [FN]. Translated by Johann Winter von Andernach. Paris, 1528.

[English translation] *On the Natural Faculties*. Translated by A.J. Brock. Harvard University Press. 1916.

———. *De placitis Hippocratis et Platonis* [PHP]. Translated by Johann Winter von Andernach. Paris, 1534.

[English translation] *Galen on the Doctrines of Hippocrates and Plato*. Translated by Phillip De Lacy. Berlin: Akademie Verlag, 2005. 2 volumes.

———. *De usu partium corporis humani* [UP]. Translated by Nicolao Regio Calabro. Basel, 1533.

[English translation] *Galen on the Usefulness of the Parts of the Body*. Translated by Margaret Tallmadge May. Ithaca, NY: Cornell University Press, 1968. 2 volumes.

[Hermes Trismegistus]. See under Ficino.

Hilary. *De trinitate*. In *Divi Hilarii pictavorum episcopi lucubrationes*. Basel, 1535.

[English translation]
(1) In *Nicene and Post-Nicene Fathers*, series 2, vol. 9.
(2) *The Trinity*. Translated by Stephen McKenna. New York: Fathers of the Church, 1954.

Irenaeus. *Adversus haereses*. Basel, 1526.

[English translation] In *Ante-Nicene Fathers*, vol. 1. The same translation is printed in book form as *Against Heresies*. Ex Fontibus Company, 2010.

Isidore of Seville. *Etymologiae*. Paris, 1520.

[English translation] *Isidore of Seville's Etymologies*. Translated by Priscilla Throop. Charlotte, VT: MedievalMS, 2005. 2 volumes.

Peter Lombard. *Sententiarum libri quatuor*. Paris, 1514; many other editions.

[English translation] *The Sentences*. Translated by Giulio Silano. Toronto: Pontifical Institute of Mediaeval Studies, 2007-2010. 4 volumes.

Plato. See under Ficino.

[Pythagoras]. *Carmina aurea*. Included as an appendix in Constantine Lascaris, *Grammatica*. Venice, 1494-95.

[English translation] Many available, including:
(1) Johan C. Thom, *The Pythagorean Golden Verses*. Brill, 1994.
(2) *The Golden Verses of Pythagoras*. Adapted from translation by Nicholas Rowe (1707). https://sacred-texts.com/cla/gvp/gvp03.htm

Steuco, Agostino. *De perenni philosophia*. Lyons, 1540.

Other Sixteenth-Century Works

Calvin, John. *Institutio Christianae religionis*. 5th edition. Geneva, 1559.

[English translation] *Calvin: Institutes of the Christian Religion*. Translated by Ford Lewis Battles. Philadelphia: Westminster, 1960. 2 volumes.

Colombo, Realdo. *De re anatomica*. Venice, 1559.

Fuchs, Leonhart. *Methodus seu ratio compendiaria perueniendi ad veram solidamque medicinam*. Paris, 1541.

Vesalius, Andreas. *De humani corporis fabrica*.
   First edition: Basel, 1543.
   Second edition: Basel, 1555.
      [English translation] *On the Fabric of the Human Body*. Translated by William Frank Richardson. Novato, CA: Norman Publishing, 2009.

Selected Secondary Works

Aird, W. C. "Discovery of the cardiovascular system: from Galen to William Harvey." *Journal of Thrombosis and Haemostasis* 9 (July 2011), 118-129.

Alcalá, Ángel. Introduction to *Obras Completas*, Vol. 1 and 3.

Ancín, Miguel González and Otis Towns. *Miguel Servet en España (1506-1527)*. Tudela, 2017.

Bainton, Roland H. *Hunted Heretic: The Life and Death of Michael Servetus, 1511-1553*. 1953; revised edition, Providence, RI: Blackstone Editions, 2005.

———. "The Smaller Circulation: Servetus and Colombo." *Sudhoffs Archiv für Geschichte der Medizin* 24 (1931), 371-374.

Cavard, Pierre. *Le procès de Michel Servet à Vienne*. Vienne: Syndicat d'Initiative, 1953.

Coppola, Edward. "The Discovery of the Pulmonary Circulation: A New Approach." *Bulletin of the History of Medicine* 31:1 (1957).

Friedman, Jerome. *Michael Servetus: A Case Study in Total Heresy*. Geneva: Droz, 1978.

Harris, C. R. S. *The Heart and Vascular System in Ancient Greek Medicine*. Oxford University Press, 1973.

Hillar, Marian. *Michael Servetus*. Lanham, MD: University Press of America, 2002.

Hughes, Peter. "The Christology of Michael Servetus." *Journal of Unitarian Universalist History* 40 (2016-2017), 16-53.

———. "The Early Years of Servetus and the Origin of His Critique of Trinitarian Thought." *Journal of Unitarian Universalist History* 37 (2014), 32-99.

———. Introduction to *On the Mysteries of the Word*.

———. Introduction to *On the Trinity and the Bible*.

Mackall, Leonard. "A Manuscript of the 'Christianismi Restitutio' of Servetus, placing the discovery of the pulmonary circulation anterior to 1546." *Proceedings of the Royal Society of Medicine* 17 (1924), 35-38.

O'Malley, Charles Donald. Introduction and commentary in Servetus Writings (trans. O'Malley).

Pagel, Walter. *William Harvey's Biological Ideas*. New York: Hafner, 1967.

Schulte am Hülse, Christine. "The Holy Spirit in the Theological Work of Michael Servetus." *Church History and Religious Culture* 101:2/3 (2021), 214-233.

Siegel, Rudolf E. "The Influence of Galen's Doctrine of Pulmonary Blood Flow on the Development of Modern Concepts of Circulation." *Sudhoffs Archiv für Geschichte der Medizin und der Naturwissenschaften* 46 (1962), 311-332.

Singer, Charles and C. Rabin. *A Prelude to Modern Science*. Cambridge University Press (for The Wellcome Historical Medical Museum), 1946.

Index

Abbreviations
The following abbreviations are used in the indexes.

A	Annotation	Reference is to book and annotation number, e.g. **A.R5.10** indicates annotation 10 for *Restoration* book 5.
Rest	*The Restoration of Christianity*	Reference is to page number in the original 1553 printing, e.g. ***Rest*: 180**
Paris	*The Restoration of Christianity - Paris manuscript*	Reference is to page number in the **printed** book, e.g. ***Paris*: 186** indicates the Paris manuscript version of text on page 186 in the 1553 printed edition. Only items that are unique to the manuscript are indexed as *Paris*.

Index of Biblical References

Genesis
1:1-3	*Rest*: 165, 193
2:7	*Rest*: 168, 178, 179; A.R5.34
6:3	*Rest*: 168
6:17	*Rest*: 168
7:15	*Rest*: 168
7:22	*Rest*: 168
9:4	*Rest*: 169, 170
16:7-13	*Rest*: 183, 184
18:2-9	*Rest*: 183
21:17-18	*Rest*: 183
22:11	*Rest*: 183
22:15-18	*Rest*: 183
31:11-13	*Rest*: 183
32:24	*Rest*: 183

Exodus
3:2-4	*Rest*: 182, 184
3:6	*Rest*: 182
13:21-22	*Rest*: 178
14:24	*Rest*: 178
23:20-23	*Rest*: 183
28:3	*Rest*: 192
29:7	*Rest*: 192
31:3	*Rest*: 192
35:31	*Rest*: 192

Leviticus
5:2	*Rest*: 192
6:27	*Rest*: 192
11:24-28	*Rest*: 192
17:11	*Rest*: 169, 170, 178
17:14	*Rest*: 169, 170

Numbers
11:16-17	*Rest*: 167
11:25	*Rest*: 167
14:14	*Rest*: 178
24:2	*Rest*: 192

Deuteronomy
12:23	*Rest*: 169, 170, 178

Joshua
5:13-15	*Rest*: 183
6:2-5	*Rest*: 183

Judges
2:1-4	*Rest*: 183
6:11-22	*Rest*: 183, 184
14:6	*Rest*: 192
14:19	*Rest*: 192

2 Samuel
22:16	A.R5.34
22:29	*Rest*: 174

1 Kings
4:29	*Rest*: 168
Chapter 22	*Rest*: 183

2 Chronicles
18:4-22	*Rest*: 183

Job
4:9	*Rest*: 178; A.R5.34
10:12	*Rest*: 168
27:3	*Rest*: 168, 178
32:8	*Rest*: 168
33:4	*Rest*: 168, 178; A.R5.34
33:28, 30	*Rest*: 174
34:14	*Rest*: 168
37:10	A.R5.34

Psalms
18:28	*Rest*: 174
31:5	*Rest*: 194
33:6	A.R5.34
33:7	*Rest*: 193
33:15	*Rest*: 179
36:9	*Rest*: 180

Psalms, continued

51:11	*Rest*: 191, 192
68:18	A.R5.33
82:6	*Rest*: 196
103:20-21	*Rest*: 183
104:4	*Rest*: 183
104:29	*Rest*: 168
104:30	*Rest*: 181
135:7	*Rest*: 193
139:13-16	*Rest*: 179

Proverbs

20:27	*Rest*: 168

Isaiah

2:22	*Rest*: 168
11:2	*Rest*: 168
29:16	*Rest*: 179
40:7	A.R5.34
42:5	*Rest*: 168, 179
45:7	*Rest*: 179
57:15-16	*Rest*: 167, 178
62:12	*Rest*: 197
63:8	*Rest*: 197
63:10-11	*Rest*: 191, 192
64:8	*Rest*: 179
65:17-19	*Rest*: 197
66:22	*Rest*: 197

Jeremiah

10:13	*Rest*: 193
10:16	*Rest*: 179
18:16	*Rest*: 179
24:7	*Rest*: 168
32:39	*Rest*: 168
51:16	*Rest*: 193

Ezekiel

9:3	*Rest*: 183
10:1-19	*Rest*: 183
11:19	*Rest*: 168
11:22	*Rest*: 183

Ezekiel, continued

14:6-11	*Rest*: 183
37:1-14	*Rest*: 166, 168, 178; A.R5.6, A.R5.34

Daniel

6:3	*Rest*: 168

Zechariah

1:9-19	*Rest*: 183
2:3	*Rest*: 183
4:1-5	*Rest*: 183
12:1	*Rest*: 178, 179

Matthew

1:20	*Rest*: 193
3:16-17	*Rest*: 182, 183, 190, 195
11:27	*Rest*: 186
12:32	A.R5.29
15:5	*Rest*: 183
15:18-19	*Rest*: 174
20:29	*Rest*: 189
23:9-10	*Rest*: 166
28:10	*Rest*: 191
28:19	*Rest*: 192

Mark

1:10-11	*Rest*: 183, 195
9:7	*Rest*: 183

Luke

3:22	*Rest*: 183, 195
9:35	*Rest*: 183
10:22	*Rest*: 186
11:13	*Rest*: 190
12:10	A.R5.29
23:46	*Rest*: 194
24:49	*Rest*: 167

John

1:9	*Rest*: 180
1:13	*Rest*: 185, 196
1:32	*Rest*: 195

Index of Biblical References

John, continued
1:51	*Rest*: 183
3:5-6	*Rest*: 192, 196
3:8	*Rest*: 198
3:15	*Rest*: 196
3:34	*Rest*: 186; *Paris*: 186
4:24	*Rest*: 167, 187
6:64	*Rest*: 196
7:39	*Rest*: 190, 191, 192, 195
8:12	*Rest*: 180
8:51	*Rest*: 197
10:15	*Rest*: 191
10:28	*Rest*: 196
10:30	*Rest*: 184, 188
10:34	*Rest*: 196
10:38	*Rest*: 190
11:26	*Rest*: 197
14:9	*Rest*: 186
14:16	*Rest*: 184, 187; A.R5.27
14:17	*Rest*: 198
14:26	*Rest*: 184, 185; A.R5.27, A.R5.29
15:14-15	*Rest*: 192
15:26	*Rest*: 184, 190; A.R5.27
16:7	A.R5.27, A.R5.29
16:8-10	*Rest*: 188
16:13	*Rest*: 185, 191
16:14-15	*Rest*: 185, 190
17:21	*Rest*: 168
20:17	*Rest*: 191, 192
20:22	*Rest*: 182

Acts

1:8	*Rest*: 167
2:2-4	*Rest*: 182, 183, 184, 190, 198
2:4	*Rest*: 168, 184, 186
2:33	*Rest*: 190
3:18	*Rest*: 167
3:21	*Rest*: 167
4:8	*Rest*: 168, 184, 186
4:31	*Rest*: 168, 184

Acts, contiued
4:32	*Rest*: 168
5:3-4	*Rest*: 167
7:30	*Rest*: 182
8:26, 29, 39	*Rest*: 183
10:1-6	*Rest*: 183
10:44-45	*Rest*: 192
11:4-17	*Rest*: 183
13:2-10	*Rest*: 183
13:9	*Rest*: 186
13:52	*Rest*: 183
16:6-7	*Rest*: 183
16:9-10	*Rest*: 183
17:28	*Rest*: 168
19:2	*Rest*: 191

Romans

5:5	*Rest*: 191
6:4	*Rest*: 192
6:23	*Rest*: 196
7:4	*Rest*: 192
8:9-11	*Rest*: 167
8:15	*Rest*: 191, 192
8:17	*Rest*: 191
8:23	*Rest*: 191
9:4	*Rest*: 191
9:21	*Rest*: 179
12:3	*Rest*: 186

1 Corinthians

2:9	*Rest*: 186
2:10	*Rest*: 185
3:17	*Rest*: 167
6:17	*Rest*: 197
6:19	*Rest*: 167
8:8	*Rest*: 166
12:4-11	*Rest*: 168

2 Corinthians

1:21-22	*Rest*: 167, 192, 196
3:17	*Rest*: 167
3:18	*Rest*: 185

Index of Biblical References

2 Corinthians, continued
6:16	*Rest*: 167
6:17	*Rest*: 188
10:13-15	*Rest*: 186
11:4	*Rest*: 187

Galatians
3:28	*Rest*: 168
4:3-7	*Rest*: 192
4:3	*Rest*: 178
4:5	*Rest*: 191
4:6	*Rest*: 167, 191
4:7	*Rest*: 191
4:9	*Rest*: 178

Ephesians
1:5	*Rest*: 191
1:10	*Rest*: 165
1:17	*Rest*: 187
2:16	*Rest*: 197
2:22	*Rest*: 167
3:9	*Rest*: 166
3:10	*Rest*: 185
3:16	*Rest*: 196
4:7	*Rest*: 186
4:8	A.R5.33

Colossians
2:9	*Rest*: 186, 190
2:12	*Rest*: 192

1 Thessalonians
4:8	*Rest*: 167

2 Timothy
1:14	*Rest*: 196
1:16	A.R5.26

Titus
3:5-6	*Rest*: 190
3:7	*Rest*: 196

Hebrews
1:1	*Rest*: 167
1:7	*Rest*: 183

James
1:17	*Rest*: 187

1 Peter
1:4	*Rest*: 196
1:11	*Rest*: 167
1:12	*Rest*: 185
1:23	*Rest*: 196
3:4	*Rest*: 196
4:14	*Rest*: 185

2 Peter
1:4	*Rest*: 196
3:10, 12	*Rest*: 178

1 John
1:3	*Rest*: 166
2:1	A.R5.27
2:20	*Rest*: 192
2:27	*Rest*: 192
3:9	*Rest*: 196
4:6	*Rest*: 183
4:13	*Rest*: 196
4:17	*Rest*: 196

Revelation
11:11	*Rest*: 178

Index of Authorities Cited

Alexander of Aphrodisas
   De anima ex Aristotelis institutione, *Rest*: 169; A.R5.8
Aristotle, *Rest*: 151-152
   On the Heavens, A.R5.25
   On the Parts of Animals, A.R5.17
   On the Soul, *Rest*: 168-169; A.R5.16
[Athanasius]
   De unitate sanctissimae trinitatis, *Rest*: 167
Augustine
   De trinitate, Paris: 183
Bereshit Rabbah, *Rest*: 193
Calvin, John, A.R5.35
Chaldaean Oracles, *Rest*: 174, 178, 180; A.R5.25
Corpus Hermeticum, *Rest*: 174, 180
Didymus of Alexandria
   De spiritu sancto, *Rest*: 185
Ficino, Marsilio
   Theologia Platonica, *Rest*: 180, 194
Fuchs, Leonhart
   Methodus seu ratio, A.R5.10
Galen
   On the Teachings of Hippocrates and Plato, *Rest*: 170; A.R5.7, A.R5.16
   On the Usefulness of the Parts of the Body, *Rest*: 169, 171; A.R5.9, A.R5.13, A.R5.14, A.R5.17, A.R5.18, A.R5.20, A.R5.21, A.R5.22, A.R5.24
[Hermes Trismegistus], *see Corpus Hermeticum*
Hilary
   De trinitate, *Rest*: 167

Irenaeus
   Adversus haereses, *Rest*: 196; A.R5.4
Isidore of Seville
   Etymologiae, *Rest*: 183
Peter Lombard
   Sententiae, *Rest*: 166; A.R5.28
Plato
   Cratylus, *Rest*: 179; A.R5.26
   Timaeus, *Rest*: 178, 194; A.R5.7, A.R5.16, A.R5.25
[Pythagoras]
   The Golden Verses, *Rest*: 174, 180
Servetus, Michael
   In Leonardum Fuchsium apologia, A.R5.10
Steuco, Agostino
   De perenni philosophia, *Rest*: 180
Vesalius, Andreas
   De humani corporis fabrica, *Rest*: 171; A.R5.12, A.R5.14, A.R5.18, A.R5.23
Virgil
   Eclogue 4, *Rest*: 197
[Zoroaster], *see Chaldaean Oracles*

www.ingramcontent.com/pod-product-compliance
Lightning Source LLC
Chambersburg PA
CBHW071959070526
44583CB00015B/1257